A Personal Guide to Living with Loss

Elaine Vail
Western Illinois University

John Wiley & Sons, Inc.
New York • Chichester • Brisbane • Toronto • Singapore

To Ron, Lanita, and Mary Lee
In Memory of
Their Beloved Wife and Mother,
Annette Marie George Herms
1956–1981

Library of Congress Cataloging in Publication Data

Vail, Elaine, 1948–
    A personal guide to living with loss.

    Bibliography: p. 207
    Includes index.
    1. Death. 2. Grief. 3. Bereavement. I. Title.
HQ1073.V34   306   81-23089
ISBN 0-471-09891-4   AACR2

Printed in the United States of America
82 83 10 9 8 7 6 5 4 3 2 1

Contents

Preface

Good grief! Aside from Charlie Brown's lamentations, just what do those two words mean? We Americans tend to deny the possibility, but I believe that there can be some good in grief. I hope this book will help others to find it.

We harbor many misconceptions and fears about death in this youth-oriented society. We feel uncomfortable around someone who is dying or someone who is grieving. At least three-fourths of us die without a will or adequate legal organization of our affairs. Embalming and cremation are equally mysterious processes, one of which we readily accept while the other is largely feared, with both opinions based on scant information and hearsay.

Our confusion over the very definition of death is unsettling. We are bewildered by the implications of medical advances which both promote and sustain life and potentially prolong dying. Euthanasia splinters our moral convictions. Suicide diminishes our humanity. The process of aging is misunderstood and feared, although other cultures proudly revere and respect their elders. At the other end of the life cycle, we feel especially uncomfortable explaining death to children.

If grief after a death is given too little recognition, that which follows other losses is virtually ignored. Divorce, amputations, mastectomies, crippling arthritis and heart disease, unemployment—these and many more losses may also require resolution through a grief process.

New research and developments in death-related areas have changed forever our ideas about dying. Cryonics, hospices, accounts of near-death experiences pique our curiosity and stretch our philosophical boundaries. Interest in reincarnation has been renewed as we struggle to make some sense of the life we think we do know about.

All of these issues and more are addressed in this *Personal Guide to Living with Loss*. The book encapsulates death and dying in the proverbial nutshell. But it is a capacious nutshell and, to my knowledge, this is the only book encompassing such a broad spectrum of topics suitable for a survey-type introduction to death and dying.

My goal in teaching "Understanding Death and Dying" at the college level for the last seven years has been simple. I want to help the individual better understand his or her own feelings about this increasingly complex part of life and society. This book was designed with the same goal in mind. In our confusing and overwhelming culture, death is ignored and abhored, but remains inevitable. This book recognizes and even explains why death is such a problem for us and provides information and practical suggestions for helping one cope and even grow through an open confrontation with the concept of death.

This is a personal and professional resource book, often referring the reader to appropriate sources of more in-depth information and even personal assistance. No one chapter is offered as the "last word" on the topic. The broad-spectrum approach is valuable, but necessitates a limit on depth. I have tried to present the heart of each issue, in true nutshell style, and not just skim the surface. My purpose is to stimulate some interest, answer some questions, encourage new approaches, provide helpful information and some good sources for more of it. If the ideas in this book inspire the reader to ask some new questions, gain a few insights, and be curious enough to pursue more study independently, it will have accomplished a great deal.

Being a great respecter of members of both sexes, I have made an effort to refer to both in the text. Most examples could refer to either sex, but one or the other was chosen merely to simplify the language, avoiding the he/she, his/her dilemma. No slights or prejudices are intended.

For you, my wish is for good reading and a good life.

Elaine Vail
November, 1981
Macomb, Illinois

Acknowledgments

Probably the greatest reward for a teacher is not the satisfaction of sharing some of your own knowledge, but the exhilaration of having students show you a new insight, a different perspective, a broadened view. My students have been my joy in teaching, and, in essence if not in ink, they wrote this book. They colored, shaped, and expanded my thoughts at least as much as I did theirs. I am grateful to them all.

When my patient husband Terry proposed this project, I doubt that he envisioned the extra effort *he* would have to expend to accomplish the task and keep our family intact throughout the endeavor. But he persisted and made the work much more pleasant than it might have been. I am grateful, too, to Brea and Birk, my understanding little ones, who endured a summer without swimming lessons or tot lot so that Mommy could finish her book. And to Maureen Frazier, Sheila Gierhan, Tracy Veronie, and Grandma and Grandpa Vail, I am forever indebted for their loving attention to Brea and Birk while I was holed up in the library.

For their friendship and sharing of special experiences which helped form this book, I am grateful to Sue Patrick, Becky Nash, Cynthia Harris, Jan Miltenberger, Sue Currie, Mary Bailey, Bridget Weber, Mildred Butt, Judy Squires, Timothy and Marilyn Kling, Drexel and Alta Sargent, and Kitty Faulkner. Dorothy Hansen was especially helpful in supplying me with resources and ideas, and Sandra Fisk, Helen Bantz, Donna Anderson, Connie Engel, and Nancy and Larry Jameson also supplied special information that facilitated my research. Mary Lou George has been an aunt and survivor *par excellence.*

Doug March and Bob McMahan provided much-needed legal and insurance expertise for Chapter 8. John Audette and Dr. Michael Gulley offered enlightening perspectives on near-death research. Winona Malpass kindly shared her time and office as we discussed her work in the local hospice program. State Representative Clarence Neff and Congressman Tom Railsback were quick to supply requested information regarding Illinois and federal laws.

I owe a very special debt of gratitude to Dr. Robert Synovitz, my department chairman and indefatigable friend. He has patiently but persistently encouraged my professional growth and involvement, even as I nursed my babes and tended the home fires. It was Bob who gently but firmly nudged me into developing the course on death and dying in the first place, and stuck by me when the first proposal was rejected. The subsequent success of the course had a special meaning for both of us.

Jan Rockwell has been a source of constant encouragement and support. An extra dose of appreciation goes to Glenda Bliss, who bravely and beautifully typed the manuscript from my handwriting.

And to Jack and Marilyn Ginn, who are excitedly about to become grandparents to a book, I give my deepest gratitude for a lifetime of making me feel special. I love you both.

I thank Nina Houlton for sharing her father's thought-provoking philosophy. The words of Leonard Poland:

> When someone dies, we should be happy. When a baby is born, we should be sad. The newborn has a lifetime of work ahead, while he who is dying has completed his life's work and is at rest.

Never Say Die: The Society That Would Be Immortal

When a new course on death and dying was first proposed to the faculty senate of Western Illinois University by the Health Sciences department, the vote was against adoption. Senators claimed that the course outline was too extensive to be covered in one term, that the course should be offered through various other academic departments, and that there probably wouldn't be much student interest in a course of this nature, anyway. There was a lot of death-denying in the atmosphere that day. When the Department of Health Sciences revised and resubmitted its proposal months later, the senators reversed their decision, perhaps because the other departments preferred to steer clear of it.

Health Education 125, "Understanding Death and Dying," was an instant success. It has enjoyed standing room only enrollment every term for several years, and student response has been enthusiastic. With typical reactions like, "This is the most helpful course I have ever taken," it seems logical to conclude that the course is meeting a need. This book grew out of that course. It is hoped it, too, will meet a need.

Why do we need a course or a book on death and dying? People have been dying since shortly after human existence began. One would think we would have it down pat by now. Apparently not. Death is probably even more puzzling today than it was in the days of our ancestors. Life and death are increasingly complex matters. This first chapter examines why we late-twentieth-century Americans exist in such a unique medical, cultural, social, legal, and ethical environment when it comes to death. Death may be universal and timeless, but it isn't quite as simple as it used to be.

Here is an excerpt from the Bundy family records:

	Born	Died
Lewis Oscar Bundy	December 7, 1867	April 22, 1944
Rosa Lewis Bundy	September 23, 1869	1917
Cynthia Bundy	June 23, 1871	1931
Ethel E. Bundy	February 7, 1873	April 18, 1876
Matilda E. Bundy	November 17, 1874	1950
Florie G. Bundy	July 18, 1877	October 9, 1878
Miranda J. Bundy	March 20, 1879	July 21, 1956
Harriet P. Bundy	November 4, 1880	June 27, 1884
Raleigh Oran Bundy	March 8, 1883	February 9, 1971
Bessie P. Bundy	August 19, 1885	November 9, 1887
Lillie Bundy	April 11, 1887	1970
Baily Bundy	April 8, 1889	August 22, 1889
Dwight Bundy	July 15, 1890	August 2, 1890
Ivan D. Bundy	July 5, 1891	March 21, 1950

This simple chronicle records the births and deaths of the fourteen children of Mary Adeline Adams Bundy and Alexander Bundy. It graphically shows the reality of living and dying in mid-America before the turn of the century. Six (almost half) of the children died before reaching their fourth birthday. Their surviving siblings had to accept death as a part of life. Its presence was simply too real to ignore. The Bundy family was typical. One could examine the records of virtually any family living at that time in this country and find a similar situation. The survivors of this kind of existence were forced to come to terms with death. And so they did.

The calm selection of "going away" clothes shows the acceptance with which many of these people approached death. It was a common practice (which lingers to this day in a few places) for persons to select the clothes they wanted to be buried in, their "going away" dress or suit. My own grandmother, Ruth Ginn, chose a dress she made herself, one which she had worn on many happy occasions. Choosing the dress was a matter-of-fact task for her, revealing her acceptance of the simple reality of her own inevitable death. Some people today might view such a custom as macabre or depressing. To Grandma, it was just a fact of life.

A Social and Medical Evolution

The pervasiveness of death has, thankfully, been dispersed to a great extent by the remarkable advances made by medicine since the early 1900s. Smallpox, diptheria, polio, whooping cough, rheumatic fever, and pneumonia, all once potent and frequent death dealers, are now, for the most part, merely bad memories for those old enough to recall the early part of this century. While rheumatic fever and pneumonia still occur, they can usually be treated most effectively and only rarely pose a serious threat to life. The virtual eradication of many of childhood diseases has, along with other factors, effected a dramatic increase in life expectancy. A newborn in 1900 could expect to live about forty-five years. A newborn today can look forward to at least three-score and ten.*

The way we spend these seventy or so years has changed just as dramatically. The Bundy children lived in a small community in Illinois and played and worked in a culture which included many family members—grandparents, aunts, uncles, cousins. Not only did they witness the unfortunate early deaths of their siblings, but they also had a very vivid understanding of aging and death. When Grandma died, she was in her own bed and someone was with her around the clock the last few days of her life. Even the grandchildren took their turns holding her hand. Today, family life tends to be confined to the nuclear family. It is quite common for employment opportunities or the lure of excitement and challenge to draw a family hundreds, even thousands of miles away from grandparents. Children today rarely have a close, personal comprehension of the natural cycle of aging and death. It is difficult to maintain an emotional relationship with a child seen only on semiannual visits. The impact of the death of a distant grandparent can't compare to that of the loving lady who always had fresh cookies in the cookie jar every Saturday morning.

Of course, there are exceptions. There are those lucky children who have frequent contact with their grandparents. But even these children are sheltered by our society from any experience with those who are seriously ill. Most hospitals have a minimum visiting age of between 12 and 14 years, and good or bad, children have very little chance to observe first hand the effects of disease, terminal or otherwise. There is, likewise, little chance to develop a sense of reality about illness and to begin to learn how to cope with this part of living. We all learn to deal with difficulties and challenges by facing them and dealing with them and by observing how others handle such situations. The problem is that we have produced an environment where recent generations have been denied the confrontation with, and therefore the opportunity to learn how to cope with, illness and death. When we grow up and are faced with sometimes cruel reality, we are at a loss for ways to handle it. There are no memories of childhood strengths and successes against crises upon which to call

---

*Life expectancy is an averaged figure. Certainly some people lived to a ripe old age early in this century. But so many people died young that the average expectancy was low.

for confidence and guidance in the present dilemma. What is youth if not a training period for adulthood?

Youth, Impatience, Convenience, Control

Ah, youth. Whatever it is, Americans seem to crave it, worship it, seek it (or at least its facade) at all costs. We are the "Pepsi generation," full of vigor and good times. Advertising constantly beseeches us to use myriad products which will, they tell us, make us look and feel younger, a goal Madison Avenue apparently believes we all have in mind. The ads for one product claim that using it will make you look "ten years younger." The fitness craze has popularized the notion that one can delay the effects of aging by maintaining a regular exercise program. We are bombarded with innuendos that we will be more attractive to the opposite sex and to prospective employers if we look, feel, and act *young.* The importance of success, ambition, and activity in our society leaves little room for the calmer wisdom of old age or contemplation of the finiteness of life. Illness and death simply aren't "in the program," and we try (often successfully) to avoid all thought and conversation concerning either of them. It is the perfect example of using the famous coping method, "Ignore it and maybe it will go away." But death is not so easily intimidated.

We are living in an age of instant everything: fast-food restaurants, twenty-four-hour dry cleaners, microwave cooking, quick-cooking rice, cake mixes, powdered instant soup, instant tea, instant cocoa, or whatever. Just add water and stir. We are accustomed to having what we want when we want it. It is staggering to recall that before World War II, families would save for months or years to accumulate the cash for the purchase of a much needed or wanted item. Now, millions of us simply flash a plastic card when we spy an irresistible product and begin to enjoy it instantly, long before we have suffered so much as the pangs of the first installment payment. We are an impatient people, geared to immediate gratification of our wants and needs. We are annoyed by waiting in line at the grocery store checkout, or the bank teller's window, or the airport ticket counter. We want attention and answers to our problems right now. Unfortunately, the problems of illness and dying are often long, drawn-out affairs with no fast answers and sometimes no answers at all. It is exceedingly frustrating to be faced with a situation over which we have no control, one which forces us to wait for difficult and even unacceptable solutions.

Another aspect of our culture and economy is the proliferation of disposable and convenience products and services. Paper dishes, plastic forks and knives, paper diapers and premoistened washcloths, flashlights, placemats, tissues, paper towels, and even thermometers come in the "use once and throw away" variety. Many products that are not intended to be disposable just don't seem to last as long as we would like, either. Appliances, automobiles, carpeting, houses, and clothing are a few of those things that apparently aren't "made as well as they used to be." Being surrounded by so many reminders of this age of disposables, perhaps we are haunted by the prospect that we, too, can be easily "disposed of," forgotten, and replaced. It is not an ego-building prospect, and it is natural that we should try to avoid dwelling on the possibility. Our convenient lives would be disrupted and inconvenienced by illness or death, either our own or that of someone close to us, and so we naturally divert our attention from that possibility, too. It just doesn't fit our lifestyle and we prefer to deny the existence of such problems.

Independence and a sense of control of our own lives are also important contemporary goals. We ridicule the 24-year-old baby still living in his parents' home. "He ought to be on his own by now," we say. We pity the weakling who allowed his father to bully or intimidate him into attending law school, when he really always wanted to be a mechanic. We like being the master of our own destiny, having the power to make the decisions that will affect our lives and the direction they will take. When a terminal illness or the death of someone close denies us this precious control, we are hurt and bewildered, if not outraged. Given the choice, we would opt against the disease, against the death. But the choice is not ours to make. At best, we can delay the event by deciding not to smoke or work in an asbestos factory or eat fatty foods. Even then, we cannot be assured of a completely healthy life.

The experience of Adele Davis, famous nutritionist and author, was a cruel example of this lack of control. An avid proponent of eating a well-balanced combination of nutritious foods to maintain optimum health and avoid disease, she was stricken with cancer which claimed her life in a matter of months. Adele Davis was almost embarassed to have gotten cancer despite faithful adherence to a lifestyle and diet she believed would protect her from such maladies. She felt somehow betrayed by the principles she had held so dear. No one is immune to disease and death and this is, at least superficially, an unpleasant concept to embrace. It might put things in better perspective, however, to contemplate what you would do with the next eight hundred and forty-seven years of your life (just for starters) if indeed you were granted immortality. Is that not at least as awesome a prospect as the thought of a natural death?

It is simply a great frustration for those of us who so keenly value our independence to know that there are some important aspects of our lives over which we have no control. We can, however, control how we will react to these situations and what impact they will have on our lives.

Perhaps the devastating potential of nuclear weapons has frightened us all, has presented the concept that perhaps not only a person but humanity itself may be disposable. If we are unsure of our personal immortality, there would at least be some comfort in knowing that human life goes on. But if *all* of humanity is but a fleeting quirk of nature, it is even more difficult to comprehend the meaning of existence.

Redefining Death

Medical science is continually improving its technology and its pharmacy, presenting us with miracles and dilemmas we have scarcely had the chance to imagine. A nineteenth-century person would probably have been horrified at the thought of removing the heart from a freshly dead body and sewing it into the chest of another.

And the idea of maintaining heartbeat and respiration with machines would likely have brought unbelieving laughter. But no one is laughing now and few, if any, are horrified by transplants anymore. They save too many lives. There are, of course, hosts of new problems and questions that surround each new medical advance. We are now more uncertain than ever about even the most basic question, "What is death?"

Defining death and being able to diagnose it correctly have always been major concerns of physicians and lay persons alike. Until the last few decades, however, it was basically pretty simple. Once heartbeat and respiration had irreversibly ceased, a person was considered dead. Now, thanks to our sophisticated equipment and the special time requirements of transplant surgery, we are trying to refine our definition of death.

Death is now conceptualized in at least eight different ways:

1. Medical or clinical death: cessation of breathing and heartbeat. The person can no longer function.
2. Biological death: cessation of functions of organs and tissues.
3. Cellular death: cessation of function of all cells.
4. Cerebral death: cessation of function of the cerebral cortex, the part of our brain responsible for thought and reason. This is the part of the brain that is uniquely human.
5. Brain death: cessation of the functions of the brain, including the midbrain and brain stem, which control the basic life functions (heartbeat, respiration) and which die sequentially

after the cerebral cortex. Other body organs may still be viable. This term is sometimes used synonymously with cerebral death.

6. Spiritual death: departure of the spirit or soul from the body.
7. Legal death: cessation of the legal rights of personhood, citizenship. A person who is in perfectly good health who has been missing for seven or more years, may be declared dead by the courts for the purpose of settling various legal and financial matters. A court decision is also sometimes involved in deaths connected to criminal cases, traffic accidents, transplant cases, and other special situations.
8. "Reversible" death: temporary cessation of heartbeat and respiration which would have become permanent without emergency medical intervention which was unavailable several decades ago. People who originally would have been declared as "clinically dead" years ago are now being revived with modern resuscitation methods. (Example: A child is electrocuted while playing with a faulty electrical cord. The emergency squad arrives and restarts the child's heart with a portable defibrillation machine.)

All of these perspectives contribute to the dissolution of a myth still perpetuated by movies and television programs. You have seen the scenario a hundred times; no wonder it seems true: The handsome young cowboy (or private eye or jilted husband) is shot (or falls seventeen flights or collapses with an apparent heart attack) and the shocked companion rushes to the body, feels for a pulse and declares angrily (or tearfully, or in a broken voice) "He's dead." The myth is that it happens in a moment. Yes, a gunshot wound or a fall or a heart attack can instantly cause the heart to stop beating, which will lead to death. But death is not just an instant in time. Death is a process, at least biologically speaking. Body cells (we have billions of them) die when they are deprived of oxygen. Some cells are very sensitive to oxygen deprivation and die rapidly. The most sensitive are the cells of the cerebral cortex of the brain. Some are far less sensitive and may continue to function for hours without oxygen. The cells which produce hair and nails may not "die" for a day or more after the person has "died." So when is a person actually dead? When the cerebral cortex (which controls thinking) dies? When the entire brain is dead? When all of the cells have died?

In most cases today, the old criteria remain valid. If the heart has stopped beating and respiration has ceased and all resuscitative measures have failed to restore them, the person is dead. An increasing number of cases, however, require a more definitive diagnosis.

For example, a twenty-three-year-old woman on artificial life support for three weeks after an automobile accident appears to have died. If life support is removed and she isn't already dead, she will likely die as a result of the removal of the equipment. But since the machines are carrying on the vital functions, it is difficult to determine if they might be maintained independently. (It is unlikely that the patient could have survived without the machines. The very purpose of artificial respirators is to provide patients with critical help when their bodies are too weak or incapacitated to make it alone; to get them over the rough spots until their strength has improved. Respirators were not designed with the intent to maintain noncognitive humans indefinitely, but rather to supply a temporary, life-saving stop-gap, to be withdrawn when the patient's condition improves.) This situation calls for the use of the electroencephalogram (EEG) to determine if the brain is still alive. The EEG measures the electrical activity of the brain. If the EEG is flat (shows no electrical activity) for a certain period of time, the person might be declared dead and artificial life support measures discontinued.

The concept of brain death is used more and more often, but there is some disagreement among physicians regarding exactly how long the EEG must be flat before brain death can be diagnosed with certainty. Several states have passed laws verifying a particular definition of death and many institutions and physicians have determined their own standard criteria for diagnosing death. Two popular ones are the Harvard Guidelines and Dr. Benjamin Boshes' criteria.

The Harvard Guidelines, developed in 1968, call for the observation of four basic areas for a period of twenty-four hours. If these four guidelines remain unchanged for that time, the patient is dead. Here are the guidelines as published in the *Journal of the American Medical Association:*

1. Unreceptivity and unresponsivity. There is a total unawareness of externally applied stimuli and inner need and complete unresponsiveness—our definition of irreversible coma. Even the most intensely painful stimuli evoke no vocal or other response, not even a groan, withdrawal of a limb, or quickening of respiration.
2. No movements or breathing. Observation covering a period of at least one hour by physicians is adequate to satisfy the criteria of no spontaneous muscular movements or spontaneous respiration or response to stimuli such as pain, touch, sound, or light.
3. No reflexes. Irreversible coma with abolition of central nervous system activity is evidenced in part by the absence of elicitable

reflexes. The pupil will be fixed and dilated and will not respond to a direct bright source of light.
4. Flat electroencephalogram. Of great confirmatory value is the flat or isoelectric EEG. We must assume that the electrodes have been properly applied, that the apparatus is functioning normally, and that the personnel in charge is competent.

It should be noted that these criteria are not applicable to patients who have evidence of having taken high doses of drugs (such as barbiturates) which depress the central nervous system or to those who have been exposed to very low temperatures of either air or water. These conditions often mimic death but can be reversed if detected in time and treated.

Dr. Benjamin Boshes directed a study of over five hundred dying patients over a period of four years. Out of the study evolved a new definition of death which he claims approaches 100 percent accuracy and can be determined in a period as short as thirty minutes. These are Dr. Boshes' criteria:

1. The patient is in a coma.
2. He is totally unresponsive.
3. Breathing has stopped for 15 minutes.
4. No brain activity is detected by EEG.
5. He has no reactions such as swallowing, coughing, and pupillary movement.
6. His pupils remain dilated.
7. His body temperature is over 90 degrees Farenheit.
8. There is no clinical or chemical evidence of drug intoxication.

The last two items guard against mistaking a victim of exposure to extreme cold or drug overdoses for dead, in the way that the Harvard guidelines allowed for these two situations.

The mammalian diving reflex (MDR) is an involuntary and potentially lifesaving response of the body when exposed to extreme cold. Circulation is cut off to all of the body except the most critical organs: heart, lungs, and brain. The lower temperature dramatically slows down metabolism so that oxygen requirements are likewise reduced, and the brain can survive on the minimal amount of oxygen remaining in the blood. This has happened to many drowning victims, some of whom were known to have been submerged in cold water for nearly forty minutes. Originally thought to be dead, several have been warmed and revived without any detectable brain damage. (Ordinarily the brain can survive only three to six minutes without oxygen before obvious damage is manifested.) The body temperature of an

MDR victim will be below 85 degrees, but above 60 degrees, below which there is little hope of recovery.

The appearance of death may also be confused with that of barbiturate intoxication. Hence, the safeguards to protect potential survivors from being declared dead in this half-hour period required for determination of death using Dr. Boshes' criteria.

Probably the most significant factor in the current controversy over the definition of death has been the advent of transplant surgery. If, for example, a dying patient is a potential donor of his heart for a transplant, the surgeons have only a short time (generally less than an hour) after the "moment" of death to remove the heart in a viable condition or to maintain a sufficient oxygen level in the blood to keep the heart viable until it can be removed from the body. It is, therefore, critical to be able to determine that point at which the death process is absolutely irreversible, but not yet completed.

It is easy to understand how we might be confused and prefer to detach ourselves from this dilemma of definitions. It is simpler to "never say die" and avoid the issue as much as possible. We would like to pretend that we're immortal and that all this doesn't directly concern us.

A Uniquely Contemporary Challenge

These are all issues new to us in the second half of the twentieth century. Never before did we have the capability to measure brain waves. Never before were we able to artificially maintain the vital functions of life. Never before have we successfully attempted to replace a diseased organ with a healthy one from another person. This generation is facing decisions and challenges for which there are no precedents in history, no record of achievements on which to base our judgments. It is both exciting and frightening to be a part of this proliferation of new knowledge and live-saving techniques.

The omnipresence of scientific discoveries has contributed to an atmosphere in which the public is seeking and receiving more information than ever before about all areas that potentially affect people's lives. We are no longer willing to swallow the medicines our doctors prescribe without knowing what they are, what they will do for us, and what the possible side effects could be. We want to know the nutrient content of packaged foods. We want to know about the hazards and potentials of nuclear energy. We want to be aware of what is going on in our fast-paced world and regain some sense of control amidst the dizzying changes. We are bravely breaking down barriers, eliminating taboos. The unspeakable is being spoken. The once timid, now bold questions are being answered. Sex has ceased to be a dirty word. And now, we want to understand even death better, too.

No other society in recorded history has had to face all of the conditions that now challenge us. We are in a truly unique position. It is no wonder that death finds us bewildered, frustrated, and perhaps reluctant companions. But we must be willing to search and learn and gain the confidence to overcome our many present hurdles. The fact that we are trying bodes well for us.

2

Death, the Ultimate Crisis

Hurricanes swept through six coastal villages this afternoon, leaving 30 persons dead, hundreds injured and homeless.

A thirty-three-year-old high school teacher was shot and killed by a bullet apparently intended for the governor, who received only minor injuries in the assassination attempt.

Saul Abernathy, great-grandfather, retired jeweler, dedicated member of the city council, passed away in his sleep early this morning at his home. He was 87.

Eloise delivered her baby this evening. He was, unfortunately, stillborn.

While horsing around on the eighteenth floor of the dormitory, Cameron Hathaway, 19, pushed in on the elevator door. It gave way and he fell down the shaft some twelve floors. He was killed instantly.

Cancer has claimed the life of Julie Swanson, age 52. She had been in and out of the hospital for nearly eleven years and the last year or so her condition deteriorated steadily. Pain and depression had been her constant companions for many weeks. She died precisely at noon.

Jay Kaufman, a brilliant young man with a promising future, was my debate partner in high school. He has been dead for twelve years, one of the soldiers who didn't make it back from Vietnam.

Richard Cory went home one night and put a bullet through his head.

Death has many different faces and yet just one. We perceive death in a certain way because of our particular experiences with death, our religious background, our philosophy of life, education, and even our "lot in life." Those who have an easy, comfortable life are more likely to view death as an evil than those who are enslaved and abused, who may see death as a blissful release. How we deal with death depends on all of these factors, on our personality, and the presence of supporting, helpful people.

Death is universal. We know that each of us will die. Yet each death has a meaning of its own and a unique influence on others. How we perceive death is probably a crucial factor in the way we live our lives. Indeed, many authors have pointed out that only because our lives are finite do they have meaning. Many times, individuals have been spurred by the death of another into a significant discovery or great accomplishment. We feel an urgency to do all we can, love all we can, "grab all the gusto" because we *don't* have forever. It is unfortunate that it often takes a tragedy, an untimely death to make us realize the truth of our mortality. If we all died only at a ripe old age, probably only a few of us would truly appreciate our lives and make the most of our potential. Perhaps what seem to us as senseless, violent, or early deaths are sometimes God's message to the survivors to make the most of our lives *now.*

We face many crises in our lives. They are all losses of some measure. We lose jobs, get divorced, move away from home, fail tests, burn our breakfast toast, and miss the bus. Learning to cope with these crises is necessary and desirable. Otherwise we would be crippled, helpless, unable to function in an environment beset with imperfections, not the least of which are often our own. Each time we suffer one of these losses and somehow adapt to it, learn from it, and grow from it, we gain some skills, some insight, and some confidence in our own ability to survive such events.

Death is probably the ultimate crisis, the ultimate loss. If lightning strikes your stereo system, you have lost some expensive equipment that will cost a lot to replace. If your pet runs away from home, you have lost a treasured companion. If the cleaners shrink your favorite sweater, you have lost a comfortable item of clothing. If your factory closes down, you have lost a means of procuring income. If your best friend dies, you have lost late night conversations, crazy parties, loving support and a source of approval. But if you are dying, you are losing your best friend, your job, your favorite sweater, your pet, your stereo *and* your second-best friend, your third-best friend, your home, your hobbies, your walks in the park, everything., It *is* an incredible adjustment to make, if granted the time to do it. Many of us wonder how we would handle our own death or even that of someone close to us. How will we react? What will we do?

The Stages of Dying

Our techniques for handling smaller crises will no doubt be our reserve when faced with a death. We call upon our experiences and our successes to help us through this difficult time. Dr. Elisabeth Kübler-Ross, a pioneer in modern death research, found what she called "the stages of dying." The stages are actually psychological responses to crisis which many of us experience many times in our lives, not just in life and death situations. She defines five stages: (1) shock and denial, (2) anger, (3) bargaining, (4) depression, and (5) acceptance.

When I first learned of the "stages," I recoiled, hating to pigeonhole people or tell them how they ought to act under any circumstances. After all, people are so different and, as the Indians say, we should not judge our brother until we have walked for two moons in his moccasins. I was relieved when I learned more about Kübler-Ross and her stages. Her primary observation was that many, but *not* all people often respond to the knowledge of a terminal diagnosis (their own or a loved one's) or the death of a loved one with some or all of these fairly typical reactions. Other authors have found three stages or four responses, or have otherwise labeled what are essentially similar although not identical conclusions. But because Kübler-Ross's contribution to this field of study is so remarkable and her work is probably best known, I like to use her stages of dying for purposes of illustration.

Before actually discussing these stages, I want to emphasize several points. First, although it is quite normal for a person to go through these stages, it is not necessary. There are many persons who, because of their backgrounds, personality, or beliefs are at ease with the idea of death and have already accomplished the mental and emotional work of the responses described. Second, the sequence of the stages may vary considerably from person to person. Some stages may be repeated or omitted entirely. That is not to say the person who repeats or omits stages is handling death better or worse than another person. We each cope in our own unique way. Third, our discussion of these stages is *not* a prescription of how persons should act under these circumstances. Our purpose here is to gain some insight and understanding of how people (perhaps ourselves) may feel and act when faced with impending death. Fourth, it is hoped that the obvious application of this information to our daily existence will help us to appreciate the similarity in our reactions to all losses, large and small. This realization may make us aware that having survived a myriad of lesser crises, our resources will get us through this most dramatic and troublesome loss of all. Let us now consider these stages of dying.

Stage One: Shock and denial   Our frequent initial reaction to unwanted news is simply to "say it isn't so." If the police arrive at the door to tell us a loved one has been in an auto accident, we say, "No, couldn't be. My sister was just here an hour ago. You must have misread the license plate number. Or maybe someone borrowed her car. She's always loaning it out to her friends." Or, if the doctor tells us we have cancer, we're sure the x-ray department got the films mixed up or the lab tests were wrong, or the doctor's a quack, anyway. Upon opening a grade report with an ugly "F" opposite a needed course, you assume an error was made by the computer, or the teacher mistakenly put another student's grade by your name, or that one page of the final exam came unfastened and it didn't get graded. When a spouse asks for a divorce, we think it is some kind of macabre joke. Sure you've argued a lot, but things aren't *that* bad. It's just the anger or the liquor talking. Our minds seem to try to protect us from this awful information by fabricating a way out of it, or even if at a loss for a fabrication, we simply refuse to believe it. Sometimes we are buffered by a state of shock which temporarily separates us from reality. It gives us some time to absorb the emotional insult and begin to adjust to its impact.

Denial, when it occurs, may last for a few moments, a few days or months or it may never go away. Some days, we may be able to deal quite openly with the impending death or divorce or the loss of three semester hours, while the next week we may be unable to face it again. We all have good days, when we feel strong and in control, and bad days when we are "down" and feel impotent and ill-at-ease. Surely you can recall one of your own "down" days, when you were already upset about one or several things going on in your life, or perhaps you simply didn't feel good. If someone walked in the room and brought up the fact that you are expected to arrange a program for the club meeting or fix the leak in the basement or bake a cake for the fundraiser at school, you would probably kick him, at least mentally, or ignore the intrusion completely. At that moment, you must deny those particular responsibilities, and you cannot or will not deal with them. There are other demands and difficulties claiming your attention, and anything else is overload and must wait. Our egos can accept only so much assault. Denial is a way of maintaining some sense of integrity. Otherwise we might just distintegrate ("dis"-"integrity").

It is not so terrible, then, to think that a dying patient, or the spouse or child of a dying patient, might be able to freely discuss a will, funeral plans, and cremation on one day and yet another day be talking of a trip to Mexico next spring or of planting fruit trees as though the present illness is only a temporary inconvenience and life will soon return to normal. When denial has been conquered, some consider a return to it a regression, but I see it as merely the human psyche wielding its remarkable powers of self-protection in an over-whelming situation.

Stage Two: Anger   After the initial denial subsides, and we can confront—intellectually if not emotionally—the terrible truth, it is quite common to become angry and bitter. Why did this have to happen to me (or my brother, or my baby)? I am a good person, an upstanding citizen, a devoted family person. It shouldn't happen to folks like us. There are derelicts and criminals who have earned some punishment, but why me? The object of the anger may be the disease or the faulty brakes or God, who, after all, could have prevented this anyway, couldn't He?

But yelling at God or a disease or a set of brakes offers little emotional satisfaction. When we have been hurt, so terribly hurt, our gut reaction is to want to hurt back, to retaliate for the wrong done us. Brakes, diseases, and even God, however, provide no visible response to our outrage. So we more often vent our anger on innocent, vulnerable people who will respond with hurt and confusion and misunderstanding, mirroring our own internal chaos. We are rewarded with a sign of the power of our words at a time when we feel generally powerless. It is small and negative, but reassuring evidence that we are still alive and capable of eliciting responses from others. We may berate the nurse for imaginary lapses in care, verbally attack our visitors for coming too early or too late or for not bringing the proper magazine, or accuse our family of avoiding us, of not really caring. Probably none of it is true. But because there is so much bitterness and hostility pent up inside, it is necessary to seek out ways to release this vicious emotion.

Most often, once given the opportunity to exercise this anger, the stage will quickly pass. Therefore, it is helpful to know that, although the storm is unpleasant and difficult to deal with, it is usually purposeful and short-lived. There is a possibility of recurring anger, as the disease and disability progress. The mere fact that others are healthy, can come and go as they please, can make plans for a new home, and live the usual allotted life span can arouse jealousy and anguish and renewed hostility over our own frailty while they seem to flaunt the vigor we once took for granted. To be able to understand the anger of others in this situation and learn not to take the verbal assaults personally is, I feel, one of the most beneficial aspects of learning about the stages of dying. It would be so easy to take the anger personally, to be truly hurt and thereafter to be constantly cautious, have our guard up and never really be able to share real feelings again. But to understand the reason for the anger, that it is normal, and to take it in stride can facilitate the future relationship with a person who probably desperately needs that relationship.

Bear in mind, too, the anger that arises from the everyday frustrations of living. I find myself venting anger at my family for totally unrelated problems for which they had no responsibility. We all do it occasionally. We're planning a dinner party and the washing machine overflows, the mailman brings an overdraft notice from the bank, and the grocery is out of fresh artichokes *and* asparagus. So I shout at my sweet five-year-old for dropping an ice cube, an otherwise benign event grown disproportionately annoying only because of the other pressures and disappointments I have endured that day. Fatigue and stress frequently masquerade as anger. Perhaps a little more understanding of our own as well as others' day-to-day anger, would be valuable for relationships, too.

Stage Three: Bargaining Once we can face the truth and have overcome most of our rage, we begin to try to figure out ways out of the situation. We make bargains, or attempt them, anyway. Sometimes physicians receive generous or even bizarre offers in return for life-saving efforts. But realistically speaking, doctors are going to do everything they can to make you well, anyway. They don't want their patients dying. It's bad for their reputation. So promises of bequests to medical clinics, testimonials, or free cars aren't likely to persuade a doctor to do anything more. He is probably already using every available medication or treatment.

Most bargains, then, are made with God. "If You will save my life, I'll become a missionary." "Spare my husband and I promise to teach Sunday school." "God, let our child live and we'll give ten percent of our income to the church forever." Occasionally, a bargainer takes his own offer seriously and, if his prayers are answered, follows through. A young father in the Phillipines prayed for the recovery of his small son, promising to personally reenact the crucification every Good Friday in return for God's blessing. The boy did regain his health. And for years thereafter the father arranged, on each Good Friday, to have his hands and feet nailed to a large wooden cross and have the cross erected to remind the world of Christ's sacrifice. This parent's faith, concern, and gratitude are unquestionably genuine if perhaps a little dramatic.

The majority of bargains made are probably far less grandiose, although this is largely a private matter and it is impossible to know the content of others' prayers. It is safe to say there are few such blatant examples of people keeping their bargains with God. In fact, many of us, once granted our heartfelt plea, tend to forget our end of the deal. We rationalize: "I was really getting better, anyway," or "God wouldn't have wanted me to leave my sick mother and move to Africa." In the movie *The End*, Burt Reynolds portrayed a man with a terminal diagnosis. Despondent, the character swims out into the ocean to die, only to change his mind several hundred yards from shore. Suddenly yearning to enjoy whatever of his life is left, he begs for God to give him the energy to make it back to land, promising everything he owns in return. He succeeds in swimming several yards towards his goal, still pleading for strength, but decreasing his offering to 80 percent. Still closer in, the bargain is further reduced to 50 percent, then lower and lower until he finally reaches the beach.

Perhaps it is human nature to risk anything when the stakes are high and the chances are slim, and for our fervor to diminish as the situation improves. Occasionally patients will bargain for "privileges" short of a complete cure. For instance, "I'll agree to these tests (or new treatments) if I can be out of the hospital in time for my daughter's graduation. Just grant me this much time and I'll do anything you say."

Bargaining is a frequent component of other crisis situations. The couple having marital difficulties often indulges in bargaining, also known as compromise. "If you'll stop playing golf every Saturday, I promise to spend less on new clothes." "I'll stop making fun of your friends if you'll try to help more to keep this place picked up." The student with a failing grade may call the professor and offer to do some extra assignments or write a paper in order to bring up his grade. So this, too, is a familiar coping technique that probably all of us have used at one time or another.

In a terminal illness situation, however, the bargaining stage is usually brief, probably because it is ultimately viewed as a futile effort. Even those who believe in miracles would likely argue that God is more concerned with the strength of one's faith and the sincerity of one's entreaty than with the "deal" we have to offer.

Stage Four: Depression   Perhaps it is the cold realization of our absolute lack of control of the situation that really gets us down. When we can no longer deny our dilemma, our rage has usurped much of our energy, and our bargains have gotten us nowhere, we are finally left with the sad truth. The reality of the magnitude of our loss begins to sink in. We become introspective, pondering the meaning of our lives, the wasted days, the mistakes, the joys which will now never be. We begin to grieve before the death. This is preparatory grief (also called anticipatory grief). We feel lonely, sorry for ourselves, sorry for our loved ones, tired, and anguished. We find little comfort in any words of comfort offered to us by well-intentioned friends and relatives. It seems that life is a cruel, bitter joke, void of any happiness or purpose. The dejection may be overwhelming at times.

Persons experiencing this preparatory grief may be very withdrawn and communicate little or none of their major concerns. It is a very personal agony and therefore very difficult for another to understand fully. It is frustrating for the observers as well, who want to help, and yet are being shunned or ignored. Hopefully, with time and patience the depression will lift as the individual gains new insights, understandings, and perspectives never before considered.

Of course, depression is hardly restricted to dying patients and their loved ones. All losses result in periods of sadness, some lasting longer than others. Lyrics of many contemporary songs are devoted to the pain of dissolution of a love relationship, such as "Breaking Up Is Hard To Do." A woman who wants to have children may become depressed upon learning she is once again, not pregnant. A young boy may be devastated at being told he has been cut from the basketball team. Parents may feel quite lonesome and useless when their youngest child finally leaves home. We may potentially experience any of a variety of such happenings every day, and we all have experienced and recovered from some measure of depression. It is good to remember the recoveries, for they do come.

The time required to accomplish the tasks of the depression stage is highly individual. It may also be a recurrent stage, as a disease progresses or other factors in the person's life change. For those wishing to help, it is a time to be especially certain to offer love, support, and reassurance without being aggressive or suggesting unwelcome pat answers. Just let them know you care.

Stage Five: Acceptance Acceptance is being comfortable with the concept of our own mortality. Our physical existence is unquestionably finite. None of us will be in this earthly body forever. As obvious and universal as this is, the number of people who have difficulty accepting their own mortality is incredible. Most of us simply delay consideration of the issue until absolutely necessary, but even the healthiest and saintliest among us are just as mortal as the terminally ill and the criminal. The terminally ill patient and the condemned criminal have, perhaps, a more urgent incentive to think through these ideas. But acceptance is a goal anyone may achieve, regardless of health or imminence of death.

Acceptance of the inevitability of death is not, however, the same as being resigned to an early death or giving up all hope of recovery. We can come to terms with the idea that our earthly treasures are not everlasting and still seek to enjoy and appreciate them for as long as possible. Acceptance can quite peacefully coexist with hope for a miracle or the discovery of a new cure. I can accept the fact that it is highly improbable my lottery ticket will be drawn as the winner in the million-dollar sweepstakes. But I can fervently hope that will be the outcome and derive great joy from fantasizing about how I might spend my new fortune. I know a young woman who has accepted the doctor's judgment that she will never have children. But she still hopes that he is wrong, or that a new medical discovery will make it possible for her to become pregnant and bear a child. Hope springs eternal, even in the breast of a man who recognizes the imminence of his own death.

Kübler-Ross has been criticized by a few theologians for suggesting that acceptance of death is a desirable goal. Among these critics is Roy Branson, who contends that acceptance of death is a denial of the Christian belief that death is not a part of the rhythm of nature but rather a consequence of sin. "The Christian . . . will expect to find the dying person rejecting the prospect of death, angry at its destructive finality, depressed at the loss of friends and family." It seems Branson would have us all fighting death to the bitter end, and abhors the "peace and tranquility" inherent in the acceptance of death as a natural phenomenon. I do not pretend to be a student of theology, but I cannot agree with his position. Indeed, I have dear Christian friends who anticipate their eventual deaths as a graduation day, as a transition from their earthly life to one of eternal joy in the presence of the Lord. Those who view death as final and total annihilation are less likely to reach "acceptance" than those who believe in some form of after-life. But even those who see death as the end can be motivated by that belief to make the most of their hours of life.

I prefer to align myself with Robert Neale's suggestion that denying death is, in fact, denying life, and that accepting death is accepting life. A vacation that has no end, no purpose, ceases to be a vacation. We would become, eventually, bored and fatigued on such a pointless, infinite journey. It is because vacations are brief relaxing respites from the work-a-day world that we so enjoy and treasure them. Only by realizing that the holiday will end do we make every effort to squeeze as much joy as possible into each hour. Only by realizing that life has an end are we driven to use and appreciate every day and every pleasure and every opportunity afforded us, "for we will not pass this way again." If we each had an eternity to accomplish our life's work, what would be the rush? Most likely, many of us would get nothing done.

Decathexis

When a patient has reached the stage of acceptance, he is able to deal calmly and openly with the idea of his death and anticipates a certain peace and release as the hour of death draws near. As death approaches, many people experience a gradual withdrawal from and loss of interest in concerns and relationships that once held great importance for them. Kübler-Ross calls this *decathexis*. It is derived from an outmoded psychology term, *cathexis*, which refers to the attachment of emotional energy to persons, ideas, and objects we find important in our lives. It is not a measurable phenomenon, but is useful in helping to understand how we behave. I "cathect" a lot of energy to my husband, my children, my home. Most of my emotional energy is connected to their needs and the joy I feel in meeting those needs and having them meet mine. I also cathect some energy to my work and derive a measure of confidence and satisfaction from that part of my life. Vacuuming the house, buying groceries, and so on, also demand some emotional energy, though far down on the list. There is a hierarchy, then, of emotional involvement. Some persons and things are understandably more important to us than others, and these are the strongest attachments, the ones we cling to most. This is often a changing hierarchy, though, as we go through life. We may buy something new and exciting—perhaps an automobile. For a while, this new car is uppermost in our thoughts. Weekly car-washing and polishing may provide us with great satisfaction. After a time, the newness wears off and other interests divert our attention. Our obsession with the car dwindles.

When my husband and I were newly married and living in a town-house, we bought a beautiful 2-½ acre lake-front lot. We had a fantastic notion that someday we would "grow up and get rich" and build our dream home there overlooking the water. For several years, we frequently visited the site, picked the wild raspberries and imagined how our lovely home would look, with the sunset reflecting on the lake. The time came when the townhouse no longer suited our growing family, so we ebulliently made an appointment with our contractor. The estimate of the building costs for our dream house would have staggered our bank account. We then decided to build another home to get us through the interim, still clinging to our plans to eventually move to the lake. As we became involved in making decisions about this actual construction—light fixtures, wallpaper, floor coverings, and all that—we found ourselves becoming more and more attached to it. When we finally moved in, we knew we were "home." A call to our realtor put our lake lot in his listings. We had gradually but definitely decathected from that lake lot and dream and put that energy into our new and lovely, if somewhat more modest home.

Actually the decathexis was gradual and unintentional but very necessary for our emotional well-being. It would have been destructive and painful to cling to an idea that was beyond our reach.

Often, but *not* always, when someone is dying, they seem to go through a similar process. Because it is so painful to leave when they have such close attachments, they withdraw the emotional energy once devoted to such relationships and interests and begin to apply it to the task at hand, that of dying. It may follow a very systematic "reverse hierarchy" pattern. A patient will ask to see certain friends, say a fond farewell and then wish to see them no more. A businessman who once insisted on reading *The Wall Street Journal* every day announces he wants the papers removed from his room and refuses to look at any others that are brought in to cheer him up. The children are called in for a final visit, then the spouse. The patient is gradually taking back his emotional energy to help him in his final journey. He is at peace and ready for his death.

This withdrawal is often misinterpreted by family and friends, who feel rejected and concerned that their loved one seems to have lost all interest in life. A middle-aged nurse who took my course was awestruck when we discussed decathexis. She said, "I wish we had known about this two years ago when my father was dying. He refused to see my mother the last two weeks of his life. They had been married sixty-one years and were very close. Mom was crushed. She wondered what she had done to anger him so, to make him shut her out at this critical time. I only wish we had known. It would have been so much easier for her to accept. To think he didn't want to see her just because he loved her so much it would hurt too much to leave with that love intact."

Sometimes, it is the family who decathect from the patient, especially in long-term illnesses. They may be so frustrated and overwhelmed watching their loved one suffer that they just can't take it anymore. They begin to find reasons to stay away from the hospital, establish new time-consuming commitments, or become involved in projects that take their minds off of this terribly painful part of their lives. In time, they find that the patient, once so intimate and important a part of their existence has become merely an obligation, and visits are reduced in frequency and poignancy, if not stopped altogether. The patient feels bewildered and abandoned, if she is not also decathecting.

Decathexis is similar to the other stages in that it happens to many persons but is not a universal experience. When it does happen, we can probably handle it better if we are aware that it is apparently a frequent and normal human phenomenon. It is also frequent and normal for dying patients to want their loved ones with them, offering emotional support and physical contact even at the moment of death. It shouldn't be too surprising that there are many normal ways of dealing with death, just as there are many normal ways of dealing with almost any life crisis.

Many Faces and Yet Just One

Death is perceived as a tragedy, a blessing, a fact, a mystery, an ending, a beginning, a crisis, an answered prayer, senseless, purposeful, enlightening, confusing, nothingness, peace, transition, agony, release. You could probably add many perceptions to the list. The point is that our view of a death is colored by our perspective, and experiences, and by the particular details of that death. The death of an unknown foreign soldier thousands of miles away elicits in us a reaction different from our reaction to the death of our 93-year-old uncle or the death of our five-year-old daughter. While death is the great equalizer and happens to us all, it happens in different ways, at different times in our life. There is no one right way to handle this ultimate crisis. We simply do our best.

The following letter vividly illustrates many of the ideas discussed in this chapter—vivid because it comes from the heart of one about to die. It was written by a young man thirty years old, who was engaged to a lovely student enrolled in my course on death and dying. They had learned he was dying, but thought he had at least several months to live. He died two weeks after the term started. He wrote her this letter only two hours before his death, suddenly aware it was happening sooner than they had expected. At his request, she shared the letter with me and others, and now we share it with you. I think you will agree it is a beautiful gift to his bereaved fiancée and for us all.

Thurs., Dec. 12, 1974

Dear Ellen,

My time here is almost over, I don't have much to do anymore. I just watch some TV, read a little and sleep a lot. I didn't think it would come so soon, but it kind of sneaks up on you before you're ready. Ellen, there's so much more I want to do! I want to marry you and raise our babies, but most of all I want to grow old and die old. This can't happen now, I'm not ready. I feel that you're more ready than I am, even though you say you can't bear it, I know you will.

There are times when I lay here at night and wish you were here with me, but I want you to stay where you are. I know you'll stay at school because it's best for you. But more often there are the times when I wish we had never met, because it's so hard to leave you.

Last time you wrote you asked me to tell you what it's like—I'll try the best I can. It's easier for me to talk about now, since it's so close. It's not scary anymore, but it makes me angry that God would take me away from here when I've just found you. Still, I want His will, not mine. I can say that easily, His will, not mine, there's still the anger, but I know God understands. It doesn't hurt, but it is a little hard to breathe at times. Susan is writing this for me, she'll probably call you later. But I don't want you here, until it's over. I know you don't understand, but it's easier for me this way, I won't have to see you cry, and it will also be easier for you. We've said everything that had to be said, I'm only sorry we can't do all we wanted to do.

Most of the time I think about what I could have done with my life, how I wasted so many years. I don't think I really began to live until I met you and Christ. Some of the time I spend thinking about the future. I know for sure that there's a heaven and that I'll be there, but still I regret having to leave here. This world may be great, but heaven is a thousand times better. I have to keep telling myself that.

I don't know that I'm explaining dying—I don't know that anyone can—I only know that to me it means leaving you, but it also means meeting Jesus.

I think when you read this you'll cry, but then you'll rejoice for me, because I'll be where I was always meant to be.

You've said you can't live without me, many times, but now you have to—you've got no choice. Your whole life is ahead of you, don't waste one second of it.

Dying is hard for me, but it's even harder for you I think.

Try not to regret anything, there's a purpose for everything that happens.

I've said all I can. This letter is very personal, but I want you to share it, because maybe someone else faces the same thing. No one should have to face death alone—you and I have Jesus to lean on, but there's at least one person who has no one, maybe you can help them.

Be happy for me Ellen, deep inside I know you are happy. Mourn your loss, but rejoice for my gain.

Be happy Ellen, finish your education, get married, have babies, whatever you decide is right. But don't ever take your life for granted, because it's never really yours—it's only a loan for 50 or 60 years, and sometimes only 30.

I love you,
Bruce

3

Death and the Medical Milieu

Because so many of us get sick before we die, the process of dying is, for many people, inextricably a part of the medical milieu. Hospitals, doctors, nurses, diagnostic tests, medications, treatments, waiting for test results, surgery, and visiting hours pervade our lives and intrude on our private space, physically and emotionally. Dramatic and rapid changes in the care of dying patients and their families have greatly improved the way these patients are approached and helped. But we need much more change. A growing public and professional awareness of the needs of the dying will no doubt nurture these advances.

Sharing the Bad News

One of the greatest dilemmas in medical care is whether or not to inform a patient of his terminal diagnosis. When individuals are polled as to whether or not they would want to be told if they had a fatal illness, the vast majority respond in the affirmative. Yet physicians display a terrible reluctance to share the bad news. Whose life is it, anyway? When such a diagnosis is found and the doctor opts for disclosure, it is often the patient's family, not the patient, who is the first to hear. Together, the family and doctor will likely conspire to protect the patient from what they anticipate will be too overwhelming a revelation. There is a conspiracy of silence or facade of deceit, which never allows any truly honest communication between patient and family again.

The bitter irony is that most dying patients don't need to be told. They seem to have some inner psychophysiological awareness of their true condition. But they are afraid the revelation will be too overwhelming to their loved ones, or sensing they already know but have not spoken of it, presume it is too painful a topic and so avoid it, too. In *The Death of Ivan Illych,* Leo Tolstoy describes the patient's resentment of his participation in this mutual deceit. Illych senses that he is dying and that his family knows it. But the family pretends that he will recover and so to avoid an unpleasant confrontation, he continues his role in the pretense. He yearns to blurt out the truth, to watch their startled faces, to destroy once and for all this aggravating artificial complacence. But he lacks the energy to do it.

Modern families, often doubting their own ability to confront the issue openly with the patient, rationalize they are doing their loved one a great service by sparing her the task of actively facing her own imminent mortality. Many physicians, too, proclaim patients get too "depressed" when told they are dying, and doctors are usually eager to go along with the family's plan of noncommunication. But the wisdom of this particular deception is questionable at best. There may be a few individuals who would truly prefer not to be aware of having a fatal illness, and if told would probably continue in a state of denial. But it is so difficult to deal with a lack of knowledge. The anxiety of *not* knowing, for most people, is most likely harder to handle than the truth.

As a student nurse in the Army, I lived and went to school in Washington, D.C. Because of our enlisted military status, my friends and I were able to fly free on virtually any Air Force plane, on a stand-by basis. So, on Friday afternoon, many of us rushed out to Andrews Air Force Base, hoping for a seat on a flight home, or to the mountains, or to visit a fiancé, or wherever, prepared to pay for commercial transportation back again, if necessary. We would sit and wait for hour upon hour, wondering if we would soon be off on an adventurous or romantic journey or whether we'd be spending another weekend in the dorm. The waiting and the anxiety were awful. If they could have just told us when we got there that no seats were available, we would have been disappointed, but at least in a position to make other plans. Having to wait it out was sometimes almost unbearable.

One summer, later in my schooling, while working in a hospital office, I received a Thursday afternoon call expressing some concern over the chest x-ray the hospital had taken as part of my employee physical. The doctor wanted to see a previous x-ray to compare with the new one. Then he wanted to see me the following Thursday (the usual day for employee physicals). It might as well have been a century away. I arranged to have the old film sent to the hospital and agonized the entire week about what was wrong with me. Maybe I had lung cancer. Maybe my heart was too big, or too small. Maybe I was dying. Maybe I had tuberculosis. Why didn't they call and say everything was okay? My medical-student boyfriend and I pondered all the possibilities and made various contingency plans, depending on the diagnosis. The pressure and anxiety were almost crippling. Without knowing what the situation was, we didn't know how to respond. Even bad news, I thought, would be better than no news. At least I would have a chunk of reality on which to base a reaction. Floundering helpless in a sea of ignorance is sheer torture. We always imagine the worst. As it turned out, I was fine. Hallelujah. But for many patients who aren't fine, they are left floundering with ambiguous statements like "serious condition," "doing all we can," and "Don't worry, we have the most sophisticated treatment available."

Why, indeed, should a person be denied information so personal, so intimate, so critical about his own life? There is no such inclination to refuse to tell a woman she is pregnant. Of course, she needs time to prepare, to make space in her life for this child, to rearrange career priorities, if necessary. It would be preposterous to withhold the truth until the swelling abdomen left us no choice but to admit it. If a patient has a hearing loss because of an infection, do we simply talk louder and hope he won't notice? Would it be fair to deny a brittle diabetic, whose condition could easily break into a coma, knowledge of her condition because she never liked shots? How absurd. The information will probably be unwelcome, but with time we can learn to adjust to even the most devastating circumstances.

What possible reason could inspire the refusal of this opportunity for final adjustment, to tie up our loose ends, write those important letters, make decisions about our own care, compose a will, make peace with God? I believe we piteously underestimate the power of the human spirit to cope with these tasks. This is our last chance to do it right. Let's have it.

Let's consider two sorrowful examples where this conspiracy of silence did far more harm than good. In the first case, a man in his late seventies had surgery in the summer for a swelling in the abdomen. He was sent home, told to take his water pills and not to worry. When he died half a year later, the surgeon confided to a family member that he hadn't expected the old man to survive more than two weeks after the surgery the previous summer. This was the *first* time the doctor had mentioned anything about the patient's true prognosis. It was probably brought up at his death to impress and comfort the family with the old man's sheer will to live. But it was too late. All those months he was losing weight, his strength was fading, and the family was convinced the water pills were responsible. They all knew he was terribly ill, but kept expecting him to come around, pull out of it. How much better it could have been for all of them to have had the chance to talk openly and honestly about what was happening.

In the second case, the family was aware of the diagnosis, but chose to keep the truth from the patient and her spouse until just a few weeks before the death. The news, when it finally came, nearly overwhelmed them. Having been married fifty-five years, the husband was accustomed to a tidy house and warm meals precisely on time. The last year of her life, he had chided his wife for her laziness and slovenly habits. He couldn't understand why she had changed so much, why she kept losing weight even though her appetite seemed good enough. When they were told she was, in fact, dying of cancer, he was stricken with unbearable guilt for his insensitivity and criticism of her, when she had truly lacked the strength to do those routine tasks. The husband spent those last weeks lavishing attention upon his loved one, attempting to compensate for the harsh words and lack of understanding of the past year. But it was not enough. For a long time after her death, he continued to bear a heavy burden of guilt, a guilt which could have been avoided had he only known the truth about his wife's condition. The children, in their supposed compassion and wisdom denied their parents those last months of closeness, of sharing. Instead, there was confusion and resentment. What a bitter gift.

There are, of course, appropriate and inappropriate ways to convey such weighty words. This is one of those skills doctors are supposed to "pick up on their own." Medical school curricula are far too crowded to include a session on handing out terminal diagnoses with grace. Consequently, we are greatly at the mercy of our doctor's personality and past experiences when, if she is honest enough to share the truth, she calls us in for the conference. It may be just a phone call, "The tests came back positive. You have cancer of the pancreas. Call my receptionist for an appointment and we'll schedule your surgery." Or if we're lucky, it may be a well-planned disclosure, with discussion of treatment options and time for answering questions.

One of my students, herself a health professional, wrote a paper about her own recent discovery of an unfavorable diagnosis.

"Doctors make me angry, too. They say things that can affect a person's life with such lack of compassion. There it was, black on white, no ifs, ands or buts. Nobody to say, 'I understand. Let me know if I can help,' only a passing 'It was lucky I could squeeze you in today,' as he handed me a bill for $55, payable on leaving."

Dr. Howard Hogshead, in an article titled "The Art of Delivering Bad News" in the anthology *Psychosocial Care of the Dying Patient.* said, " . . . perhaps there is no right way, only varying degrees of wrong ways." He gives nine suggestions for physicians to consider when faced with this task, with the hope that the disclosure will be handled in a compassionate and supportive fashion so that if the patient reacts with depression or unbridled emotion, at least he will not feel isolated or left totally to his own resources.

The truth is that in many cases, rather than the depression, self-pity, and sorrow that we might expect the knowledge of a terminal diagnosis to elicit, ample time for assimilation may produce quite the opposite effect. Orville Kelly (who founded the organization Make Today Count), Lois Jaffe, and Charles Wertenbaker all expressed a certain heightened awareness and appreciation of life after reconciling themselves to their fatal cancers. All three have said they truly enjoyed life more after being told their diagnosis than they ever had before. Also, many patients rally when they realize what they are fighting and direct their strength and energy toward the conquest of their disease. This strength might never be tapped in the conspiracy of silence. We are all terminal. If each of us could come to terms with this today, how much more we all might get out of life.

Doctors and Nurses and Death

Sometimes it is difficult to understand the workings of a hospital ward. It may seem that the staff is so cool and efficient, just when we need warmth and time. While this situation is changing for the better, nurses and physicians have traditionally avoided dying patients, going in their rooms only when absolutely necessary. Until recently, it was rare for the subject of dying patients to be discussed at all in doctors' or nurses' training. In fact, medical and nursing students are often admonished, "Don't get involved with your patients!" Approaching a patient when simple human presence may be more comforting than any medication or treatment that could be offered is, ironically, professionally threatening to medical personnel.

Persons who pursue careers in nursing and medicine train for years to learn all about anatomy and physiology, chemistry, diseases, and, most importantly, the methods for treating or curing the ills of the human body. They receive innumerable satisfactions as patients get better, return to their jobs, resume a normal life. It makes all those years at the books worthwhile. But now, here is a patient who challenges the healer's purview. The terminal patient is, by his very existence, a reminder of the limitations of medicine and those who pursue its practice. It must seem the ultimate put-down when a scrubwoman can offer such a person more with her listening and caring than can the physician, whose bag is essentially empty for this patient.

Viewed from this perspective it is not so hard to understand why doctors and nurses might stay away from terminal patients as much as possible. A salesman prefers to spend time with his good customers and will eventually give up on the recalcitrant retailer. None of us would seek out situations which remind us of our failures, our weaknesses. A doctor may well contend that his time would be better spent tending to those patients who have a chance of recovering.

There is, however, another perspective, one that is finally being presented in nursing and medical schools and hospital in-service programs nationwide. There is a heightened awareness of the special needs of dying patients. Health care professionals are being taught ways to meet those needs without compromising their life-saving ideals. They learn new, appropriate skills for dealing with dying patients when the healer's skills are no longer of value. Some hospitals have hired special nurses as "patient advocates" whose job it is to see to those important, but not necessarily medical, personal concerns of dying patients. Joy Ufema held the first such position at Harrisburg Hospital in Pennsylvania. She has since opened her own hospice. Also, nursing students are finally being taught to view a patient as a "whole person" and not the "gallbladder in 207." The interrelationship of physical, emotional, and spiritual health is being more widely recognized, especially in innovative programs like the hospice movement. This wholistic approach to medical care will no doubt have far-reaching benefits for all patients, whether or not they are near death.

However approached, the stress of working with life and death every day can get to be unbearable. Hence, the rule, "Don't get involved with your patients." If you establish relationships with all of these people, only to lose them eventually, it can become a terrible strain. So, many doctors and nurses who work in critical areas such as intensive and coronary care, oncology, and neurosurgery, soon learn not to care too much. Function efficiently, do everything correct medically, but don't spend any unnecessary time chit-chatting with the patient, learning about her daughter in Schenectady who is about to have the first grandchild in the family, or why Hesse is her favorite author, or about the time she got stranded in the Rockies for a week waiting for the car to be fixed. Knowing these little details of a patient's life can make it much harder on the care-giver when the patient dies. And remember, this is *not* the nurse's only dying patient. Getting to know patients well and watching them die is emotionally painful.

As a means of self-protection, nurses may deny the emotional needs of the patient. They may deny even more than that. As a naive young nurse on a pulmonary ward, I was surprised by the brusque business-like attitude of the older nurses who had been there for years. About 90 percent of our patients had lung cancer. The prognosis for most of them was about six months to live following diagnosis. Consequently, we saw many patients dying. If these older nurses had a few free minutes, did they try to do something special for a patient? Of course not. They went to the staff restroom and smoked a cigarette! Talk about blatant denial. Here they were surrounded by dying people, most of whom probably paved their way to the hospital with cigarette butts, and they had to run off for a smoke every chance they got. I was appalled and internally quite hostile about it for a long time. In the first place, they weren't giving the best patient care they could have. In the second place, they were purposely and frequently exposing themselves to the same poison that caused most of our patients' fatal illnesses.

My hostility has diminished over the years and I can almost understand their behavior now. These nurses had been there, day after day, year after year, watching patients die, new patients come in, only to see the cycle repeated time and again. Then I walked onto the floor, all shiny and idealistic, unscarred by this cycle of attachment and loss, ready to right the wrongs of the world. And I left there for another position after several months, really too soon to be dissuaded from my ideals of good nursing. Perhaps that is the answer, or at least part of it. Maybe we should give nurses a break from such demanding duties. After a few months on oncology (cancer treatment) transfer them to the outpatient clinic for a while. They deserve an emotional respite from the trauma of consistent confrontation with death.

Physicians, unfortunately, would find it much more difficult to change positions for a while. Their speciality training is so intensive and consuming that they either have no desire to trade practices or would find it simply impractical to do so. Would you want your neurosurgeon to be temporarily replaced by an obstetrician? Not if it happened to be the week you needed brain surgery! Because a doctor chooses and excels at his speciality, even enjoys its challenges and successes, does not mean he is immune to stresses anyone would face in his position. Just because a chef loves to cook, it doesn't mean he doesn't sweat in a hot kitchen.

There are, of course, some sensitive and caring physicians who have made their own peace with death and take the personal time and effort to help patients who are struggling with the imminence of the inevitable. In his *Hope: A Loss Survived*, Richard Meryman discussed just such a satisfying relationship that he and his terminally ill wife shared with one of her doctors. The doctor's consistent openness and honesty seemed to bolster his wife's ego at a time when self-confidence was often precarious. The doctor had the honorable attitude of approaching his patients as competent persons who had the capability and the right to know what was happening to themselves and to participate actively in the treatment, rather than assume they were little helpless lambs who wouldn't understand the truth, anyway.

Physicians may also find indirect ways to talk about a patient's approaching death. I especially like the story of an Iowa physician who, upon entering his patient's room, was appalled to see that a once lovely plant was withering and dry. When questioned about it, the woman responded. "Why should I take care of the plant? I'm going to die, anyway. Why not let the plant die, too?" The perceptive young doctor walked over and examined the plant. "Well, we would have to take off this section, and that section, but if we watered it and put it in the window it could still be quite lovely and give us a lot of enjoyment." The dying woman, who had lately been quite despondent and shown no interest in anything, must have sensed that he was talking about her own life, as well as that of the plant. She did salvage the remainder of both of them and went home to enjoy a few more months with her family and plant before returning to the hospital to die. Those few months were a precious gift from a doctor who cared enough to take the time to share some of his philosophy with his patients.

Doctors are people, too. We tend to idolize them, thinking they are somehow less vulnerable than the rest of us. But they, too, are members of the same society, this society that denies death, glorifies youth, ignores old age. As a cross-section of our culture, they share our fears and anxieties about death. Recent studies have shown that, compared with members of other professions, medical doctors and medical students fear death more. Perhaps that is why they choose to become the preservers of life. For whatever reason, they have selected careers which bring them into contact with death fairly often. This, combined with the other stresses of medicine, puts doctors at the top of all professions when it comes to burnout, alcoholism, marital problems, and suicide. If physicians allowed themselves to be compassionate and involved with every patient, we might lose even more of them! Or perhaps, if they allowed themselves to express those emotions they deny, some of the tension would be dissipated.

Room 1

Lots of hospital wards have a "room at the end of the hall," where a patient is moved when his death appears to be imminent. Often, there is a practical reason for the move. The room may be closer to the nurses' station so that they may more easily check on the patient's status, more quickly answer the call light and respond to requests for pain medication, and other needs. On the hematology unit of a large military hospital, the young soldier leukemia patients knew what it meant when one of their friends was moved to Room 1, and dreaded the day when their turn would come. The word would spread quickly through the ward, where the patients were more like fraternity brothers than strangers brought together by a deadly similarity in lab tests and bruises. Hushed anxiety and preparatory grief spilled into the corridor from each of the rooms as these "brothers" waited for news that their number had, in fact, diminished by one. That news was followed by open sorrow and a sharing of community spirit, each silently wondering who among them would be the next brief inhabitant of Room 1.

As awesome and macabre as this ward policy might seem, there was a certain sense of security in it. These young men knew that as long as they weren't in Room 1, there still might be a chance for them. Perhaps theirs would be the bone marrow that would respond to these treatments and stop making cancer cells. As long as they were in Room 14, there was a possibility they would be in that fortunate percentage of patients who recovered completely. There was some comfort, too, in knowing that the "brothers" who were taken to Room 1 were at least given extra TLC by the nursing staff, most of whom were pretty young lieutenants. So, despite its shortcomings, it was a policy that worked for most of the patients and staff involved.

The type of care given to terminal patients is now receiving much more attention. New ideas and dimensions are being introduced and the overall effect has been a more caring, humane approach to the dying patient. Many patients are asking to be allowed to die at home, surrounded by loved ones and cherished possessions, and away from the tubes, schedules, monitoring, and sterile smell of the hospital. Even in hospitals, visiting hours are being relaxed or completely opened, so that someone close may stay with the patient at all times. Some hospitals go so far as to allow members of the patients' family to sleep in an adjoining room to ease the strain of the death-bed vigil. Numerous hospital in-service programs are directed specifically toward helping nursing and other staff members come to terms with their own feelings and attitudes about death, so they may be able to better aid patients and families who are facing this crisis.

The SHANTI project in Berkeley, California uses a pool of trained volunteer counselors who, upon request, deal directly with patients and families who feel they need assistance. These volunteers work with persons as they are facing a life-threatening illness, with those close to the dying patient and continue to offer counseling to survivors after the loss of a loved one.

Hospice care of terminal patients involves services on either an in-patient or home care basis and have the goal of keeping patients comfortable, lucid, and free of pain as they approach death. The family as a unit is the "patient" in most hospice settings and much effort is extended to help each family member cope with the actual or impending loss from his or her own perspective. As with the SHANTI project, care continues for the survivors even after the death. The hospice concept is discussed in greater detail in Chapter 13.

Medical After-Thoughts

One of the most poignant memories of my clinical nursing days was the observation of a resident instructing an intern to ask the family of the deceased for permission to do an autopsy or remove organs for transplant. It was a task no one wanted, certainly not this forlorn intern. Here was a family, who less than an hour ago learned of the death of their loved one, in the throes of grief, and someone was being told to pierce that grief with what may seem like a request to violate the body of someone they loved. But time is very critical, particularly in the case of obtaining organs for transplant. Also, the family often leaves the hospital premises soon after the death, and it is very difficult to reach them later to obtain such permissions. So, if the autopsy is considered critical or a potential transplant recipient is waiting, the family must be approached at this very vulnerable time.

Autopsies are no longer done with the frequency evident several years ago, when hospitals were required to do a certain number of them each year to maintain their accreditation. In instances of sudden death and coroner's cases, autopsies usually answer the mystery of what caused the death. In coroner's cases, an autopsy may be performed even without the consent of the family. Otherwise, the next-of-kin must give consent for the procedure. Even in cases of death after a lingering illness, an autopsy can reveal much valuable information both for the physician and the family. For instance, discovery of a hidden hereditary disorder may prove helpful when another member of the family begins to show symptoms of the same disorder. Autopsies of motor vehicle accident victims may show consistent types of injuries that will eventually lead to better design of cars and their safety equipment. Often, autopsies of children reveal injuries that were inflicted by abusive adults.

Today, most autopsies are performed by pathologists, although occasionally other physicians may be called upon by the coroner. The television program "Quincy" has popularized the duties of the medical examiner (a forensic pathologist) and dramatized the value of his special techniques. A properly done autopsy will not disfigure the body or seriously interfere with the embalmer's task. It is quite possible to continue with plans for a regular visitation and funeral after the completion of an autopsy. The potential value of the information gained makes it an option worth consideration.

A person may arrange before his death to donate certain organs for transplant or his entire body to a medical school, for instance. In most instances, however, even if the donations have been prearranged, the next-of-kin may refuse to allow them. If you do wish to donate organs, discuss this with your family so that they understand your wishes and the sincerity of your motives. The organs most often used for transplant are the kidney, liver, and cornea (the front part of the eye). Unless removed from the body less than an hour after death, the organs are no longer viable and useless to the transplant team. More rarely, heart and skin transplants may be requested. Temporal bones from the hearing-impaired are used in ear research. The Uniform Anatomical Gift Acts of 1968–1970 established criteria for these donations. These are effective in all fifty states with only minor differences such as minimum age or witnesses required, etc.

1. Any person eighteen years or older may donate all or part of his body after death for transplantation, research, or placement in a tissue bank.
2. A donor's valid statement of gift supersedes the rights of others unless a state autopsy law prevails.
3. If a donor has not acted during his lifetime, his survivors, by a specific order of priority, may do so.
4. Physicians who accept anatomical gifts, relying in good faith on the documents, are protected from legal action.
5. Time of death must be determined by a physician not involved in the transplant.
6. The donor may revoke the gift, or it may be rejected.

The National Kidney Foundation, 315 Park Avenue South, New York, New York 10010, will supply, upon request, free Uniform Donor Cards. Some states note willingness to donate organs on an individual's driver's license.

Even though one has made prearrangements with a medical school for donation of one's body, some problems may arise after your death. They may decide they no longer want your body (the ultimate rejection), perhaps simply because they already have enough at the time or perhaps due to the particular cause of death or condition of the body. There may also be problems with respect to the transportation of the body, even if the medical school or research center is across the street from the hospital. For full information about this, consult the closest medical school or see *A Manual of Death Education and Simple Burial* by Ernest Morgan.

The Week After

4

After a person dies, there is a period of several days when the members of the family are more or less expected to participate in a fairly standard sequence of events. The death rituals observed in the United States are nearly universal within our national borders, but quite different from those in most other parts of the world. Other countries watch in amazement as we select elaborate and expensive caskets, embalm and dress up our deceased for display, and finally inter them in magnificent stainless steel and concrete underground vaults in a garden-like cemetery. Jessica Mitford's *The American Way of Death* created quite a furor when it exposed the "greedy" American funeral industry in 1963. But in the nearly twenty years since her number one bestseller was published, very little has changed in our national funeral customs.

Although it has become more common to do so in recent years, few Americans give any thought at all to funeral arrangements until it is urgently necessary to make some. Without any forethought or planning, a bereaved relative must look to others for assistance with a task that is both unfamiliar and unwelcome. Most often, we turn to the funeral director. He does this all the time and knows what needs to be done. It can be most reassuring to know that the minor details and the major problems are being handled properly and we needn't worry about having forgotten something. Contrary to Jessica Mitford's characterization, most funeral directors are sincere in their desire to provide comfort and help to families at a time when they are in definite need.

Although many times last-minute funeral preparations will result in a perfectly satisfactory funeral, there are certain drawbacks to resorting to this procrastinator's way out. As in every occupation, there is, no doubt, an occasional charlatan in the funeral home business out there waiting to take advantage of the unsuspecting bereaved. By using only referrals from trusted friends or advisors, you can hope to avoid this type of establishment. Another disadvantage is that, when freshly bereaved, you are in quite a vulnerable state emotionally and probably not thinking too clearly, either. It is very easy to get carried away in the grief and possible guilt of the moment and perhaps spend far more than you would have under less stressful circumstances. We hear the funeral director say, "This is the last chance you have to do something for your mother," and we think tearfully of the times we forgot her birthday or didn't take the extra time for a visit or hurt her terribly in what seems now to have been a silly argument. Many an unspoken word of kindness or neglected responsibility has been assuaged by a thirty-two ounce copper casket with tufted velvet lining. And perhaps there is nothing wrong with that. The point is that these are expensive decisions being made at a time when we are possibly precariously balanced between reason and emotion.

A further problem with after-the-death planning of a funeral, is that, in plain terms, you have no opportunity to shop around, either for the type of casket you're selecting or the atmosphere of the funeral home and personalities of the individuals who are working with you. By waiting until the need arises, you are pretty much limited to the merchandise and environment of the one place you select. There realistically just isn't much time for prudent comparison, even in the unlikely event that you felt up to it. A funeral is the only fairly large expense that most of us will probably make without having really considered our options. If we were going to spend $2,000 on a stereo system, we would probably do at least some research on the advantages of certain types before making a choice. Ordinarily prudent, coupon-clipping, ad-watching, option-conscious American shoppers somehow forget all that in the emotion of making funeral arrangements. It is an interesting dichotomy in our economic values.

Now, unlike Jessica Mitford, I am not about to contend that Americans are getting ripped off at our friendly neighborhood funeral homes. It is true that we spend far more money on funerals than do our foreign friends. But we also spend far more money on cars, fuel, make-up, and food. We Americans live and die affluently. If there weren't a big market for $1,500 caskets, funeral homes wouldn't have them available. Whether we buy them because it is truly our choice or simply because we don't preplan and think we don't have a choice is perhaps the issue. Unless our national economy takes a real nosedive, however, I doubt that we'll see a very rapid disappearance of the typical American funeral. There will probably be an increasing variety of alternatives available, though, as more of us do more planning and give more thought to our values with respect to death rituals.

When the need for a funeral is imminent, the funeral home can be a tremendous help in performing required tasks that we could not or would choose not to do. The funeral director will most likely also advise and assist in many details, the necessity of which we were totally unaware. The funeral industry unquestionably meets a social need, but it is a business, not a social service. Funeral directors have to pay off mortgages, pay utilities, buy and maintain expensive vehicles, and in some places, hire staff available 24 hours a day, as well as many other normal operating expenses. As of 1981, a basic hearse cost about $40,000! Funds to meet these expenses come not from the public coffers, but from the pockets of those who use these services. So, when you purchase a casket, much of what you pay goes for the routine expenses any business must meet.

The following itemization of standard funeral charges was obtained from Dodsworth-Piper-Wallen Funeral Home in Macomb, Illinois in 1981. It will provide some insight into the way funeral costs are determined. Most funeral homes include all of these services in one lump sum, which is included in the price of each casket. It is easy to see why funeral homes are reluctant to push the $300 pine box usually reserved for charity cases. They simply couldn't meet expenses if everyone chose the pine box.

Itemization of Standard Funeral Charges

Professional services

1. Removal of deceased from home or hospital	$50.00
2. Professional care and preparation	70.00
3. Restorative art and dermi-surgery	30.00
4. Embalming and posing	110.00
5. Services of lady attendant	15.00
6. Dressing and arranging hair	20.00
7. Attendant on duty 24 hours to receive friends and relatives	40.00
8. 24-hour daily attention to all details	25.00
9. Newspaper notices of service	15.00
10. Writing obituary for newspapers	5.00
11. Telephone and telegrams to relatives and friends	10.00
12. Recording of vital statistics	10.00
13. Securing doctor's and/or coroner's certificate of death	20.00
14. Securing burial, cemetery, and removal permits	20.00
15. Arranging of floral tributes	15.00
16. Listing of floral tributes	15.00
17. Care of condolence cards	10.00
18. Assistance with legal and insurance papers	10.00

Arrangements made with:

19.	Clergyman	7.00
20.	Musician	3.00
21.	Singer	5.00
22.	Casket bearers	15.00
23.	Cemetery, crematorium, or mausoleum	20.00
24.	Lodges	5.00
25.	Churches	5.00

Supplies furnished, including:

26.	Printed acknowledgment cards and envelopes	25.00
27.	Floral tribute cards	5.00
28.	Clergyman cards	5.00
29.	Casket-bearer cards	5.00
30.	Printed memorial folders	15.00
31.	Visitor's record book	15.00
32.	Spiritual bouquet cards	10.00

Total professional services $630.00

Facilities

33.	Operating room	$80.00
34.	Chapel	100.00
35.	Visitation room	50.00
36.	Lounges	10.00
37.	Offices	10.00
38.	Display rooms	25.00
39.	Public address system	10.00
40.	Equipment for church services	10.00
41.	Metal marker	5.00
42.	Prayer rail	5.00

Total facilities $305.00

Motor Equipment

43.	Funeral coach	$45.00
44.	Family limousine	45.00
45.	Casket-bearer car	35.00
46.	Flower car	35.00

Total Motor equipment $160.00

Total Standard Funeral Charges $1,095.00

Funeral directors will also advise the bereaved about various financial benefits, such as veteran's, union, and social security payments. They will also assist in filing insurance papers, making arrangements for out-of-town guests; help with travel plans if the body is to be buried elsewhere, and coordinate schedules with the cemetery.

It is my strong belief that persons should give real consideration to their own and their family's feelings regarding death rituals. A few of the issues in question include routine embalming, display of the body for visitation or funeral, appropriate expressions of sympathy (flowers, donations to charity, etc.), type of casket to be used, choice of burial vault, type of funeral service or memorial service desired, and disposition of the body. I hope the following brief discussions will serve as a spring-board for your further investigation of these matters.

Embalming

Preservation, Restoration, and Sanitation is the creed of the modern embalmer. While it is *not* required by law unless the deceased had one of a few specific contagious diseases or if the body is to be transported a great distance, *embalming* is almost always routinely done as soon as possible after the death. The primary purpose of embalming is to *preserve* the body for the week or so of the visitation and funeral. This is accomplished by draining the body of all the blood and replacing it with a formalin solution. Other specific procedures are also involved. The *restoration* involves shaping and cosmetology work to make the deceased appear as life-like as possible. Sunken cheeks can be filled in; fluid removed from swollen areas, etc. It is a surgical procedure. The *sanitation* value of embalming is questionable. But unless embalmed or frozen a body will begin to decay within twenty-four hours. In many American cultures, if the family wishes to have the body present at the funeral, embalming would be necessary.

As normal and expected as embalming seems to us in the United States, the routine practice of the procedure is virtually unheard of elsewhere in the world. Are we so shaky in our belief in the survival of the soul that we feel compelled to attempt to immortalize the shell? Our incredible awe of empiricism has both perfected the technique of embalming and perhaps dwarfed our faith in beliefs which do not lend themselves to scientific experimentation. We know we can preserve the body, at least for a while, and we don't know what else of us will survive. We scientific Americans are more comfortable with what can be proven.

How long does the preservation last? It depends on the condition of the body at death, the skill of the embalmer, and the type of fluid used, as well as the type of casket and vault selected. In some cases, the preservation may last no longer than a few days after the funeral service. Some bodies have been exhumed thirty or more years after the death and are still in "very good condition." Eventually, however, the body will decay. Ashes to ashes, dust to dust. If the preservative lasted for a thousand years, still, eventually the body will decay. When the body is dead, it is dead forever. We may postpone the inevitable for a while, but we can't keep the body intact indefinitely. And if we could, to what end? The body has served its purpose. What truly mattered about the deceased was not found in the sinew and artery and cartilage. These were merely the vehicle for the person who has left for a journey with another means of transport.

Unless you specifically request that it not be done, the funeral director will probably assume the family wants the body to be embalmed. Not embalming requires immediate disposal of the body by cremation or burial. If the death happens to occur on a weekend when the crematory and/or cemetery employees are not on duty, the body may have to be embalmed or frozen anyway to await the reopening of these facilities on Monday, or in the case of a holiday weekend, Tuesday.

Open Casket Visitation and Funeral

This is a uniquely American custom. There are ardent, educated persons who disagree quite heatedly regarding the value of this practice. It is, essentially, the cornerstone of the American funeral industry. If we did not display the body, we would have little need of embalming and beautiful caskets and expensive burial vaults. The funeral directors claim, and are supported by millions of believers, including many psychologists and clergymen, that seeing, even touching the dead body is an important part of grief therapy, of making the death seem real. Stories of widows of soldiers who died and were buried in foreign countries are replete with unresolved grief because they "never saw the body." Persons who watched a loved one suffer a long illness, wasting away, looking terrible with all the tubes and bandages of hospital procedures, are often relieved to see the "restored" body of that loved one appearing more normal and restful than in the memories of the hospital experience. This can be a comforting memory picture.

Opponents of the practice argue that it is yet another way we Americans deny death. We go to great lengths to make dead people look "pretty" and "normal" and "comfortable"—"not so dead." Some clergymen are concerned that we are placing too much emphasis on the corpse, when our minds should be with the spirit. Bereaved relatives bemoan the fact that the most immediate memory they now have of the deceased is of him lying there in the casket. Students have told me, "I try to remember Grandpa out in the garden or taking us fishing, but I always just see him there in the casket. I wish I'd never looked at it." Some people prefer their memory pictures to be of a living person, not a corpse.

The controversy will not soon be settled. At least we live in a tolerant, free country where we may do what seems best for us without fear of persecution. The "wake" originally began as a 24-hour vigil at the side of the fresh corpse. Family and friends would rotate the duty of watching the deceased to be certain that if there were movement, someone would be "awake" to notice and call the doctor. It was a way of insuring that no one was buried alive. Social customs and diagnosis of death have changed a great deal since then. No one is concerned that the bloodless, sanitized body will suddenly leap to life. Today's wakes or visitations are more an opportunity for friends of the family to share their sympathy and extend condolences. The "laying out" of the body is intended to facilitate the grief process and is especially valuable for those out-of-town relatives to have a last chance to see this individual whom they may have been unable to visit for years.

Often, even when the casket is open for the visitation or wake, the funeral service is conducted with the casket closed. The procedure here is highly variable. At some funerals, mourners are encouraged to file past the open casket one last time before it is finally closed for the procession to the cemetery. Circumstances and personalities vary so widely that there truly isn't one "right" way to arrange it. But a little pre-need discussion of the possibilities may eliminate the need for a hasty, emotional, and possibly regrettable decision later.

Appropriate Expressions of Sympathy

Flowers have been the traditional American expression of sympathy since the mid-1800s. Since World War II, there has been an increasing trend for families to request donations to charities rather than excessive floral displays. These suggestions are a source of great consternation for the florists of the country, who derive more than half of their income from orders for funeral arrangements. Certainly, flowers are lovely and have a softening, comforting effect in the stark experience of the death of a loved one. Yet, it may likewise be comforting to know that donations to a research fund in the memory of this individual may help to develop a cure for a debilitating disease or perhaps that, in this person's name, children at the local orphanage may enjoy the use of new playground equipment. Many families establish scholarship funds in the name of the deceased or a trust fund for the young children of the decedent. There are many fine, creative and helpful ways of expressing sympathy.

Sometimes, friends who have a personal reason for not wanting to contribute to the Adams County Alcoholism Recovery Program or the Unification Church Building Fund, for instance, may resent being told that is the proper way for them to express their sympathy.

Perhaps the comforter feels most comforted by sending flowers. Some persons always send flowers or always send donations to their own favorite charity, regardless of who died and the expressed wishes of the family.

I have a good friend who has told me she wants no flowers at her funeral, but would *love* to have them now. "If anyone cares enough about me to send flowers when I'm dead, I wish they would send them to me this week, instead. I love flowers and want to enjoy them in this life! Roses will be useless to me when the light has left my eyes and the fragrance wafts to a senseless olfactory nerve." It seems like a spendid idea to me, and one which would no doubt please the Society of American Florists as well. In fact, if we all sent the flowers and said and did the nice things we want to but never get around to saying and doing, there would undoubtedly be a sharp decline in the anguish of guilt that perhaps motivates a great deal of funeral spending.

The expression of sympathy is a highly individual matter. If the family feels very strongly about a special charity and wishes to have their departed member honored by the growth of that charity from donations made in the person's name, it is hard to find fault with their reasoning. If, however, certain individuals wish to express sympathy but feel uncomfortable supporting a given project, their wishes should be respected, too. We can be sorry someone died without having to agree with all of her philosophies.

One option most often ignored in our materialistic society is the true *personal expression of sympathy* through a sincere letter to the family or the performance of some direct service to the family or community in honor of the deceased. This requires a giving of self rather than money and is truly the most meaningful form of sympathy. One might wish to plant a tree on the school grounds or hospital campus, permission from authorities properly obtained, of course. A monthly visit to a friend of the deceased in a nursing home might be an appropriate gift to her memory. The possibilities are limitless. Brainstorming with others about them may give you some wonderful ideas for things to do for the living, too!

Type of Casket Used

The use of elaborate metal caskets is also pretty much an American curiosity. Until the early 1800s, use of any sort of a burial receptacle (other than a shroud) was generally reserved for princes and saints. Not only are they now considered virtually indispensible, but there is a vast array of styles and types from which to choose. There are lovely polished solid hard woods, lead-coated steel, copper, and bronze in a variety of designs and weights. The weight of the metal (and the durability of the casket) is expressed by a gauge number. A 14-gauge steel is thicker and heavier than a 20-gauge steel. It is impossible to tell which is which by simply looking at the casket. "Only the pallbearers know for sure." Casket interiors come in velvet, satin, or linen, tufted or embroidered, and in a myriad of colors. And of course there always is the cloth-covered pine box.

On the more expensive models, other options are also available. For instance, some have sealing gaskets, which keep air, moisture, and external bacteria and fungi from entering the casket. The idea is to assure greater protection for the body, although anaerobic bacteria do thrive under the conditions in the interior of a casket thus sealed. Another option is the personal history capsule. Vital information about the deceased is written on a piece of paper, which is then rolled-up scroll fashion and inserted into a plastic tube. The tube then screws into a special opening at the foot of the casket. This feature provides for accurate identification of the deceased should natural disaster or freeway construction result in a relocation of the cemetery.

The price of a casket ranges from $300 (for a plain box) to, gulp, $30,000. You won't see samples of either extreme in the selection room, but they are available. Most families spend from $1,000 to $3,000, but this varies considerably depending on the part of the country and the overhead expenses of the particular funeral home. Most funeral directors will not encourage you to purchase a casket you cannot afford, primarily because they want to be confident they will be paid for it. Uncollectable accounts do not pay the power company. However, as a friendly, small-town funeral director points out, some people like Volkswagons and some like Cadillacs. He likes to have, therefore, merchandise available to suit every taste.

What are the real differences in the various caskets? I think our small-town funeral director put it pretty well. It basically comes down to a matter of taste. Some people find the natural beauty of the polished hardwoods somehow more warm and comforting than the cold, hard metals. On the other hand, the assumed durability of the metals is appealing to others. In the long run, and I mean the Long Run, the casket and the body will eventually return to the elements, no matter the composition of the box. It is, therefore, primarily a matter of what color, style, and price are most suitable for the bereaved. The St. Francis Center in Washington, D.C. sells kits for coffins starting at $160, if you are one who finds satisfaction in inexpensive do-it-yourself endeavors.

Every term, I take my "Death and Dying" students for a tour of a funeral home. The field trip is anticipated with great fear and trepidation, but invariably turns out to be one of the highlights and most instructive sessions of the course. The students look at the caskets, compare prices and styles, see the operating or preparation room where the embalming is done and ask whatever questions they wish of the funeral director. One of the funeral directors and his wife even complete the tour with an invitation to their living quarters directly above the funeral home, where punch and cookies are waiting for the group! The whole experience usually imparts a far more positive attitude about the entire funeral process, as well as the confidence of improved knowledge and understanding. I heartily recommend the idea to everyone, to be done at a time when there is not an imminent need nor the emotion of a recent loss. A call to the establishment(s) of your choice should suffice to arrange a convenient time when you and perhaps a few friends would be allowed to examine the caskets, ask questions you might be embarrassed to ask if actually planning a funeral, and gain some insight into how the whole business operates. Okay, so it sounds like a strange thing to do. You might plan the trip as a program for a sorority meeting or civic club, if you prefer not to go privately. But I honestly believe that this pre-need introduction to the funeral industry will remove some of the awe and confusion that often accompanies the first trip of the bereaved to the funeral home.

Perhaps a word should be said about burial clothes. Occasionally, a casket is selected because the color is compatible with the garment the deceased will be wearing for burial. Other times, clothes are purchased or selected from the deceased's wardrobe after the casket has been chosen. Funeral homes usually carry a selection of clothes, made for the purpose. Some families prefer to bury their loved ones in attire befitting their lifestyle. For instance a farmer may be "laid out" in bib overalls and a work shirt. Often, families will go out to stores to purchase something, only to find that nothing is quite appropriate. The selection at the funeral home may be limited, but all dresses will have high necks and long sleeves, a style which suits the purpose but is most often hard to find in fashion-oriented stores. Maybe Grand-ma's selection of her own "going away dress" is the best solution, after all.

Choice of a Burial Vault

There are two broad uses for the term "burial vault." One refers to the above-the-ground mausoleum-type vaults, such as the one at Monticello which houses the remains of Thomas Jefferson. This discussion pertains to the underground, single-casket boxes which have become quite popular lately. These vaults are made of reinforced concrete, fiberglass, stainless steel, or other mixtures of materials. The base of the vault is placed in the grave before the casket is lowered, after which the top of the vault is placed on, and if it is a "sealer," sealed. The purpose of the vault, ostensibly, is to protect the casket from the elements. Nowhere is it required by law, although certain privately owned cemeteries require the use of one. It helps to keep the ground level and, therefore, easier to mow. When a casket begins to decay, in the normal course of events, the ground begins to sink in above it. A burial vault will cost from $250 to over $1,000. There is quite a variety of "attractive" colors and styles from which to choose. This cost is in addition to the casket and may be sold either by the funeral home or directly by the cemetery. Check with the cemetery you have chosen to see if it is required.

The Funeral vs. the Memorial Service

The primary, perhaps only, distinction between a funeral and a memorial service is that the body of the deceased, "casketed" of course, is present at a funeral but not at a memorial service. As with the issue of closed vs. open caskets, there is considerable difference of opinion as to which is the more beneficial. The funeral is by far the more popular to date, and its proponents insist that the presence of the body has therapeutic value for the mourners, makes the death seem more real. Howard Raether and Robert Slater write, "it is difficult for many survivors to disassociate themselves immediately from the lifeless body. The finite mind requires evidence that an earthly existence has ended." Funeral services, formerly almost always held in the place of worship or even in the home of the deceased, now are most often conducted at the funeral home itself.

The memorial service is used most often when there has been a direct disposition of the body, usually by cremation. Sometimes, when the body cannot be recovered, there is no choice in the matter. Many clergy and laity alike prefer the memorial service because the focus is on the spirit and life of the deceased, rather than on the body itself. Some Christians feel that this service more clearly reflects the Christian belief in after-life. Others quite simply feel it makes more sense, since the body is now useless. Occasionally, the family will have a funeral and burial at one location, and a few days later there may be a memorial service at another location for friends and relatives who were unable to attend the funeral.

Probably the single most important factor in determining which type of service is better is our expectation. If we expect to feel unsatisfied without the body present, that will most likely be our reaction to a memorial service. The reverse is also true. Our expectations are probably based on our previous experiences and upbringing, as well as our religious beliefs. Again, there is no one right answer. We can only try to do what seems most appropriate to us.

One of the disadvantages, I feel, of expounding on the great therapeutic value of either the funeral or memorial service is that it feeds the myth that grief can be completed by virtue of having sat through a meaningful, inspirational service. Grief, like death, is not an event, but a process which requires some time to resolve. In our typical American fashion, we would like for people to "hurry up and get through" their grief and get on with their lives. I do not intend to belittle funerals nor deny the important function they serve. Indeed, there are far too few occasions in our hectic lives when we are encouraged to pause and ponder the meaning and value of life. Rather, I want only to avoid the tendency to imbue a half-hour ceremony with magical curative powers which do not exist. Funeral rituals are valuable in "marking" the death, giving importance to the change that has occurred in the lives of the survivors. But these rituals only facilitate the beginning of the grief process. It is a mockery of the meaning of human relationships to presume the events of a few days could effect a completion of grief.

Disposition of the Body

When someone dies, it is most often left to the survivors to decide what shall be done with the body. (The exceptions are those cases where the deceased has prearranged his own funeral or cremation or donation of his body to science and, of course, those situations where the body cannot be recovered, as in a drowning.) And, most often, the body is embalmed, put in a casket, and buried underground. This is the traditional disposition in this country, and we usually do it this way because it has always been done this way, if for no other reason. Following tradition also allows us to avoid having to think about it and make a decision. There are, however, a number of alternatives available which, given some consideration, we might actually prefer.

Americans are quite preoccupied with their bodies. Fortunes are made by health clubs, manufacturers of diet pills and plans, athletic equipment suppliers, and purveyors of numerous health and beauty aids. We are almost obsessed with keeping our bodies attractive and youthful. Perhaps it gives us the illusion of immortality we want to maintain. Certainly, to some extent, we are the victims of Madison Avenue in this regard. There is a great deal of money made by companies convincing us these are worthwhile values. Given similar propaganda regarding the development of mental and spiritual capabilities, we could probably be convinced to devote a great deal of effort to those endeavors. Alas, there is little money to be made in the exercise of mind and spirit. But *muscles*—now there's a tangible fortune-builder.

The point is that, having placed such a high value on our physical nature in life, there is a great reluctance to so readily dismiss its importance after death. Perhaps that is why we are so taken with the idea of embalming, heavy caskets, and burial vaults. Having devoted so much attention to our bodies during life, we like the notion of indefinite physical survival, albeit without motion. This post-death glorification of the body, declared by some to be instrumental in helping us realize the finality of death, may in fact be only a tacit denial of the meaning of death and, maybe, life.

Assuming we are open to other suggestions, let's consider some of the alternatives. One of the popular concerns over underground burial is the eventual problem of running out of space. While there is already enough committed cemetery land to get us well into the next century, there will sometime come the dilemma of whether to use a given acre for an apartment building, park, corn field, or burial plots. When the planet becomes more crowded, these decisions will have to be made. Many efforts at more judicious use of burial land are already in practice. In some cemeteries, plots are rented rather than bought. If, at the end of the twenty- or forty-year lease, a member of the family wishes to renew the lease, they may. By then, the natural recycling processes will have taken place and, if the lease is not renewed, the grave may be rented to a new occupant. Other cemeteries routinely make multiple use of graves as a wife may be buried on top of her husband, a child with its parent, etc. This stacking of graves is common in Arlington National Cemetery in Washington, D.C. Another option is vertical burial, which requires less land space than the usual horizontal placement of the casket.

The construction of large, impressive mausoleums for above-ground placement of caskets is now quite common. These structures, often beautiful and marble-faced, can house many bodies in a comparatively small area and appeal to many persons who abhor the idea of being underground. Specific spaces in the mausoleum are purchased much as one would purchase a cemetery plot.

Some individuals have a strong desire to be buried at sea. While this is a relatively rare practice, and one which must be accomplished far enough from the coastline to avoid the body being washed ashore, it certainly eliminates the need for space in a cemetery.

Of course, donation of the body to medical and research institutions is another possibility for those with altruistic inclinations. Arrangements for this can be made by contacting a medical or research institution directly. A complete listing of these schools, including phone numbers, addresses and other pertinent information is included in Ernest Morgan's *A Manual of Death Education and Simple Burial*, Celo Press: Burnsville, North Carolina. There is a need for body donations, but they are not universally accepted. It is wise to investigate the matter thoroughly if this means of disposal interests you. Your generous gift will be appreciated by medical students and their future patients, as well.

Probably the least understood and yet most significant alternative to traditional burial practices is cremation. Cremation effects a clean and rapid oxidation of the body, as opposed to the slower, but equally destructive decomposition of the body which follows earth burial. There is considerable resistance to the idea of cremation, in large part due to the general lack of knowledge regarding the process and the disinclination to pursue the study of death-related topics. Cremation is used in only about five percent of all deaths in the United States, and most of those are done on the West Coast. In contrast, countries like Japan and England, with more of an immediate land-use problem, find the majority of deaths are followed by cremation.

The first crematorium was built in the United States scarcely over a hundred years ago (1876). The practice is slowly growing in popularity and is now available within reasonable distance of even most small towns. In the Midwest, the few cremations that are done usually follow the regular visitation and funeral and then, rather than going in a procession to the gravesite, the body is taken directly to the crematory by the funeral director. In cities where a crematory is available locally, the services may be held at the crematory itself. Some crematories are operated as part of a funeral home, some are owned by cemeteries, some function as separate entities which include a columbarium (a building with niches for the storing of the ashes), and a very few are government-owned.

The process of cremation is simple. The body must be in some type of receptacle, usually a casket. There is no law requiring this, but most crematories insist on something more than a shroud. There is a heavy gauge rubber pouch that is sometimes used if the family chooses not to purchase a casket. If a casket is used, it will be destroyed in the heat of the furnace. There are two types of cremation now carried out in this country. The newer retorts operate on the principle of intense heat, like an oven. There are no flames that touch the body. The moisture of the body evaporates and the remaining tissues disintegrate, much as a roast would if left in your kitchen oven too long. What remains after the cremation is the inorganic ash of the bones. The older retorts, some of which are still in operation, produce the intense heat necessary by means of gas or oil flames. If a metal casket is used, the metal fragments that may be mixed with the ashes are removed with a magnet. If a wooden casket is used, the ashes from it are light and will float up the chimney. The "cremains" or human ashes are then sometimes mechanically crushed to a consistent size and returned to the funeral director or placed in an urn selected by the family. The average cremains weigh about six pounds and fit easily in a shoebox.

The ashes may be buried in a cemetery, if desired, or kept in a niche at the columbarium with a memorial marker. They may also be scattered at sea (as is frequently done off the coast of California) or, except in California, Washington, Nevada, and all national parks, they may be scattered over land. Some persons prefer to keep the ashes at home in an urn. In England, it is a common practice to mingle the ashes with the soil in rose gardens established for the very purpose.

The very first term we offered our death and dying course, Ellen signed up for the class because her fiancé was dying of cancer. (Bruce's letter to Ellen is at the close of Chapter 2.) His wish was to be cremated and have his ashes scattered over Alaska, and she personally flew the nearly six-thousand mile round trip to do just that. She felt a deep satisfaction in knowing she had carried out his wishes.

One elderly couple, deciding they preferred cremation to burial, bought a double urn, so that their ashes could be kept side by side. One of them died and the ashes were placed in one side of the urn. In time, the surviving spouse remarried and the new couple came to the funeral director with a novel request. They had decided that when one of them died, the ashes would be put in the other side of the urn. Upon the death and cremation of the final spouse, they wanted all the ashes to be removed from the urn, comingled with each other and the most recent cremains, and then have the resultant mixture divided equally between the two sides of the urn. Eternal togetherness of three good friends!

If cremation is used as a means of direct disposal, that is, without embalming and visitation, it is considerably less expensive. The cremation itself costs usually little more than a hundred dollars. If the body must be transported to the crematory, that expense would be extra. Scattering is free if you do it yourself (unless you have to fly to Alaska). If the cremains are kept in a columbarium, the cost is roughly the same as for a cemetery plot. If you choose to keep the ashes on the mantle or bookcase, there are many urns (in bronze and other materials) available, costing from about fifty to several hundred dollars, or you may use any container you like. If cremation is done simply as an alternative to underground burial, after the regular visitation and funeral service, the cost difference is not as remarkable, although you would save the cost of opening and closing the grave, which itself varies considerably depending on the community and the day of the week and the cemetery. (When my grandmother died recently, the funeral had to be on a Saturday. Had it been on a Friday, it would have cost $275 to open and close the grave. Since it was on a Saturday, however, the charge was $375. This was in a medium-size town. In large cities, the cost is sometimes much higher.)

If cost were the only consideration, the most inexpensive disposal would probably be a direct cremation of the body, followed by a memorial service and either scattering or keeping the cremains at home or burying them yourself. Of course, cost is *not*, or should not be the only consideration. There are many times when families have found much comfort and peace of mind being able to view the body. Many people derive a serene satisfaction in choosing the type of casket and burial vault that seems most appropriate to them. The funeral rituals we practice have a purpose. To take them too lightly would be a disservice to us all. But to consider our options and make a decision based on forethought, knowledge, and discussion of alternatives will probably result in more meaningful and personal methods of handling this crisis in our lives.

Memorial Societies

One of the relatively recent developments in this area is the formation of "memorial societies" established for the purpose of providing people with the opportunity to have relatively inexpensive funeral and burial services. There are more than a hundred of these societies in the United States and Canada, each of them serving from as few as 20 to as many as 4,000 or more families. These funeral and memorial societies strive through education, preplanning, and special arrangements with funeral directors to obtain simplicity and dignity in funeral practices for their members. The Continental Association of Funeral and Memorial Societies, Suite 1100, 1828 L St. NW, Washington, D.C. 20036, has a list of member organizations. This list is also available in Ernest Morgan's *Manual*, previously mentioned. The *Manual* also contains much helpful information for groups interested in forming new memorial or funeral societies.

One of the beautiful things about our country is the tolerance for a wide range of beliefs and practices in virtually all areas. We are an incredibly heterogeneous society with different needs and customs and resources. That we permit excesses along with frugalities, and the broad range of styles in between, is a credit to us all.

Good Grief—
What Good Is It?

Good grief. How often have you heard or used this expression without considering the meaning of the words outside their use as an exclamation of surprise or disgust? Grief, after all, is that very difficult process of learning to adjust to the loss of someone (or even something) very important. What could possibly be good about it? A little-appreciated fact is that we all have ultimate control over our own grief and that we can transform the experience of grieving into a positive one.

Americans tend to have a negative attitude about grieving, feeling that it is something we should get over with as soon as possible. Grief, whether our own or that of someone in our social or business life, is an inconvenience, an interruption in our hectic schedules. We harbor many misconceptions about the grief process and scarcely comprehend or appreciate its value and purpose. We can hope to begin to recognize the necessity of grief and allow more space in our lives to go through this potentially profound and beneficial experience.

Defining Terms

Three terms are commonly used to refer to the plight of the survivors following the death of someone close: bereavement, mourning, and grief. Occasionally, we hear them used almost interchangeably, although there are some subtle and significant shades of difference in meaning.

Bereavement is a statement of fact. It is a simple acknowledgement of your relationship to a person who has died. Bereavement connotes nothing of the way you react to that death. For instance, if your beloved husband or wife dies you are bereaved. You are also bereaved if your wealthy bachelor brother, of whom you have never been too fond, dies in a distant state without benefit of a will, thereby leaving you, as next of kin, sole heir of the estate. Obviously, the feelings in response to these two deaths would be quite different, but bereavement occurred in both cases. Often, persons who are bereaved are also grieving, but this word does not give us this information.

Mourning refers primarily to social behavior following a death. Our culture discourages these outward displays of inward emotion. In many cultures, however, including earlier periods in mainstream American history and among many ethnic groups in America, the bereaved are or were allowed a time for the grief to be socially acknowledged. Family members wear black garments or armbands, as if to announce, "I am sad and vulnerable. Please be nice to me and understand." We put our flags at half-mast as a symbol of national mourning when one of our leaders dies. There are a great variety of cultural, ethnic, and religious norms for mourning, and we might do well to allow them greater expression.

Grief is that Pandora's box of emotion that should, and usually does, follow the death of a loved one. How one experiences and expresses this emotion is a highly personal matter, but there are some recognized similarities in the ways many of us grieve. It should also be noted that the experience of grief is not limited to losses caused by the death of a person. Many losses induce a grief reaction. Divorce, debilitating heart disease, moving to another home or city, one's child going away to school—these and many more events are occasions to reevaluate our lives and goals and develop new relationships and interests in our lives as the old ones are taken away or no longer suit our needs. Indeed, to some extent, this is a continuous process, or should be, for our lives are always in a state of flux. Some of us have to make more frequent and significant adaptations than others, but we all make them. These "deathless deaths" are discussed more fully in Chapter 10.

The Tasks of Grief

Grief tasks are important to the emotional, mental, and physical health of the survivor. There are two major psychological tasks to be accomplished by the bereaved. The first is so simple and obvious that we might assume it would not take any effort—that is to accept the fact of the death, intellectually and emotionally. It is, however, a difficult task for many bereaved persons. The second task is to reinvest, or recathect the energy once devoted to the deceased to other persons and ideas, things and activities. Robert Neale describes grief as dying and being reborn. When we grieve, we do, in essence, die as the person we were when we shared this significant relationship. We realize that, because that person or part of ourselves is gone, our lives will be forever changed. We must then be reborn as the person we will become in our new existence.

While there is a tendency on the part of society to hurry the bereaved through their grief, to urge them to "get on with their lives," there is a tendency on the part of the bereaved to want to cling to their grief. The bereaved may feel that if they can survive this loss and be happy again, maybe the relationship wasn't as important as they thought it was. We remember the sweet lover's vows, "I will love only you forever," "I can't live without you," "You are my reason for living." Having said and meant those things, how can we now go on as if we still had a reason for living? Perhaps this is why grief is so painful. The bereaved often say, "I feel as if part of me has died." Indeed, part of us does and must die when a significant relationship has been severed, whether by death, divorce, or simply geographical separation. We must change, but becoming reconciled to that change is never easy. Life will never be the same.

Grief has been likened to "cleaning out our closets." We slowly, item by item, go through our memories and emotions. We relive the significance of each bit of the past relationship we have lost and then put it away, retaining only the essence. As we go through the closets of our minds, we discard the worn-out ideas and commitments to make room for new perceptions and involvements. The effect of this cleaning process is, appropriately, "cleansing." We slowly begin to feel renewed as we assess and appreciate the value of our previous experiences and begin to see the potential for a new and necessarily different future. We make room in our "closet" for a fresh wardrobe of interests and relationships, to be integrated with the mainstays which have survived the years. We are reborn.

Unresolved grief is quite a common phenomenon in this country, since we deny the importance of the process. Failing to take time out for grief, however, can have disastrous results. An example that many may be familiar with is the bereaved mother in Judith Guest's novel, *Ordinary People.* Although obviously quite shaken by the drowning death of her first-born son, this woman was much too proper and sophisticated, her life too neat, to accommodate the disruption grief would bring. Rather than acknowledge and work through her feelings, she simply lashed out at her surviving son and husband, destroying her relationships with them. Rather than admit she needed support, she isolated herself from her support system. This is a perfect illustration of the need for control described in Chapter 1.

The character may have been fictional, but her reactions and behavior are all too familiar. Unfortunately, she has many real-life counterparts. There is no getting out of grief when someone we truly love dies. We may obscure or delay it, but eventually it will happen, unless, of course, we die first. Some people immerse themselves in work, hoping, "if I'm busy I won't think about it so much." You have to think about it some time.

"I'm Going Crazy"

It is one thing to accept that a given project may be worthwhile. It is quite another to endure the means to that worthwhile end. Running a marathon, doing the spring cleaning, building a new home, even writing a book are quite satisfying once done. But there will probably be great periods of agony to endure before we reach our goal. And so it is with grief. When the pain finally begins to recede, we may be rewarded with insight and understanding and even a greater appreciation of life. But we must go through that pain.

Because of our contemporary distaste for the tasks of mourning, we often attempt to hide our grief or even deny to ourselves that these feelings are real and normal. A newspaper survey of a large midwestern city revealed that most respondents thought that a normal period of mourning for the loss of a loved one is between two days and two weeks! What inspiring American efficiency! Most researchers in the area have found that one and a half to two years is the average time required for the resolution of grief, and the most difficult period is often four to six months after the death, when the man on the street assumes we have long since returned to normal. We hesitate to label ourselves as weak or incompetent, yet these feelings persist. We may wonder, "Does no one else go through this? Why am I so strange?" The frequent battle with puzzling and painful emotions may well lead the bereaved to conclude "I'm going crazy!"

Of course, those who allow themselves to experience the gamut of emotions are probably the least likely to actually go crazy. It is those of us who attempt to suppress, deny, and displace grief who eventually have real problems coping with the loss. The intensity and variety of our feelings may surprise and alarm us, indeed it may seem we have lost our senses as well as our loved one.

Several researchers have studied the characteristics of mourning and grief. For the purposes of our discussion, I will refer to the work of two British psychiatrists, John Bowlby and Colin Murray Parkes, who have pioneered much of the research in bereavement.

Bowlby and Parkes describe four dimensions of grief, all of which may be present when the bereaved first learns of the death. These are: shock and numbness, yearning and searching, disorientation and disorganization, and resolution and reoganization. While the four dimensions coexist throughout the grieving process, they vary in intensity, each tending to dominate the others for a time. Following is a description of each of these dimensions.

Shock and numbness: feeling stunned; bursting out in extremely intense panic, distress, or anger; impaired judgment; resistance to stimuli; incapable of functioning; concentration almost impossible.

Yearning and searching: impatience and restlessness, ambiguity and reality testing; overwhelming anger and guilt, extreme sensitivity to and confused perception of stimuli, a feeling of wanting to "do something." In this dimension, there is a struggle to defy and test reality. A widow may mistake another's footstep for that of her late husband and expect to see him come around the corner. A mother may think she hears her dead child call her and search for the source of the call, or momentarily think that a child on the playground is her own. A widower may come home from work expecting the usual warm greeting from his wife, or finds himself calling out to her, only to realize she is no longer there.

Disorientation and disorganization: depression, loss of appetite, feelings of guilt and responsibility for the death, unavoidable recognition of reality, sleep disturbances, lack of interest in doing anything. This is the most difficult and most dangerous dimension of grief, in terms of the vulnerability of the bereaved. Because this often peaks months after the death, mourners are inclined to pretend to really be all right or become physically ill, which is more socially acceptable than lamentation.

Resolution and reorganization: a feeling of a sense of release from the loss, renewed energy, improved ability to cope and make judgments, and resumption of normal sleeping and eating patterns. Although the bereaved will retain vivid memories of the deceased, there is a functional adaptation to the loss. It is not unusual for an adult to take up to two years to reach the peak of this dimension.

How each of us experiences grief is a highly individual matter, and we should not feel strange if we react differently than our friends or family members react to their own losses. Each relationship is unique and the death of one individual will be perceived uniquely by a spouse, mother, father, sister, brother, daughter, son, or best friend. While we may share our grief with others who feel the loss, too, no other person can know exactly the impact this loss has on our own life.

Like Kübler-Ross' stages of dying, Bowlby and Parkes' dimensions of grief provide us with some insights, a framework to help us understand the many possible normal reactions to any loss.

Stress Reactions

Other normal, but not necessarily universal components of grief elaborate upon the findings of Bowlby and Parkes. Surviving the death of a loved one, especially a child or spouse, ranks very high on the list of stress-producing life events. A moderate amount of stress motivates and stimulates us, but a high level of stress is potentially harmful to our health. Those who are bereaved have a decreased resistance to infections and other diseases, such as high blood pressure and even cancer. Carl and Stephanie Simonton's research has revealed a striking relationship betwen severe stress and the development of cancer. A bereaved person is likely to get more colds and flus than he usually would. This stress is also likely to lead to problems in other relationships. The incidence of separation and divorce in parents who experience the death of a young child is exceptionally high. The death rate, in fact, for bereaved persons is significantly higher than that of their social and age peers who are not bereaved. This is especially apparent in the first year following the death. It should be obvious that this is a critical phase in a person's life, with incredible potential for the development of further problems which may only serve to compound the grief. It seems foolish, even dangerous, to refuse to acknowledge the presence and significance of the grief process, even long after the death.

"He Was Here with Me"

Many bereaved persons report having sensed the presence of the deceased, even speaking with and receiving counsel from them. This is more likely to occur within the first days and weeks after the death, but occasionally occurs late in the grief period, even years later. Often, but not always, this encounter takes place in a dream. One widow reported several such visits from her husband while she struggled with her loss and some ambivalent feelings about their relationship. After nearly two years she had resolved most of the conflicts, was settled in a new home and job, and began to feel comfortable in her new life. It had been several months since one of these "visits," when her husband appeared in a dream for the last time. He said, "You don't need me anymore. I'm going now," He began to leave, then turned around and peacefully reported, "I have such riches." She was reassured in her own mind that he felt she was "doing okay" although before she had wondered if he would have approved of the things she was doing. This dream symbolized the completion of her grief. Similar experiences have been reported by others, as well. This type of experience is probably far more common than we realize, simply because there is an understandable reluctance to reveal such a thing. Society mocks and ridicules these mystic or spirit encounters. Yet they seem so very real to the mourner, who does not want his sanity or the validity of his perceptions to be questioned by others. So he keeps the experiences to himself.

Guilt

Many of the problems with grief stem from unresolved guilt. More often than not, the guilt is purely imaginary. We chide ourselves for not having somehow prevented the death. A million possibilities flood our minds. If I had only done this, if I hadn't done that. The mother whose child dies of the Sudden Infant Death Syndrome often feels responsible, although told repeatedly that even had a physician been present the death could not have been prevented. A husband feels guilty for allowing his wife to go out in the storm on a silly errand, although she was strong-willed and could not have been stopped anyway. A child feels guilty for wishing he didn't have a sister, assuming his wish somehow made her run out in front of the car. We plague ourselves with torrents of unjustified guilt. It serves no useful purpose and only magnifies our anguish. Sometimes the guilt is for all those things we had left undone or unsaid. The flowers we meant to send, the "I love you's" we meant to say; these haunt us. It helps to verbalize these feelings with a sympathetic friend who can point out the errors in our reasoning and assure us that the deceased knew we loved them. It is important to resolve these agonizing conflicts, though, and not gloss over them, for they will eventually resurface and must be dealt with.

If, indeed, the individual is somehow responsible for the death or some other misdeed during the life of the deceased, that guilt should be dealt with in some constructive way. Allowing the guilt to fester only intensifies the self-depreciation. The guilt cannot undo what has been done. Ideally, we can learn from our past oversights and misjudgments and, at the very least, resolve not to repeat such indiscretions. Perhaps the specific nature of the deed or omitted act might lead to a more mature direction in one's lifestyle or inspire a project or concept that might benefit the entire community.

For example, rather than to continue to berate himself for failing to put the snow tires on his wife's car (the lack of which caused the car to skid out of control and strike a tree), a widower might routinely offer to perform this service for neighbors or others for whom it is an unusually difficult chore. Or, he might decide to establish a trust to pay for seasonal radio announcements reminding members of his community to put snow tires on their automobiles. This constructive approach to guilt still will not bring back his wife, but it may prevent one or several similar tragedies, and he might derive a measure of comfort from that knowledge. Another person, distraught and guilty over the unsaid "I love you's" might resolve to be freer with sincere affection and expressions of gratitude and concern, thus avoiding future pangs of guilt for these omissions. The point is that guilt can be handled in a constructive fashion which, although it cannot benefit the deceased, may serve as a blessing to many others.

Negative Feelings about the Deceased

An often neglected feature in a description of the grief process is the recurrence of negative feelings about the loved one who died. The bereaved are often surprised and bewildered when they find themselves in the midst of a negative memory. They may feel guilty and mentally berate themselves for even allowing such thoughts to surface.

One widow was confused by repeated thoughts of her husband's tirades on finances. She had hated these episodes. They lived comfortably, but not extravagantly. Yet they had often had arguments regarding the budget. While he was alive, she strongly disagreed with his financial priorities. Since his death, however, it bothered her to remember this, even though her intellectual position on the matter had not changed. She was now free to spend her money the way she chose. Couldn't she just forget that unpleasant aspect of an otherwise satisfying relationship?

Yes, she could and she probably will. At the least, she may reconcile herself to accepting her memory of her husband intact. He may not have been perfect, but he was special and human. There are no perfect relationships. None. Loving people intensely and being committed to them are not synonymous with submissive agreement with each and every one of their ideas. We allow ourselves these human differences in living persons, but we feel a reluctance to think ill of the dead.

This is, nevertheless, a normal part of grieving. We will remember the bad along with the good. Just as we may have failed the deceased, they probably failed us, too. There may be resentment for unkept promises they made us, just as we regret the unkept promises made to them. There may be resentment for the mere fact of their death, as if the deceased had made a conscious choice to die. The ultimate reconciliation of all of these memories is a major accomplishment of grief. Let it happen.

Notions of Suicide

Awesome flirtation with the notion of suicide is not at all unusual during bereavement. It may be motivated by guilt and feelings that "I don't deserve to live any longer," by a simple loss of interest in living or by the insatiable yearning to be with the deceased once again. The mother of a stillborn boy repeatedly expressed a strong interest in suicide. Fortunately, her husband's support and his need for her love while *he* was grieving kept her from ever going through with it. Her private anguish was so powerful that she was alarmed to discover she could feel so intensely and so negatively.

There are many who, when confronted with these frightening experiences, feel all alone. They don't know where to turn for help, or, turning for help are met with meaningless platitudes, superficial conversation, and, maybe, a prescription for tranquilizers. The support and concern of others are important in helping the bereaved recover. No one can replace the deceased in their lives, but other caring persons can help the bereaved eventually to realize the potential for joy and meaning from other sources. Those who are left without this support system are most vulnerable to these ideas of suicide. When this self-destructive desperation is accompanied by the availability of a "suicide cache" of pills, the results may not be pleasant.

While the idea of suicide may occur to nearly everyone who has lost someone they loved very much, usually the thought does not persist. In fact, the person often lacks the energy and organization to accomplish the feat until she progresses through her grief to a point where her life is beginning to take a new direction and the desperation has diminished. The self-destructive behavior of grief often takes on more subtle tones. Lack of interest in eating, neglect of routine health habits, and loss of sleep are frequent manifestations of grief. There just doesn't seem to be a reason to go on anymore. With the gradual resolution of grief, this behavior usually diminishes.

The Spending Binge

As bizarre as it may seem, many grieving persons help to assuage their grief by buying things. At a time when it is difficult emotionally to get involved with other persons, there is an inclination to become attached to new objects—toys, if you will. Sid Cato, a Chicago man who lost several members of his family in an auto accident that he survived, reported almost a compulsion to buy. He acquired stereo equipment, a car, and clothes, and traveled a lot. Material comforts, of course, cannot replace the deceased, but they do afford a distraction. And the new "things" provide an opportunity to find some pleasure in life again, if only of a temporal nature. It is, too, a fairly safe pleasure. If objects are broken or destroyed, they can be replaced.

Although this may be another distinctly American phenomenon, "bereavement buying" is well-recognized here, especially by certain entrepreneurs hoping to lure a share of the insurance money. Many schemes have been directed at the bereaved, since many of them *do* have money from insurance as well as a tendency to splurge. For lots of people, the insurance check represents the largest sum of money they have ever had at one time, and there may well be a certain anxiety about what to do with it. The bereaved should rely on trusted financial advisors and be wary of attractive young salespersons who appear on the doorstep with investment plans or expensive merchandise.

There is nothing inherently wrong in this spending, so long as the individual has the resources to pay for his purchases and the ways he chooses to spend his money are of his own design and not the plan of a charming unscrupulous charlatan. Otherwise, the bereaved may find themselves in debt, victimized, and with even more grief than before.

Grief Following Abortion, Miscarriage, and Stillbirth

In a society reluctant to acknowledge the need for grief at all, the plight is even worse for those who survive the poignant deaths of persons who never really "existed." Only recently has there been professional recognition of the significance of these losses to some parents. While we may gratuitously allow the mother of a stillborn a few days to adjust to the shock, those who undergo abortions or miscarriages are assumed to be able to return to normal by the end of the day. After all, it was only a physical problem. There was no emotional involvement with a person not even born yet, or so we have deluded ourselves. And, of course, we *never* allow the father to grieve in these situations.

Of course, there is great variation in the amount of involvement expectant parents have with the anticipation of their unborn child, just as we vary with respect to how attached we are to our siblings. Often times, even when an abortion is sought by both parents, the motivation may be danger to the mother's health, lack of funds to care for the child, or the presence of other demanding personal obligations which lead them to believe they could not adequately devote themselves to rearing this child. Even so, there may be waves of guilt and self-doubt and a decided yearning for this person who now never will be.

Miscarriages may or may not be "convenient" or desired by the parents. Sometimes, a miscarriage is a relief. Sometimes, it is as difficult to accept as any other death. A wished-for pregnancy is full of hopes, dreams, and fantasies; plans, anticipated role changes, and abundant love. An eager parent needn't meet a child to know it will be loved. When the expected child does not survive, the loss and the grief are very real. It may well take as long to recover from the death of this anticipated person as it does to recover from the death of a living, breathing child.

An atmosphere of understanding and support is most helpful in permitting these bereaved parents to acknowledge their grief and work through its resolution. All too frequently, even those directly involved may deny the impact of this loss. The grief is then postponed, only to reappear later, perhaps on the occasion of the birth of another child or the anniversary of the abortion or miscarriage or stillbirth, or perhaps when the child of a friend dies. Eventually, something will trigger the flood of emotion denied at the time of initial loss.

Delayed or Prolonged Grief

There are a number of reasons why grief might be delayed or prolonged. The parents whose child miscarried may delay their grief because grieving seems socially inappropriate. Individuals engaged in a host of seemingly important activities may think they don't have time or even need time for grief. Grief may be delayed simply because the effect of the death hasn't sunk in yet. Sometimes, we lack the physical or emotional strength to handle grief and subconsciously put it off until we are stronger.

Bridget was 29 years old when, on Father's Day, her baby girl died of hyaline membrane disease within 30 hours of her birth. Six months later, days before Christmas, Bridget's father was in a fatal automobile accident. For many months, she told herself "it was meant to be," and really didn't let the pain of the loss surface. But in time, she began to question the too-simple answer and resented the suffering that grew as her conscious admission of the losses increased. She started asking, "Why was it 'meant to be'? What sense does it make to lose a baby girl and an adored father in one year? What possible good could come of these tragedies?" Once a very organized wife and mother of two sons, Bridget lost interest in meal preparation and the creative tasks of mothering. "What does it matter, anyway," she rationalized, "if this can just happen to you. Why bother?"

A house full of children had always been Bridget's dream. Her third pregnancy seriously endangered her own health, not unusual for a woman with diabetes, and having more children of her own was out of the question. So she and her husband applied to adopt more children. Bridget still yearned for babies, but couples with two healthy children are far down on the list at adoption agencies. After three long, anxious years, her husband openly suggested they remove from the house the "baby things" she had been saving and recognize the reality that no one was going to give them a baby.

At long last, Bridget resolved her grief. She had lost her baby, her father, and her dream of a large family. Once she finally accepted the fact of those losses, she was able to go on and make the most of the life she now had. She has resumed her menu planning and organized housekeeping and special times with the boys. But it took a long time before the joy of those tasks returned.

Some time after Bridget's father died, she learned of the death of the father of one of her sister's friends. She wrote the girl a letter expressing her sympathy and advising to treasure all the good things about her father and dismiss the unpleasant memories she had. Bridget was perplexed when the girl wrote back saying she had been doing all right *until* she got Bridget's letter. Bridget's advice had brought on a rush of memories and tears, the first she had shed for her father. Sometimes a gentle nudge from a friend can facilitate the expression and, hence, the resolution of grief.

Grieving Before the Death

The news of a terminal diagnosis induces all kinds of reactions in the patient and the people who are close to the patient. Frequently, patient and family alike, if informed of the prognosis, will start to anticipate the impending loss. This is called preparatory or anticipatory grief. It is actually grieving before the death. The feelings and behaviors may be much the same as might be expected to follow the death of a loved one. In rare cases, the grief process is completed by the survivors before the patient actually dies. This decathexis was described in Chapter 2. More often, it merely affords the opportunity to begin to grieve and work through some of the emotional turmoil a little sooner. Parkes' study of widows showed that the post-death grief period was shorter for those who had at least two weeks' warning that death was imminent than it was for those whose husbands met with a sudden death.

Anticipatory grief, however potentially valuable, is not without pain and is not a guarantee of an easier adjustment after the death. In fact, many persons who have been through it remark that "it didn't help at all" knowing the death would come and that the death was still a shock and surprise, even though they were expecting it. There are so many extenuating circumstances that it is futile to attempt to predict the outcome of grief based on the gathering of a few facts.

When it occurs, anticipatory grief should be accorded the same respect as postdeath grief. Caring friends and family should try, within the limits of their own grief process, to help the individual cope with these feelings.

Help for the Bereaved and Prebereaved

We are a self-sufficient, innovative, and resourceful society. But often we concede that we might make even more headway by utilizing our best national resource—people. We join countless special interest groups to share our expertise and glean advice from others. It is an ingenious and popular American way to do a better job, whatever our task.

This eruption of self-help groups has found its way into the lives of those who are bereaved. The new national awareness of death and the significance of grief has encouraged many mourners to join with others who share their plight. There are generic "grief recovery groups" sponsored by churches or community organizations and there are more specialized groups dealing primarily with survivors of a particular type of death. Madison, Wisconsin has two groups offering practical and psychological support for the widowed. One is named KAYRA, for the Greek word meaning widowed. The other is NAIM, named after the biblical town where Jesus raised the widow's son from the dead. Detroit has a group called "First Sunday" comprising parents who have lost a child to death. KAYRA provides social activities every Saturday night and plans "coffee and sharing" in individual homes for the recently widowed. NAIM has monthly meetings. The "First Sunday" group gathers for Mass the first Sunday of every month and shares the common experiences of bereaved parents and families. Similar local groups operate or are being formed in many communities. You might consult your community mental health center, hospital chaplain, or clergy for information about any groups in your area. Or start your own group, perhaps writing to one of those listed for assistance.

A number of national organizations have a network of local chapters, counselors, or both. Write to the individual group headquarters for more information.

Make Today Count, P.O. Box 303, Burlington, Iowa 52601. This organization now has nearly 300 chapters. It was founded by Orville

Kelly, now deceased, a victim of terminal cancer who decided to make the most of each day remaining in his life. Membership is open to anyone who wants to improve his or her appreciation of life. The organization's newsletter is available for $10 per year.

National Association of Widows, P.O. Box 109, New York, New York 10024. Lynn Caine, author of *Widow* and *Lifelines,* started the association after discovering the value of sharing common feelings and experiences. Write to her at the above address.

Widowed Persons Service, c/o American Association of Retired Persons, 1909 K Street, N.W., Washington, D.C. 20049. WPS was founded by present coordinator Leo Baldwin. There are currently over 100 chapters, with trained volunteers who call on widowed persons starting about six weeks after the death. Single copies of an excellent booklet called "On Being Alone" are available free. The WPS will also provide information and cooperate with communities interested in forming a WPS program. A listing of programs in your area is available, too.

The Compassionate Friends, Inc. Box 1347, Oak Brook, Illinois 60521. This nationwide organization offers support to families grieving the death of a child. Local chapters provide monthly sharing groups, "telephone friends," and educational programs. Send a self-addressed, stamped envelope for a list of chapter addresses.

The National Sudden Infant Death Syndrome Foundation, 310 South Michigan Avenue, Suite 1904, Chicago, Illinois 60604. The SIDS Foundation provides service programs for families of SIDS (crib death) victims, supports medical research on SIDS and offers education of health and emergency personnel as well as the public. A network of volunteer counselors, many of whom are themselves parents of SIDS victims, calls on new SIDS families to help them cope. Enclose a self-addressed, stamped envelope when requesting information and addresses of local groups.

Ray of Hope, 1518 Derwen Drive, Iowa City, Iowa 52240. Organized by Ms. Elnora (Betsy) Ross following her husband's suicide, *Ray of Hope* endeavors to help survivors cope with the special agonies of having a loved one end his own life. A helpful booklet is available for $3.50.

I Can Cope: contact your local or state office of American Cancer Society or write American Cancer Society, Director of Service and Rehabilitation, 777 3rd Avenue, New York, New York 10017. Each locally sponsored program provides a series of educational and supportive classes for persons with a diagnosis of cancer and for another important person in their lives such as a spouse, child, sibling, or good friend. I Can Cope provides an excellent approach to living with such a diagnosis.

Candlelighters Association, 123 "C" Street, S.E., Washington, D.C. 20003. Formed by and for parents of children with cancer, Candlelighters is a rapidly growing organization providing a broad spectrum of educational and supportive services.

Mothers Against Drunk Drivers (MADD), 5330 Primrose, Suite 146, Fair Oaks, California 95628. Started in May, 1980, by Candy Lightner, MADD already has thirty chapters nationwide. Mrs. Lightner's 13-year-old daughter was killed by a drunk driver, and her grief has inspired this massive effort to reform laws on drunk driving, educate the public about this number one killer of young men and women, and provide survival assistance for victims and their families. Individual memberships are $10, family memberships, $25. The MADD newsletter keeps members informed about pending legislation, accomplishments of the organization, and the services available. This group is an outstanding example of the potentially constructive power of grief.

Parents of Murdered Children, 1739 Bella Vista, Cincinnati, Ohio, 45237. POMC was founded by Robert and Charlotte Hullinger, who discovered that the grief process for parents of murdered children is prolonged and aggravated by media exposure and frustration with the criminal justice system. The group's two goals are to help families through their grieving period and to educate society to the needs of the survivors of this horrendous experience. There are more than thirty chapters now in operation.

Other groups organized to help specific groups of cancer patients are listed at the end of Chapter 10.

Grieving as Growing

There are some things that happen in life that are so terrible that it would seem almost sacriligious to suggest that there might have been some redeeming value in the tragedy. Assume, for example, that a great fire destroys most of the business and civic buildings in a small town. The financial losses sustained are overwhelming, and the town is virtually wiped out. We curse the fire and the dry weather and the wind that fateful day. As the citizens struggle to rebuild their community, they discover a surprising sense of camaraderie and find that they can work quite well together. In the course of the planning and reconstruction, they learn to appreciate the others' skills and ideas. When the work is completed, the townspeople have learned a great deal. Together, they grieve for the loss of the familiar environment, the records, documents, art, and merchandise which is forever unrecoverable. But because they shared that loss and the responsibility for adapting to that loss, they develop an even greater sense of pride and involvement in the community. The tragedy was real, the losses were undeniable, but there was also a redeeming value in their collective experiences of grief. Because of that fire, the residents of that town have gained a cohesive spirit and confidence which otherwise never would have evolved.

It is so difficult to forsee the evolution, though. Whatever we are experiencing now—rainy day, sunny day, depths of depression, unbounded joy—*seems* as if it will last forever. The more intense the experience, the more likely we are to assume it has enduring qualities. One of my students, Susan, shared her feelings about the death of her adolescent brother. She titled her paper "A 'Grade A' Person" and closed with these remarks:

> When is enough time spent for grief and when have enough tears fallen and the cheeks stop being chapped from wetness? When does this pass? I don't know. In my case, I don't think that my tears will ever stop, because then that would mean that my space has been filled, thus making me a hypocrite, because we all know "Grade A" persons' spaces are never filled by time, and that is a philosophy of mine.

I truly hope that Susan's paper might have a different tone if she were to write it today. Sometimes it feels essentially disrespectful to allow ourselves to have a life, especially a good life, without that person who was at one time so much a part of how and why we lived. But we needn't be burdened by this self-made guilt. We have the capability to learn to cherish the memory of the deceased, ponder and retain their positive qualities and influence in our lives without letting their memory control our lives. Adjusting to the death of a loved one is most often a long and painful process, but it can be a time of profound introspection, reassessment of our values, and renewed appreciation of life. We can, if only we allow ourselves, grow through our grief. We can take the grain along with chaff, to modify an ancient axiom. Would not this growth be a tribute to the memory of this very special person? Even Susan, still in the midst of her pain, remarked:

> The experience I went through was more than just a tear jerking experience. It was an experience that changed my life a great deal. The experience matured me a great deal, which was a blessing in disguise, in that sense.

As profoundly as I believe that grief can have a positive outcome, I would *never* suggest to a grieving person that someday they'll be glad they went through it. May flowers are of little concern or comfort to the rain-soaked April picnicker. The bereaved need help, love, support and patience, not platitudes. Given that atmosphere, they will eventually discover their own peace and new direction.

I recently talked with a father of four whose wife had died several months ago following a long illness. He is in his late forties. He asked me, "You know how you prepare for this? You start in high school with a hard-nosed track coach who teaches you how to gut it out. Or you get a demanding band director, drama coach, whatever—all those 'frills' school budgets can't quite accommodate anymore. You have to learn early and often how to make it through rough times. Then these skills in handling small crises pay off when the big ones come."

The only ways to avoid the grief that follows the death of loved ones are to (1) die before they do, thereby imposing the agony on them, or (2) never get involved in the first place. I believe both methods are undesirable given a choice. A favorite passage of mine is from *The Little Prince* by Antoine de St. Exupéry. It chronicles the adventures of the sole inhabitant of another planet who embarks upon a journey seeking friends and truth. He leaves his own little globe and his only friend, a beautiful rose. After a while, he comes to the Earth and happens upon a fox, who beseeches the boy to "tame" him. The curious little prince asks the fox,

> "What does that mean—'tame'?"
> "It is an act too often neglected," said the fox. "It means to establish ties."
> "'To establish ties'?"
> "Just that," said the fox. "To me, you are still nothing more than a little boy who is just like a hundred thousand other little boys. And I have no need of you. And you, on your part, have no need of me. To you, I am nothing more than a fox like a hundred thousand other foxes. But if you tame me, then we shall need each other. To me, you will be unique in all the world. To you, I shall be unique in all the world. . . ."
> "I am beginning to understand," said the little prince. . . . The fox came back to his idea.
> "My life is very monotonous," he said, "I hunt chickens; men hunt me. All the chickens are just alike, and all the men are just alike. And, in consequence, I am a little bored. But if you tame me, it will be as if the sun came to shine on my life. I shall know the sound of a step that will be different from all the others. Other steps send me hurrying back underneath the ground. Yours will call me, like music, out of my burrow. And then look: you see the grain-fields down yonder? I do not eat bread. Wheat is of no use to me. The wheat fields have nothing to say to me. And that is sad. But you have hair that is the color of gold. Think how wonderful that will be when you have tamed me! The grain, which is also golden, will bring me back the thought of you. And I shall love to listen to the wind in the wheat . . ."

The fox gazed at the little prince, for a long time.

"Please—tame me!" he said.

"I want to, very much," the little prince replied. "But I have not much time. I have friends to discover, and a great many things to understand."

"One only understands the things that one tames," said the fox. "Men have no more time to understand anything. They buy things all ready made at the shops. But there is no shop anywhere where one can buy friendship, and so men have no friends any more. If you want a friend, tame me . . ."

So the little prince tamed the fox. And when the hour of his departure drew near—

"Ah," said the fox, "I shall cry."

"It is your own fault," said the little prince. "I never wished you any sort of harm, but you wanted me to tame you . . ."

"Yes, that is so," said the fox.

"But now you are going to cry!" said the little prince.

"Yes, that is so," said the fox.

"Then it has done you no good at all!"

"It has done me good," said the fox, "because of the color of the wheat fields."

Perhaps the story of the little prince and the fox is merely an eloquent restatement of "it is better to have loved and lost than never to have loved at all." Living a life devoid of attachments merely to avoid the pain of a possible separation would be preposterous and a terrible waste. The sweet sorrow of parting is a testimony to our courage to live and to love.

6

What Do You Say After You Say "I'm Sorry"?

Practically no one enjoys going to a funeral or wake. On the contrary, one would question the mental health of someone who looks forward to such occasions. Despite our professed aversion to them, great numbers of us are drawn to these rituals and there are some very good reasons why. These are the special times society has arranged for us to acknowledge publicly our respect and admiration for the deceased, to ponder and appreciate our own mortality, and to express sorrow and concern for the survivors. But what do you say after you say, "I'm sorry"? Many of us feel uneasy around someone who is grieving and find it difficult to say the right words, as if there were some such magical combination of nouns and verbs that could erase the discomfort, even the agony of the moment. Does this sound familiar?

"Cathy, I'm so sorry. Phillip was a great guy. We all loved him." Heather choked out the words at the funeral home. She was obviously uncomfortable, but felt obliged to come. After all, Cathy and Phil had been her good friends for years.

"Thank you, Heather. Thank you for coming." Cathy paused to stifle a sob. "I just don't know what I'm going to do without him. I can't believe he's really gone." Cathy had found herself a widow only the day before, when Phillip was in a car wreck that killed him instantly. She was still in shock.

"Well, you know I'm always here if you need me. Just call if I can do anything for you, anything at all." Heather was nearly in tears herself and quickly turned, ostensibly to sign the visitor book. When Cathy wasn't looking, Heather made a quiet exit in search of some fresh air and a less depressing environment.

The depressing environment and the feeling that there is nothing we can do about it are probably responsible for a large part of our discomfort. Nobody *likes* being around depressed people, confused and tearful people. The help of loving and supportive friends can be immensely valuable in the long and painful process of trying to build a new life without that special person whose loss seems insurmountable. But because we feel uneasy around those who are grieving, we usually spend less time with them at the precise period in their lives when they need us most. A bereaved mother who was a student in my class said, "I have been so hurt and so bitter over the insensitive things people have said and the lack of caring they have shown by staying away, because they 'didn't know what to say' . . ."

Those unfortunate enough to find themselves bereaved may also often feel abandoned by their friends. This needn't be so. If we can accept the sadness as a temporary but very real part of the situation, we can become a very useful and significant source of comfort for our friends who are bereaved. In our often fruitless search for the right thing to say, we frequently forget that there are lots of things that we can *do* to help our friends through a period of mourning and readjustment. Following are some simple, but important thoughts to consider if you have a friend who has lost someone dear to her.

Simplicity and Sincerity

Express your sympathy simply and sincerely. You aren't expected to come up with clever or polished rhetoric. Your presence alone is a sign you care, and that means more than anything you could say. Feelings are more important than fancy phrases. If you find it difficult to express your feelings aloud, write them in a letter, even for a friend who lives just across the street. It may make it easier for you to say what you really want to say, and the gesture will be treasured by your friend for a long time.

Whether or not you can attend the visitation and funeral, it is a nice gesture to send a sympathy card. After recovering from the death of her father, Bridget went out and bought scores of sympathy cards to have on hand. She was so touched by all the people, many of whom she hadn't seen in years, who remembered her and cared when her father died. Now she is especially careful to send a card when she learns of a death in the family of any friend, wanting to extend the same comfort to others that she felt in a time of need.

There are probably a number of things you would like to tell your friend, either in person or in a sympathy card or letter. This is the time to share those positive, but often neglected facets of your friendship. You might wish to recount an especially fond memory you have of an event, such as the neighborhood picnic or a football game or birthday party in which the deceased was involved in a special way. Or, perhaps, you might mention a particular quality the deceased possessed (a wonderful sense of humor or terrific culinary talent, for example) that you found admirable or even inspiring. When you are grieving the loss of a loved one, it is comforting to know that others admired the person and are thinking of him or her, too.

What Not to Say

Would-be comforters of the bereaved have often been known to say, with the very best of intentions, many things that are inappropriate, if not cruel, under the circumstances. I think this is another major factor which explains our tendency to shy away from friends who are grieving. We are unsure of what to say and afraid we will say the wrong thing. None of us is perfect, and these social blunders happen occasionally to even the best of us. With a little forethought, however, we can avoid the majority of these unintentional *faux pas*. Discussion of a few examples should be sufficient to guide us away from the more common and obvious unsuccessful attempts to comfort.

In an effort, perhaps, to establish a bond between the bereaved and the comforter, the latter can often be heard to say, "I know *just* how you feel." Ridiculous. Outrageous. No one knows *just* how any other person feels in any situation. *Only* the bereaved knows the exact and many-faceted relationship he or she had with the deceased. *Only* the bereaved knows the intimate and personal details of the relationship, the kept and unkept promises, the arguments and how they were resolved, the goals, the plans, the special memories that only those two people shared. *Only* the bereaved knows exactly how he or she feels about death and after-life and, possibly, how the deceased felt about them. While we may know that they are sad and that, in their place, we, too, would be sad, no one truly knows the very special and private grief they are called upon to face by the loss of this special person in their lives. It is natural and fitting that we should let them know that we feel a loss, too; that we share their grief. But it is preposterous to pretend that we actually know just how they feel, even if we have been through what seemed to be a similar experience. (Try to recall the darkest moment in your own life, the deepest depression you have ever known. Could anyone else have possibly known just how you felt at that time? Did you believe them if they said that they did?)

Another frequent mistake is to try to make light of the tragedy, to emphasize the over-simple solution. A very dear friend of mine gave birth to a beautiful but stillborn baby boy some ten hours after the doctor told her the child was dead. (She had already been in labor a couple of hours.) Although they knew there was no heartbeat, the doctor advised Sue and her husband to continue to go through a "normal" labor and delivery rather than to have the baby taken surgically. A normal delivery would hasten her physical recovery and mean that Sue would have a chance to have future deliveries using the Lamaze techniques she and Dave had practiced for weeks. I went to visit Sue that day. She was exhausted, tearful, and shaken. She described her son, whom she had seen a couple of hours after the delivery.

"He was so sweet; so tiny and so sweet."

I ached for her, as I had a small infant at home and could easily imagine my own agony in her place. As I was leaving, Sue's parents came into the room, having driven several hundred miles after they heard the news. They are very nice people and a loving family, but I will always remember what Sue's mother said to her as soon as she came into the room.

"Sue, we love you, honey. We are just so grateful that *you* are all right. We are sad about the baby, but you can always have other children. We are just so glad that you are okay."

It was a natural and truthful thing to say. Of course, they were relieved that Sue was all right. Any loving parent would be first concerned with the well-being of her own child. And, as it turned out, Sue did go on to have two healthy, active, lovely children. But at that moment, having just suffered the loss of a long-awaited, full-term baby of her only pregnancy to date, it was almost as if her mother were saying, "I'm sure glad I didn't lose my baby [29-year-old Sue] but your baby doesn't matter." I *know* she didn't mean it that way. And Sue overlooked it. But many mothers of stillborns are hurt by such statements, however well-intentioned. It might be more helpful to say something like, "You must be so sad to have lost your baby. We love you and will help you any way we can." But don't act as though babies are as easy to replace as living room chairs.

Let's take the issue one step further. I have often discussed this incident with my "Death and Dying" classes. To clarify my point— that is, not to make light of the loss—I suggested that no one would ever go to a new widow and say, "Don't worry. It's only a husband. You can always get married again." To my amazement, a middle-aged woman in the back row named Louise Tabor interrupted me with a simple, emphatic "Oh, yes they do!" Louise told of several friends who tried to speed her recovery by assuring her that there were "lots more fish in the sea." They surely meant well. But Mrs. Tabor was mourning the loss of the greatest love of her life and she didn't appreciate people telling her that her husband and the relationship they had taken years to develop could be easily replaced. Yes, people do often remarry after being widowed. It is, however, inappropriate to mention it so soon after the death of a spouse.

Another group of not-too-helpful comments come under the general heading "it's all for the best." Sue recalls a quiet anger and agony every time someone would tell her there was "probably something wrong with the baby, anyway," as if she would have loved him less or that life with a handicapped child would be worse than having the child die. On the contrary, she was hurt to think that others assumed she had produced a defective child. She was already wrestling with many erroneously-based guilt feelings about not having done whatever it was she should have or might have done to assure her child a live birth. The it's-all-for-the-best approach only accentuated and prolonged her existing feelings of inferiority and grief. As it turned out for Sue's baby, the autopsy and lab tests revealed no birth defects or metabolic abnormalities. The cause of his stillbirth remains a mystery. But even a mother who has lost a child with an obvious birth defect is not likely to take comfort in the knowledge or implication that she was responsible for an imperfect baby. She is not likely to feel that her baby's death was "all for the best" when most women, even her own friends, give birth to beautiful, healthy, vital, bouncing babies.

Probably, the most frequent situation which prompts this sort of comment involves a person who has been ill for a long time and suffered a great deal of pain. A close runner-up would be the person who, having recently been given the aforementioned prognosis, dies suddenly of a heart attack, for instance, thereby escaping the anticipated agony. Under these circumstances, the death may, indeed, seem like a blessing for all those concerned. But it might not. There may still have been unresolved tensions between patient and family, or there may be nightmarish financial problems ahead for the survivors, or the death may have come at a time when the family needed the advice and counsel of their now departed member to help them face a simultaneous, but unrelated crisis. What seems like a blessing from one person's point of view may seem like a bitter, cruel blow from a closer perspective.

Susan, a junior in college, was still grieving over the death of her fourteen-year-old brother. He had a brain tumor and she had been with him through several years of surgery, chemotherapy, weight loss, baldness, and general agony. In a paper for my class, she recalled bitterly the people who told her it was "all for the best." "How can it possibly be all for the best when my fourteen-year-old brother is *dead*? Other fourteen-year-olds get to be fifteen-year-olds and fifty-year-olds. How can they possible say it is for the best? Is it for the best that he had a tumor and suffered? I just don't understand how they could say that."

If the bereaved comment first that they feel a sense of relief at the death, you should support and encourage their positive attitude. But don't suggest to a grieving friend that the death of their loved one was really the best possible thing. There may well be lots of reasons why they would disagree with you. If you feel really compelled to be optimistic, you might say something like, "At least his suffering is over." Better yet, just express your sorrow and your support. And be there when they need that support.

Another common tendency is to tell the bereaved about our own problems. It is almost as if we're saying, "As long as we're on the subject of personal tragedy, let me tell you what I've been going through lately." Everyone has problems and yearns for help and sympathy, but this is *not* the time to ask the bereaved to provide them. Get help for *your* problems elsewhere and don't unnecessarily overload the bereaved.

A Specific Offer of Help

Almost everyone says, "If you need anything, don't hesitate to call me." It is nice and polite to say that, but grieving people almost never call someone and ask for help. Perhaps they feel as if they would be imposing. Maybe they don't even think about calling anyone. At any rate, the offer usually goes unaccepted for whatever reason. A better approach is to follow up your offer by calling them several days later and making specific suggestions as to how you would be willing to help. Here is a partial list of things you could do to help your grieving friends:

1. address their "thank you for the sympathy" cards
2. write to their out-of-town friends and holiday correspondents who do not yet know of the death
3. bring over a meal or fresh-baked cookies
4. go to the grocery store for them
5. wash dishes
6. run the vacuum cleaner
7. take them to dinner or a movie
8. ask them over for coffee (or something stronger)
9. take care of the children for a day
10. help sort through the deceased's belongings
11. offer to take them shopping for a new outfit
12. suggest you get together for some golf or tennis
13. mow the grass or shovel the snow
14. if you are able to contact the family soon after the death, you might offer to stay at the house during the visitation and funeral, to ward off potential burglars who check obituaries and prey on

empty houses. Also, the family may be in need of someone to watch small children during the services.

15. make sure their car has a full gas tank on the day of the funeral.

Get the idea? There are many things that need to be done, and they will vary somewhat depending on the individual's situation. Try to offer to do at least two or three specific things, things you would feel comfortable doing. They may still refuse your help, but at least they will know you are sincere in wanting to help and that alone can be a comfort. A specific offer goes a lot farther than "Call me if you need anything." Repeat or alter your offers of help every few days, so that they can gracefully change their mind about accepting and so that they know you are not just making a superficial gesture of assistance.

A few years ago, an acquaintance of mine lost her husband, who had suffered a sudden stroke at age forty-two. I liked her a lot, but was not a close friend, and she lived about thirty miles away. I sent her a note about a month after her husband's death, inviting her for coffee, and enclosed a stamped, self-addressed postcard with the following options for her to check:

_____I will come for coffee on Friday at 10:00 AM

_____I will come for coffee on_____at_____

_____I won't be able to come over

_____Leave me alone for awhile

_____Other_____

She never did come over for coffee. But she did return the postcard with a note saying that my offer had made her realize that she should accept some of the offers her close friends had been making. That was worth my effort. This sort of communication would be appropriate for someone you would like to help or do something for, but to whom you are not close enough to pick up the phone and have a casual conversation. The postcard makes it easy for them to respond without an awkward phone call. Sincerity is the key. If you don't mean it, don't say it. If you really don't want to help in a certain way, don't offer.

Listen and Share

Be a good listener. You may be uncomfortable. You may even rationalize that it is bad for your friend to talk about the deceased. But many times, a bereaved person feels compelled to recall the deceased or the death event itself many times over, as if repeating it aloud will somehow impress its reality on his or her mind. They may want to talk at length about that special person, about things they liked to do together, about things they'll never have the chance to do now. Curb your desire to keep changing the subject. The expression of these thoughts and the knowledge that someone cares enough to listen are important parts of the healing process. Of course, you may have great conversations about lots of other things, too. Even bereaved persons have to pay taxes, cope with the weather, and cook.

Cindy, a close friend of mine, widowed in her mid-twenties, complained that people always clammed up around her or avoided her entirely. She didn't plan to depress them with talk about her husband, she just wanted someone to acknowledge her existence and intellect, apart from her widowhood. She just wanted to *talk* to someone. Cindy was desperately lonely and alone. Listening requires so little effort and can mean so much, it seems quite selfish to deny this outlet to our friends.

Let your friend cry. Our tendency is to say, "Now don't start crying on me. You'll be all right." They will be all right, eventually, but it will probably happen sooner if you allow the grief to pour out as it will. Cry along with them, if you feel like it. It won't last forever, and it is a wonderful, natural way to relieve tension and pent-up feelings. Crying is a virtually inevitable aftermath of death and about the worst part of it is that your face gets wet. So get a box of tissues and a nice shoulder and be available.

Anger and Guilt

Don't be alarmed if your friend is angry or expresses tremendous feelings of guilt. Almost everyone experiences some degree of guilt when someone close to them dies. Listen to these feelings and try to help your friend work through them. Most guilt feelings are not based on fact, but grieving persons don't always think very clearly. "If I had only insisted he not make the trip that day; if only I had made her go to the doctor sooner; if only I hadn't fed him so much cholesterol, he wouldn't have died."

Many guilt feelings relate not specifically to the death, but rather to things they feel they should have done or said while the loved one was alive. "I promised her we'd take that trip to the mountains, but I was always too busy to go." "I should have written to Mom more often. There were so many things I should have told her; so many things she would have wanted to know." "I never really told him how much I loved him. And now it is too late. He'll never know how much he meant to me." Assure your friend that all these "ifs" and "should haves" are only useless speculation. In the highly unlikely event that your friend was somehow partly responsible for the death, the guilt feelings are still useless. They cannot bring the person to life. They cannot promote a healthy life for the living. Wayne Dyer, in his book *Your Erroneous Zones*, agrees that guilt is a wasteful expenditure of emotional energy. It *is*, however, often difficult to deal with, and a friend's unwavering reassurance can be most helpful. The lesson for us all is to do and say *now* those things that are important so that someday we won't have to be sorry for not having done and said them.

Anger is difficult to handle, too, because we usually take it personally and get defensive. Your friend may well be mad at the doctors, the driver of the "other" car, or even at God. Somehow, we feel compelled to blame someone or something for the tragedy. Maybe we think that the assignment of responsibility elsewhere would in some way diminish our own anguish. One of the problems with anger is that it often gets displaced. If you are handy and the doctors, driver, and God are unavailable for confrontation, you are probably going to receive the anger intended for them. Try not to let it get to you. This angry period usually passes quickly if the person can get these negative feelings out as they arise.

Gentle Suggestions

Eventually encourage your friend to get involved in new activities and meet new people. Don't do this the week after the funeral, but maybe in a couple of months, after she has had some time to regain her composure. She may be very reluctant at first, but developing new interests is crucial to her recovery. Don't be forceful, but do be persistent and make a real effort to find something your friend could truly enjoy. You might encourage a latent interest in photography, or suggest that she write about her recent experience. Perhaps she has postponed a project that could use some renewed interest. You might look into evening classes on a subject of special interest to her, or suggest she join a church group or community theater or even an exercise class, and make an effort to go with her, if at all possible, at least at first.

Also, you might suggest she contact one of the appropriate grief recovery groups mentioned in Chapter 5. These groups have helped many persons cope with their loss. There is something special about the empathy and guidance of one who has "been there."

Respect your grieving friend as an adult with a host of coping resources of his or her own. respect a wish for privacy and call again later. Don't be overbearing in your desire to help. Be sure he is aware of your concern and availability. He will accept as much help as he can while maintaining his own dignity.

Remember that the most important thing is caring enough to be available after the funeral. Too many people pay their respects and then go their way, avoiding the bereaved, in the painful post-funeral months. Especially critical times are birthdays, anniversaries, and holidays. Make a special effort at these times not to let them be alone. Helping friends through a painful loss can take a lot of time and energy and even tears on your part. But your labors of love will no doubt not only augment your friendship, but also help you learn about loss and life and love and coping. And that's a lot to learn.

A Plea from Someone Who Has Been There

I think it was said most eloquently by Mary Bailey, a lovely lady whose cherished teenage daughter was killed in an accident.

Please dear friend
Don't say to me the old clichés
Time heals all wounds
God only gives you as much as you can bear
Life is for the living . . .
Just say the thoughts of your heart
I'm sorry, I love you, I'm here, I care
Hug me and squeeze my hand
I need your warmth and strength.

Please don't drop your eyes when I am near
I feel so rejected now by God and man
Just look in my eyes and let me know that you are with me.

Don't think you must always be strong for me
It's okay to cry
It tells me how much you care
Let me cry, too
It's so lonely to always cry alone.

Please keep coming by even after many weeks have passed
When the numbness wears off the pain of grief is unbearable.
Don't ever expect me to be quite the same
How can I be when part of my being is here no more.

But please know, dear friend, with your love, support and
    understanding
I will live and love again and be grateful everyday that I have you—

dear friend.

7

Talking with Children About Death

"Mommy, why did they cut off Grandpa's legs? Was something wrong with his legs? I wish they hadn't cut them off!" Mark's half-frightened inquisition startled Jeanne, whose father had just died of a heart attack two days earlier. The funeral was to be that afternoon.

"Mark, what a thing to say. Of course they didn't cut off Grandpa's legs. Why would you ever say such a thing?" Jeanne tried not to be too harsh with her eight-year-old, but her sorrow had shortened her temper. What could he be thinking? It was probably something he saw on one of those creepy TV shows. She resolved to be more diligent in screening what he watched.

"But, Mommy, did you see him in the box? You can only see the top of him. If his legs are there, why don't they let us see them?" Mark was obviously troubled and the problem was the half-couch casket.

"Oh, Sweetie, now I see what you mean. Yes, Grandpa's legs are there. When we get back to the funeral home, we'll have Mr. Sargent show you. It's just the way they usually have the casket. They close the bottom half for some reason. I don't really know why. It's just the way they do it. But Grandpa's legs *are* there. I'm sorry I didn't know what you meant at first. Yes, the rest of Grandpa really is there. I'm sorry you were worried, but I am glad you asked me about it, so you won't need to worry any more." Jeanne was relieved to find such a simple explanation for what appeared to be a horror movie type of question. She hoped all the future questions would be as easy to answer.

Children are full of questions. It is only natural. The questions are not going to stop when someone in the family dies. But most people would rather answer a hundred questions about elephants, peanut butter, dump trucks, and airplanes than to respond to a single question about death. Children are so open and vulnerable. We hate to see them unhappy and try to protect them from any sadness in life. Although the intentions may be honorable, our children deserve more—an opportunity to learn to deal with the many aspects of life. It is a most important part of growing up. Isn't that what growing up is—learning to handle life on your own? Often, it is our own lack of understanding of death that causes us to avoid the issue with children, with everyone, for that matter.

The first step toward being honest with children about death is to learn to be honest with ourselves. Reading this book and others like it, and discussing your feelings with those closest to you are good ways to begin. Having resolved your own feelings about death, you will be a far more helpful guide for your child when the need arises.

There are several important things to remember when discussing death with children. Probably the best advice is to *think* about a child's questions before answering. Be sure to understand what it is the child wants to know and respond with special consideration of the child's age, level of understanding, and personality. Very young children tend to think of death as some sort of temporary condition, from which the victim will return. (Television portrayals of dead heroes who later appear on other shows no doubt lend to the confusion.) Older children may personify death as a ghost who comes to take people away. Some developmentalists contend that most children don't really conceive of death as a permanent and universal fact until at least age seven. The most often quoted study, however, was done in Hungary in the 1940s and I question the applicability of those findings to contemporary American life.

Children vary considerably with regard to the age at which their understanding reaches a certain level. Their experiences with death and the explanations of death given to them also have an incredible influence on the development of their concept of death. A very precocious youngster, or one who has had to personally deal with death may demonstrate an amazing clarity of the concept at the age of four, while another child, following his own normal developmental pattern may have difficulty understanding it at age eleven. Obviously, the most important guidelines will be given to you by your child. Be alert to the cues they give you about their own understanding and help them to progress to a higher level.

Forget the Fancy Phrases

It is imperative to use plain English when speaking to children about death. In everyday speech, we use phrases and clichés that are unfamiliar and unmeaningful to children. You might say, "Daddy is really irritable. We'll have to walk on eggs around him today." *You* know that "walk on eggs" means to be careful not to do something to make Daddy upset, but a child only thinks of smashing yolks and shells on the floor.

Nearly all of us use euphemisms when we talk about death to anyone. But "passed away," "laid to rest," and "met his Maker" are only confusing to children, who take language quite literally. "Passed on" may mean a play in a football game, or perhaps advancing to the next grade in school. A concerned adult, trying to be honest and open, once told a little girl that death was, indeed, permanent. She responded with her own version of "permanent"—her mother's new curly hairdo! Is a dead person just "resting"? Is a resting person dead? Some children have developed tremendous sleep problems, and even feared their parents going to bed at night, after being told that someone they loved is now "asleep" and will never awaken. Be very careful about what you say and the words you use to say it. Then ask the child to tell you what you said in his own words, just to be sure the message was understood.

Be Honest

Please be truthful. Don't tell a child that a dead relative or friend has gone on a long vacation. In time, they will only learn to mistrust you or to fear having anyone go on a vacation, because their loved one never returned from "vacation." Don't send the child away for a few days when someone dies, only to have him return and find the person mysteriously missing. Children deserve and need our trust in their ability to cope with the problems of life. Deceiving them about something so important, *however good* the intentions, can seriously deflate their self-image and permanently interfere with the relationship between the child and the perpetrator(s) of the deceit. Resentment and a sense of betrayal almost always result from such an important deception. Facing the truth, however bitter, with loving, supportive adults is far better for the child than the possible temporary peace but awesome sequelae the lie would bring. The child is part of the family and deserves to share in its experiences, joyful or tragic. That is how children learn about life, from experiencing it, not from being shielded from it.

Feeling Alone

Children often feel abandoned when someone they love dies, as if the person wouldn't have left if they had really loved the child. "Why did Mommy go away and not even say goodbye? Didn't she love me enough to even say goodbye?" Assure the child that the person did love them and that they can treasure the memories of that love all of their lives. Also be certain that he understands that he is still loved very much by the people who are still living. The assurance that other adults continue to love him helps to reinforce the concept that the child is still lovable and important, even without the beloved parent, sibling, uncle, or grandparent. The grieving period is a time to be especially free with affection, in words and in actions, and to show the child some extra attention and genuine concern and interest.

Sometimes, when one parent dies, a child worries about who will care for him if the surviving parent should also die. This fear may even extend to children not directly involved. Lisa, a college sophomore, realized for the first time, when taking a course on death and dying, the reasons for her protective behavior toward her mother when Lisa was about ten years old. The mother of a friend of hers had committed suicide. For months after the incident, Lisa wouldn't let her mother out of her sight, subconsciously fearful that her mother, too, would take her own life, leaving Lisa motherless. At the time, she was unable to verbalize this fear, although it directed her behavior for a long time.

When a child has already lost one parent, the concern over the survival of the remaining parent will be uppermost in his mind. "Who will take care of me if Mommy dies, like Daddy did? What will happen to me?" If, in fact, the surviving parent is in good health and has every expectation of a long life, assure the child of this. Also, and this is very important, make definite plans for the guardianship of the child and inform him of those plans, even include him in the making of them, if possible. Be certain that the prospective guardians are people to whom the child is very close and are people who would raise your child with a philosophy similar to your own. Usually, these simple steps will easily relieve that child's anxiety about this matter. (It is a good idea to have these plans made long before any hint of an illness or accident. It is a responsibility of parenthood far too often neglected.)

Assuming Guilt

Children are quick to assume they are responsible for anything that goes wrong (maybe it is because we are always reprimanding them). It is not at all unusual for them to feel guilty when someone dies, even when there is absolutely no reason for them to feel this way. Children often engage in "magical thinking," believing that their wishes can suddenly become reality. Under most circumstances, there is no danger in this playful pretense. But to a child, it can often seem very real, and he is sometimes frightened if an event in the world coincides with his wish for the event. Denied a predinner treat, a child may declare, "Mommy, I hate you. I wish I didn't have a mommy! I wish you were dead!" If something later happens to Mommy, he assumes that his brief, angry wish made it happen. Perhaps no one else even heard the outburst and no one suspects the child feels this way. And he may be too frightened and ashamed to admit what he considers to be the "truth" regarding the cause of his mother's death. The source of guilt may be even more subtle, for children learn early not to verbalize all their hostile, bitter feelings. Please don't let them go through life thinking they killed someone at age seven.

Jason, a shy, withdrawn third-grader had been characterized by his teachers as "hard to teach," "hard to talk to." He rarely played with other children. He must have sensed his new teacher was special, though, for the very first day of class he went up to Miss Clabaugh and said simply, "I killed my brother." Miss Clabaugh tried to discern the reason he felt this way, for Jason was obviously very serious, but the boy had no details. He only knew that he had killed his brother and he was a bad boy.

A talk with Jason's family unraveled the mystery. Three years earlier, when Jason was five years old, his infant brother died, a victim of Sudden Infant Death Syndrome. Unfortunately, Jason was in the room where the crib was when his grandmother came in, saw the baby and gasped, "What did you do to your baby brother?" Jason didn't know what he had done, but he did know he must be responsible. For three years he assumed he was a murderer, but never told anyone until Miss Clabaugh. After the family-teacher conference, the situation was explained to Jason and he finally understood he was not to blame for the death. A tremendous burden of hidden guilt was lifted. Jason blossomed, did well in school, made many friends and became a successful athlete, later even winning a college scholarship. But if his third-grade teacher hadn't been the sensitive, caring Miss Clabaugh type, it might have been many more years before he shared his terrible secret. It has happened to many others, who finally end up on a psychiatrist's couch.

Explain to a child simply how the person died, emphasizing the fact that it was an illness or accident that made them die, and that no one deliberately caused it to happen or could have kept it from happening. This can be touchy, because if they don't already feel guilty (and it is likely that they won't tell you anyway, if they do,) you certainly don't want to suggest that they might. The most important thing is to be sensitive to the child's feelings and listen to any clues they may offer about how they feel.

Sharing Religious Beliefs

Use extreme caution when giving religious explanations of death. A simple statement like "God wanted Mommy to be with Him in

Heaven" can make a budding atheist out of an innocent little person. A child might wonder how God could possibly need Mommy more than he does. A small child's world is also small, and a parent represents a huge chunk of that small world. A god who takes away a central figure in a child's life is not likely to be thought of too fondly by that grieving youth. If Heaven is such a lovely place and Mommy is there, a child may sincerely want to die to see this wonderful place and be with his mother. Certainly, share your religious convictions with your children, but try to do it in a way that will not confuse or alienate them.

Explaining Death Through Nature

If a pet dies, don't try to hide the fact or immediately replace the animal with a double, hoping the child won't notice the switch. In the first place, the child probably *is* going to notice the change and wonder why his pet suddenly reacts differently to him. "Doesn't Spot like me any more? Why didn't he run to greet me when I came home?" Once again, the temporary illusion of normalcy provided by the deception is a small gain, compared to the child's loss of trust in you and the loss of the opportunity to learn to deal with life on its own terms. This is a natural chance for the child to learn about death. You might have a small "service" for the animal and bury it, or at least seize the opportunity to introduce the concept of death by having a simple talk about what happened.

The seasonal change of flowers and trees offers another simple and familiar illustration of life vanishing in the winter only to renew itself in the spring. Take advantage of these smaller crises to begin to teach your children about death. Not only will they learn about the nature of death, but they will learn about themselves, what it feels like to be sad when a pet dies, and what it feels like to have the strength to cope with such losses. When a more serious death touches their lives, they will have acquired some insight into the tragedy and some confidence in their own ability to get through it.

The Dilemma of the Funeral

Consider letting a child attend a funeral, if the child expresses a desire to go. It is important for a child to learn about funerals; that it is normal for big people to be very quiet and sad, even cry. Each child is different emotionally and behaviorally and should receive individual consideration when it comes to attending the services. Don't force a reluctant child into going and don't allow children to go if they might disrupt the service for others.

An especially good idea is to have a separate, shorter service for the children in the family. It can and should be a time when they can ask questions about what is happening and what it all means. You might have this in the morning before the regular funeral. The minister, funeral director, and parents or very close adult relatives should be present to help answer the children's questions. They may want to know why Grandpa is so cold and hard, what will happen to Grandpa after the funeral, why he is in a box, why he died, why Grandpa won't come home, even what it is like to be dead. Children sometimes imagine all sorts of weird things (like Grandpa's legs being gone) and are relieved to have someone listen to them and set their minds at ease with reasonable explanations. This separate service has worked well for several families and is certainly worth considering if you have young children in your family.

A Child's Grief

Allow children to grieve. Just like adults, they need to go through the grieving process when they lose someone they love. Also like adults, children express their grief in different ways. Some will cry; some will withdraw for a while; some will have discipline or academic problems in school, or both; some may not eat or sleep well, or not even want to play with other children and pursue their otherwise normal activities. Children may glorify a dead parent or sibling and even express the wish that a surviving parent or sibling had died in their place. On the other hand, the deceased may become the object of the child's resentment and anger.

Given an atmosphere of patience, understanding, and unconditional love, the storm will gradually clear. Avoid the tendency to say "Big boys don't cry." Rather, let them express their feelings and work through their loss. Don't be tempted to believe "children soon forget these things." Children usually have vivid and lasting memories of the deceased and have grief work to accomplish. Let them talk about the dead person and how they feel and felt about her. Suppress your desire to change to a more pleasant subject. A child will soon discover when his thoughts and feelings are not welcome and will only harbor them silently, sometimes for many years, until they finally erupt with even greater magnitude and destruction. Cry with the child until the tears have dried into accepting memories.

Remember They Are Small

Let a child remain a child. Of course, when someone in the family dies, everyone else has to pitch in and assume some of the tasks and responsibilities that the deceased once had. But don't make a ten-year-old or even a fourteen-year-old be the "mommy" or the "man of the house." They should know that more is expected of them in terms of household chores, but they should know that it is okay to be ten or fourteen. The experience will have helped them mature a lot, anyway. Don't force it further by denying them the opportunity to still be a child.

Don't be afraid to talk about the deceased with your child, and let them share their memories. Recall Aunt Linda's favorite song and the way she always made everyone laugh. Let children know that it is good to remember people after they have died, that we can treasure the lessons and joy they brought us for all our lives. And we can share them with people who never even met the person. Talking freely about the deceased will help the child to see that you have special insights and will foster a closer relationship between the two of you. Honest sharing always does that.

There are several lovely books available which help interpret death to children. One of my favorites is *The Two of Them* by Aliki. It tells the story of a little girl and her grandfather, the love they share, and the memories she treasures after his death. My own preschoolers love *The Two of Them* as much as I do. Reading this and similar stories with your children provides a good opportunity for them to ask questions and consider the values of life and the impact of death in a non-threatening atmosphere. Check your local bookstores and libraries for other titles.

Be an open, loving, supportive adult. Be available. The period following a death in the family is a very important time to share yourself with your children. You may be surprised to discover that as you were comforting them, they have helped to ease your pain, too. Let them offer you their comfort, and you can learn and grow together.

8

Legal Matters

As we go through life, most of us accumulate some property. Some of this may be real estate, called realty, and the rest of it (cars, money, fur coats, pianos, thimble collections) is personal property, or personalty. Put all together, your realty and personalty comprise your estate. The big dilemma, and the source of numerous court battles, not to mention family arguments, is what to do with this estate once the owner has died (you can't take it with you) and how to do whatever should be done.

Specifically, an estate includes a person's home or homes and other real estate holdings; money in bank accounts and "under the mattress"; stocks, bonds, and other securities; business interests, life insurance, items for personal use and enjoyment—in short, everything a person owns. Arranging for the transfer of ownership of all this property becomes an incredibly complex task in many cases. In an effort to understand and simplify the process, let us examine some of the most important issues involved. This chapter cannot answer all your questions, but rather can help you learn what questions to ask when planning your own estate. Federal Estate Tax law applies to residents of all fifty states, but other laws regarding wills and inheritance tax, although they share certain similarities, vary somewhat from state to state. Because it would be too cumbersome to include all the states' laws, I have chosen to use Illinois law for illustrative purposes and encourage you (including residents of Illinois) to consult your attorney for specific information and guidance pertaining to your particular situation.

What Happens to an Estate

When a person dies, the distribution of the estate will be determined and directed in one or several of the following ways.

Last Will and Testament

If a person has prepared a valid will, it will be used to determine appropriate distribution of the estate upon that person's death. A person who writes a will is called a *testator*. Part or all of the estate may be included in the will and parts of the estate may be transferred in other ways.

If a person has not prepared a valid will, he or she is said to have died *intestate*. In cases of intestacy where there are heirs, the states have a law typically called the "Statute of Descent and Distribution" which legislators have contrived in an effort to surmise how persons might choose to divide their worldly goods, if only they had written a will. In essence, if you don't write a will, the state has written one for you.

The problem is, the legislature has one law to cover all intestacies and most likely will not have anticipated your exact wishes. For instance, in Illinois, half of the estate will go to the surviving spouse, half to the children in equal shares, regardless of age or number. In the case of a young widow with very small children, it would have been easier to have the entire estate in her name. Since the children own half of the dead father's property, the mother must now go to court to ask permission to sell the car, get money from the estate for dental work for the children, and other needs. Few people are aware of the details of their state's statute of descent and distribution, yet a good *three-quarters* of all estates are settled this way, by virtue of intestacy. One of the most serious flaws of intestacy for parents of minor children is that, in failing to write a will, they relinquish to the courts the very personal and critical task of selecting guardians for their children.

In cases of intestacy where there are no heirs, the estate *escheats* or reverts to the state government after a stated number of years (in Illinois, seven years). Even a person without relatives might have wished to name another person or charity to receive his estate after his death, but without a will it goes to the government—no doubt a very worthy cause!

Trusts

Trusts involve the transfer of property to a trustee for the benefit of another person. Trusts may be made effective during one's life—an "inter vivos" trust, or become effective upon death—a "testamentary" trust.

Survivorship

If one owns property in joint tenancy with another person, the survivor assumes full ownership upon the co-owner's death. The fact that the property was transferred without benefit of a will does not exclude it from the inventory of the estate for tax purposes.

Life Insurance

Life insurance is paid to a beneficiary by contract. It may or may not be mentioned in a will or testamentary trust. The beneficiary may be a named person or organization, or may be the estate of the deceased. As with joint tenancy, although the property transfers directly, taxes may still be due, depending on a number of variables.

Where There's a Will There's a Way

Writing a will is probably one of the nicest things you can do for the people you love. An effective will can insure financial security, name a preferred executor of the estate, minimize costs of settling the estate, minimize estate taxes, and provide peace of mind for the testator during his life and for his heirs upon his demise. But the complexity of modern law places certain restrictions upon preparation of the will and almost eliminates the opportunity for a do-it-yourself last will and testament. Even in small or modest estates, legal counsel can provide helpful perspectives and advice that can result in a far more suitable document for all concerned.

Preparing a Valid Will

Illinois law requires that a will be typewritten. Some twenty-three states accept a holographic will (one written entirely in the handwriting of the person signing it). Illinois does not. It is best to follow formal procedure to avoid possible problems. Most states, including Illinois, require that two witnesses, who are aware that this is a last will and testament, sign the document in the presence of each other and the testator. They need not, and probably should not, know the contents of the will, only that it *is* a will. Five states require that three witnesses sign the will. These witnesses will be called upon to testify regarding the validity of the will when the testator dies. It is best for the testator to be known to the witnesses, but that they not receive property through the will. In twelve states, a witness may "take under the will," but in the rest they cannot. Minimum age for writing a will is eighteen in most states. Property of minors automatically goes to the parents. The testator must be of "sound mind and memory."

Changing or Revoking a Will

Having written a will, there will probably be occasion to change or add to it as your life circumstances change. A will may be changed by adding a page or two, called a *codicil*, which must be prepared with the same formality, including witnesses, as the will itself, and should be attached to it. If the changes are important or extensive, however, it is best to simply rewrite the will. Codicils have a way of getting misplaced when their content is not to the liking of the person finding the will.

A will may be revoked in several ways. Writing a new will revokes an old will if it says it does. A later will without a declaration of a revocation of an earlier will revokes the earlier will to the extent it is inconsistent. The testator can execute an instrument (with the same formality as a will) declaring that the will is revoked. Or the will can be burned, torn, canceled, or obliterated, preferably in the presence of witnesses.

In a number of states, certain situations automatically alter or revoke a will. In Illinois, divorce or annulment revokes a spouse's interest under the will. A legacy to the convicted murderer of the testator is void. (How appropriate!) A child born after his parent makes a will can take a share under the will unless it is clear from the will that the parent desired to disinherit the child. The child's share is equal to the share he would have received had the parent died without a will. In Alabama, marriage automatically revokes the will of the woman, but not the man!

Location of the Will

A will can be a powerful legal instrument—but only if it is found and filed with the appropriate court official. If the will cannot be found, it is worthless. Take care to keep your will in a safe but not obscure place. Inform your executor, lawyer, and family members of the location of the will, as well as the location of insurance policies, stocks and bonds, and burial instructions, if any. All too often there is a frantic, perhaps fruitless, search for these papers. "I know Dad said he had five insurance policies, but where are they?" Some families choose to keep these items in a safety deposit box in a bank, which is fine. The best place to keep such documents is in a truly fireproof safe in your home or, perhaps, your lawyer's office. Wherever it is kept, be certain to inform several key persons of its location.

Provisions of a Will

Typical provisions of a will may include some or all of the following and possibly many more, depending on the size and nature of the estate, legal requirements, and testator's desires.

1. Clear, unquestionable identification of testator and of this document as last will and testament, revoking all others.
2. Specific bequests of property—either individual items (the antique oak table) or a percentage of the estate.
3. Instructions regarding method of payment of taxes (taken from each bequest proportionately or from residual of estate).
4. Naming of executor; waiver of requirement of posting bond.
5. Establishment of trusts.
6. Naming of guardians for minor children.
7. "Thirty-day survivorship clause," which states that beneficiaries receives nothing from estate unless they outlive the deceased by at least 30 days (can be up to six months). This prevents the estate from being taxed twice (in testator's estate, then primary beneficiary's estate) before reaching the secondary (contingent) beneficiary. For instance, if husband and wife are in a common accident, he dies and leaves everything to her. She dies of injuries three weeks later, and so does not ever inherit the estate, which then goes directly to the children. This saves a lot of double-handling of the property.
8. Signatures of testator and witnesses, noting date of signing.

There are many other possibilities, but the foregoing ones are basic. Limitless variations exist on how one might choose to have an estate distributed. We will mention only a few examples. One may divide property among one's descendants by allotting a specific amount to each ($5,000 for Alicia; $10,000 for Gordon, who manages the household; $1 for Karen, who has not written or called me in fifteen years), or by dividing the estate in shares either *per stirpes* or *per capita.* In per stirpes distribution, each child receives an equal share. If a child should predecease the parent, the child's "issue" (testator's grandchildren) divide the deceased parent's share equally, while children of surviving aunts and uncles receive nothing.

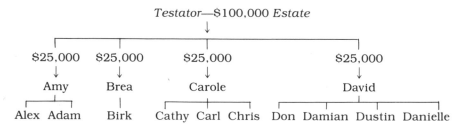

Testator—$100,000 Estate

In a per stirpes distribution, if Amy predeceases her father, her $25,000 share of the estate will be split equally, $12,500 each to Alex and Adam. If David predeceases his father, each of his children would receive half as much, $6,250. Some persons, however, want to provide equally for grandchildren and prefer a per capita distribution. For example, a person may establish a trust, the income from which will benefit his children as long as any of them lives. When the last of the testator's children dies, the trust may be dissolved and the money divided in equal shares among the then-living grandchildren. In the example above, assuming the $100,000 estate remained intact in a trust, Amy, Brea, Carole and David could use the income from that trust in equal shares so long as they lived. When the last one died, the $100,000 would be divided equally among the ten grandchildren, assuming they all survive. An only child would prefer the grandparent's choice of per stirpes, while his cousins with many siblings have more to gain by per capita assignment.

Other factors will be considered, too, such as the financial status and career plans of the children and grandchildren. Sometimes a trust is established granting the trustee "sprinkling" privileges, that is to use the funds as seems appropriate without specific regard to equality of distribution. Perhaps one child needs years of expensive medical treatment and physical therapy following a serious automobile accident. The parent wants to give the trustee the flexibility to properly meet this child's needs without the obligation of giving siblings equal funds since they do not share the agony and expense of their less fortunate brother.

It should be noted that to avoid problems if and when a will is contested, all who are descendants (and therefore potential heirs) should be named in the will. If testator chooses not to make a bequest to any one or more of them, a brief explanation will facilitate the later judgment of the validity of the will. Sometimes, when an individual is intentionally omitted, that person may claim that the omission was merely an oversight and contest the will. A statement in the will regarding the omission leaves little doubt regarding testator's true wishes. There may still be claims that the testator was not of "sound mind and memory" or he would not have done this cruel thing; or was coerced by a third party to so write his will. Of course, all this must be proved in court.

The object is to make your will as explicit and detailed and legal as possible in every respect. In that endeavor consult your attorney. "If something is worth doing, it is worth doing well," is especially true when it comes to wills, because you can't come back and correct your errors. If you do care what happens to your belongings, invest the time and money to ensure that your wishes will be followed.

Trusts

Many persons of means (or anticipated post-mortem means) wish to share their monetary blessings with others without making an outright gift. Trusts are established as a method of accomplishing this goal. Funds are placed in a trust held by a third party, such as a bank, trust company, or individual experienced in managing and investing property, and the income and capital of that trust is distributed to the beneficiary in accordance with the guidelines established by the benefactor. Motivation for establishing trusts as opposed to making outright gifts may be a desire to be assured the funds will not be squandered or mismanaged by a beloved but immature child, or that the money will be used only for the expressed purpose, such as a college education. Also, it gives the donor greater control over the timing of the distribution of funds.

A trust may be set up and operate while the benefactor ("trustor") is still in good health, or he may choose to arrange to have the trust established after his death according to the instructions in his will. My discussion primarily concerns the latter type, called a testamentary trust.

Flexibility is one of the major advantages of trusts. A testator may design a trust virtually any way he wishes. For instance, in providing for minor children, the trust may be set up as a single fund for all the children or in separate shares. In a *single fund* trust, the trustee is directed to provide for the needs of all children until the youngest child reaches twenty-one (or whatever age the parents name). This assures that, although the youngest child did not have benefit of the parents' love and counsel as many years as the older siblings, at least their financial support will be available until the child reaches the specified age. If, for whatever reason, the expenses of rearing this child exceed what might "normally" have been his share of the estate, the parent's desire is to have these needs met. After the named age, the trust is divided into equal shares, and the share of each child is separate for accounting purposes. The shares will then be distributed at the ages the parents designate. For example, each child may receive one-half at age thirty, and one-half at thirty-five, or one-tenth of a share each year for ten years—however the parents feel would be wisest and in the best interests of their progeny.

Parents may choose to have a *separate share* trust set up immediately upon the death of the parents. This may give older siblings a larger share than would be their due under a single fund arrangement, but may not be as fair to the younger siblings. There may still be restrictions regarding disbursing of income and, eventually, perhaps the principal of the trust at designated ages or life events such as marriage, birth of a child, purchase of a home, or graduation from college.

Money from the trust may come from the existing estate or may be created by a life insurance policy. Most often, trusts are managed by trust departments of banks or by trust companies, which invest the capital wisely, we presume, and for their trouble take as a fee a small percentage of the income. The trustor, however, may name anyone as trustee, himself included so long as he is alive. (Successor trustees may be designated to assume the duties upon the death or incompetency of the original trustee.) Consider the trustee assignment in a situation where small children are involved. The testator names a loving and responsible couple, Tom and Ann Manor, as guardians for the tots. The trust for the children, funded by a life insurance policy, amounts to well over $200,000. The Manors are comfortably situated, but not financial wizards. Testator may name the Manors as trustees as well as guardians, hoping they make sound investments, realizing it would be simpler for them to gain access to the money for the children's benefit if they had control over the trust. The testator "trusts" the Manors to use the children's money wisely, not squandering it on foolish whims, but actually would not mind if some of it found its way into some airline tickets for a trip to Acapulco for the Manors. They are, after all, assuming a monumental responsibility and deserve to benefit somewhat from the arrangement. If a bank is named as trustee, the jaunt to the coast of Mexico would most likely not happen. On the other hand, $200,000 is a sizable sum which could grow considerably if wisely handled. The Manors may prefer not to take on the financial as well as custodial duties for the children's welfare, or the testator may feel more comfortable knowing a bank is handling the investments, despite the occasional inconvenience to the guardians.

One may begin to appreciate the versatility and efficiency of the trust arrangement. Properly handled, it may also result in considerable tax savings. There are at least fifty types of trusts, each developed to meet a particular need. The trust option is well worth your consideration when planning your estate and last will and testament.

Probate

Probate, from a Latin word meaning "to prove," refers to the in-court proceedings which may be required to settle an estate. In Illinois, the purpose of probate as strictly defined is to establish the legal status of a written instrument as a will and to furnish the means of establishing, by record, evidence of the validity of an existing right (as to a portion of the estate). Some estates, because plans were made for all assets to be passed outside the will, will not require settlement by probate. Understandably, among those estates settled through probate are some which are quite involved and lengthy, but also others which are handled quite simply.

When someone dies, a person possessing the deceased's will is required by law to file the will with the court. A person who knows that he is named as an executor in a will has thirty days to file the will with the court. Following court acknowledgment of the will, the executor will be authorized by the court (through issuance of letters testamentary) to administer the estate. The executor must then inventory the assets of the estate and file this inventory with the court within sixty days. Notices are published stating that all creditors who have claims against the estate must file them within six months (in some states, four months). After that period, no further claims will be considered.

The *probate estate* includes only property held in the deceased's name alone—joint assets are not included. Real estate owned only by the decendent passes through probate (in Illinois). Probate is a court proceeding that takes place in the county of residence of the deceased. In addition to the above-mentioned procedures, it will handle guardianship arrangements, name an administrator in the case of intestacy, and ultimately decree that the assets have been distributed lawfully, and that taxes have been paid, "closing the estate." This final decree relieves the heirs of any subsequent claims against Grandpa's farm.

At this point, I want to reemphasize that discussion in this chapter has merely touched on some of the legal aspects of estate settlement and planning. Many huge volumes have been written on each of the concepts mentioned herein; this discussion is by no means intended to be an in-depth view of any of them. However, I have been equally impressed by (1) the need for individuals at least to anticipate the types of potential problems and solutions relating to death laws and (2) the amazingly widespread lack of knowledge in this regard and I have therefore felt compelled to skim the surface. I hope that the reader will begin to appreciate the need for careful planning and the value of legal counsel with special expertise in this area of the law.

Death Taxes

Governments, always in need of funds to carry on their pursuits for the public good, seem to seize every opportunity to extract a portion of that public's resources. Legislators got together and decided that death would be as good an occasion as any to add to the public coffers. It would likely be a far greater burden to tax parents upon the birth of a child, just when financial responsibilities are multiplying rapidly. It was deemed more appropriate, in essence, to tax the child upon the death of the parent.

Of course, it isn't the child who is taxed, per se. There are usually two types of taxes to pay, depending on the size of the estate and to whom the property transfers. Some estates are small enough, or have bequests that have been handled in such a manner that taxes need not be paid. The Federal Estate Tax (FET) is a tax on the total assets of the estate. The individual state inheritance tax is a tax on the transfer of property at death. Let's look at each a bit more closely.

Inheritance Tax

Thirty-seven states, Illinois included, have a law by which the transfer of property at death is taxed according to the relationship of the heir to the deceased. This is called an inheritance tax. Twelve states impose a tax on the entire estate, with exemptions for spouse, children, and charitable groups. Nevada, rich from gamblers, is the only state which has no "death tax."

In Illinois, the *inheritance tax estate* includes all of the probate estate, half of joint tenancies, payable-on-death accounts, most retirement accounts, insurance policies payable to the estate, and any gifts made within two years of death. The Illinois inheritance tax taxes each share of the estate based on the closeness of relationship of the beneficiary to the decedent. Beneficiaries are classed into three groups.

Class A	Class B	Class C
father, mother	uncle, aunt	all others, except
lineal ancestor	niece, nephew	exempt institu-
husband, wife	lineal descendant	tions
child	of above	
brother, sister		
wife / widow of son		
husband / widower		
of daughter		
descendant		
mutually acknowl-		
edged stepchild		
legally adopted		
child		

Personal exemptions are allowed to each class of beneficiary. This exemption is the amount of inheritance the individual may receive tax-free.

Class A	spouse and children	$40,000 each
	brother and sister	$10,000 each
	all others	$20,000 each
Class B	all	$500 each
Class C	all	$100 each

Bequests to charitable organizations are wholly exempt from the inheritance tax.

Beyond the exemptions, bequests are taxed on a graduated scale which is lowest for Class A beneficiaries and higher for both Class B and Class C. For instance, a Class A beneficiary is taxed two percent on the first $50,000 in excess of the exemption, and four percent on the next $100,000. A Class B beneficiary pays six percent on the first $20,000, eight percent on the next $50,000 and twelve percent on the next $80,000. For Class C, the rates are ten percent for the first $20,000, twelve percent for the next $30,000, sixteen percent for the next $50,000, and twenty percent for the next $50,000. The percentages continue to escalate in each class as the size of the share of the estate increases.

Let's compare what the tax on a bequest of $150,000 would be for a person in each class.

	Bequest			**Tax**
Class A	$40,000			exempt
spouse or child	50,000	@	2%	$1,000
	60,000	@	4%	2,400
	$150,000			$3,400
Class B	$ 500			exempt
	20,000	@	6%	$1,200
	50,000	@	8%	4,000
	79,500	@	12%	9,540
	$150,000			$14,740
Class C	$ 100			exempt
	20,000	@	10%	$2,000
	30,000	@	12%	3,600
	50,000	@	16%	8,000
	49,900	@	20%	9,980
	$150,000			$23,580

Obviously, the state of Illinois would be better off if Uncle Joe left his fortune to a kindly neighbor (Class C) rather than to his own offspring. Of course, if he leaves it all to the Congregational Church, there is no tax to pay to the state at all. It might seem that $23,580 is a big chunk to send to the governor, but on the other hand, $126,420 is a big chunk to keep, too. And an inheritance is not taxed as income, so the $126,420 will not be further diminished by income tax. I doubt I would complain.

A well-advised and careful testator may so write his will that the taxes levied on each bequest will not be deducted from the bequest but paid by the "residual funds" of the estate, presuming, of course, the estate is large enough to do so. Even the most careful plans don't always work out, though. A generous soul may misjudge the value of certain properties and make large bequests to friends and family totaling $500,000. When the will is probated, the executor discovers the estate to be worth only $200,000. Each bequest must then be reduced to conform with the available funds. In such a case, the executor, with the court's permission, may determine it to be best to have inheritance taxes paid out of each share, since the "residuary" is virtually nonexistent. If the persons receiving specific bequests are not the same persons who receive the residuary, the appointment of the tax liability is one of the most important decisions that should be considered when the will is made.

In Illinois, inheritance tax is due ten months after the date of death. The amount of money gained by states through death taxes is considerable, although it actually represents a small percentage of the total income of any state. A sampling of revenue from death taxes in fiscal year 1979 shows the following figures: California, $409 million; Pennsylvania, $173 million; New York, $155 million; and Illinois, $136 million. That would no doubt build a lot of schools and highways, although it actually accounts for only a very small percentage of overall state income.

Federal Estate Tax

The federal government and several individual states place a tax on the estate itself, rather than the amount of specific bequests. Deductions are allowed for the surviving spouse, children under twenty-one, and charities. The Federal Estate Tax, (hereinafter abbreviated FET), is based on the total assets of the estate (minus, of course, its debts). The FET is applicable only to large estates. In fact, one need not file a return unless the estate is valued at over $225,000, with the use of the marital deduction, even larger. The marital deduction applies if decedent is survived by a spouse. Using it, one spouse can transfer an unlimited amount of property tax-free to the widowed partner.

The Economic Recovery Tax Act of 1981 revised many aspects of the Federal Estate Tax, including a six-year progressive increase in the minimum taxable estate. The following table shows the new minimums.

Year of death	Minimum taxable estate
1982	$225,000
1983	275,000
1984	325,000
1985	400,000
1986	500,000
1987 and thereafter	600,000

While the FET does not tax small estates, its rates are quite high for those estates it does tax. The schedule starts at thirty-two percent for all practical purposes, and the percentages escalate rapidly. For a taxable estate of $600,000 in 1982, the tax would be $145,800. An estate larger than $5 million would be taxed $2,550,000 plus seventy percent of the amount over $5 million. By 1985, the maximum rate will be decreased to fifty percent, which will apply to all estates over $2,500,000 in taxable value.

The FET is now unified with the Federal Gift Tax. Many people think they will avoid paying estate taxes by giving away their assets before they die. No such luck. Gifts exceeding $10,000 per person per year are taxed at exactly the same rate as estate tax. For example, if Grandpa chooses to give his $640,000 farm in equal portions to his four children before he dies, $10,000 per child is exempted, but gift tax must be paid on the remaining value of the gift, or $600,000. The gift tax on $600,000 would be $145,800. Husband and wife together may make a nontaxable $20,000 gift to any person or persons each year, but any gifts in excess of that are taxed at the same rate as legacies.

To determine total value, the following are considered as parts of the FET estate:

all of the probate estate

most of the inheritance tax estate, but not retirement accounts

full value of property held jointly, unless survivor can *prove* percentage of contribution to purchase price

insurance policies to named beneficiary owned by decedent.

If an estate is found to hold assets in excess of $225,000 ($600,000 after 1987—see table above), the FET return must be filed within nine months of the date of the death. By wise use of trust instruments and preplanning, death taxes can be minimized. As with the inheritance tax, testator may direct the FET to be paid out of the residual of the estate, thereby not affecting the value of specific bequests. Compliance with that request depends on the solvency of the estate.

Payment of Claims

Before bequests can be distributed, other claims against the estate must be met. In Illinois, these claims are divided into seven classes, and are payable in the order listed. That is to say, class 1 claims are paid first. If funds remain, class 2 claims are paid. If funds remain, class 3 claims are paid, and so on throughout the classes.

1. Funeral expenses; expenses of administration of estate, including court costs, legal fees.
2. Award to surviving spouse or child. Spouse—$5,000 minimum; child—$1,000 minimum.
3. Debts due the U.S. government, including current and delinquent income tax and federal estate tax.
4. Money due employees of the decedent, not to exceed more than $800 per employee; expenses of last illness.
5. Money or property held in trust by the decedent for another, but which cannot be traced.
6. Debts due the state, county, city, or school district.
7. All other claims.

In other words, the executor is not free to pay the contractor for the recent remodeling of the deceased's kitchen unless and until he is certain there will be sufficient capital to pay the first six classes of claims. We all have our priorities, and so do the courts. (It is interesting to note that court costs are a class 1 claim!)

Life Insurance

When a person signs a contract with a life insurance company, he is essentially placing a bet. The company wagers that the person will have a long life, while the person anticipates the prospect of dying before having paid sufficient premiums to the company to cover the face value of the policy. Life insurance can be of tremendous benefit in the settling of an estate for the security of the survivors. But here, too, are many options, and it pays to study the possibilities and consult an expert in the field before buying a policy.

Depending on one's station in life, a good life insurance policy can meet many diverse needs. We'll mention some of the basic benefits, but there are many more.

Create an Estate

The young family with small children is often concerned about the family's future financial security should the breadwinner die. Often there is actually little estate to distribute at this stage in the family's life. The couple may have purchased a home with many years of mortgage payments ahead, or perhaps lives in an apartment with no equity at all. Except for a small savings account and an almost-paid-for automobile, there may be virtually nothing to inherit.

To take a traditional situation, let's assume the father of three small children dies very suddenly, leaving his widow "all his worldly goods," a hefty mortgage, and a legacy of love. Had he envisioned the consequences, they would no doubt have caused him great sorrow. He and his wife had always felt strongly about one of them being "home with the children" until they were all in school. With no income, his widow would have to shuffle the little ones off to a day care center and enter the work force at a salary very likely much lower than his own. She would probably have to give up their home, since child care for three children and a secretary's wardrobe would whittle her meager income to a point where the mortgage payment would be out of the question.

Alas. What could he have done? Despite his potential, he simply didn't have enough time in his career to accumulate sufficient investments to leave his family well off. There is no estate as such to transfer. But he could have created a sizeable estate at the moment of his death through life insurance. He could arrange for the insurance money to be paid all at once, in monthly installments, or put in a trust with monthly interest payments to provide income for his family. That, combined with social security payments, should be enough to help them through those first few years, if he has planned well.

Conserve an Estate

It happens more often than it should. The family farm is about all Dad has to leave when he dies, but he wants the kids to have it. He had three hundred acres which he bought way back when for about $200 an acre. It was a big investment at the time, but had been well worth it over the years. Now, he hopes his children will continue to prosper from the land.

What Dad hadn't thought about was Federal Estate Tax. He may have paid only $200 an acre, but the current value is over $3,000 an acre. That puts the amount of his legacy very close to the $1 million mark. With no surviving spouse, FET on that size of an estate is going to be more than $300,000! The family would have to sell about a third of the farm to pay the estate tax! Then, of course, there's inheritance tax, too. That would break Dad's heart.

Life insurance to the rescue. Here is a case of a large estate about to be considerably diminished by death taxes. A carefully studied estate plan could result in the purchase of a life insurance policy large enough to handle most, if not all, of the expected death taxes. The estate would be then conserved intact, relieving the heirs of the heavy burden of taxation.

Improve an Estate

Many situations fall somewhere between the young man with many obligations and few material assets and the "land rich," cash-poor farmer. There may be some investments, some equity in a home, perhaps some valuable silver or art. Despite the inherent worth of this estate, there is not enough that is liquid for the survivors' day-to-day subsistence.

The estate may be improved by balancing investments, minimizing taxes through the establishment of trusts, diversifying the portfolio, making proper use of dividends, and moving policies around to the advantage of the estate and its potential beneficiaries. Here, life insurance can be employed to continue to provide the family the financial security that would have been assured had the deceased not died.

Other Uses and Benefits

Life insurance may also be used as a specific means of paying final medical expenses or as a means for one partner to buy the other's share in the business should either of them die. Mortgage life insurance is available to assure the surviving spouse needn't worry about the mortgage payment should the insured die before the house is paid for. Many well-intentioned but inconsistent savers use the regular life insurance premiums as a means of saving a little money. (See "whole life" on page 106.)

Proceeds of life insurance are payable outside the probate process, and so are usually available for the family in a short period of time following the death. This is a time when an urgent need for cash may be met with a virtual lack of funds, especially if most or all of the family's accounts were in the name of the deceased.

If a life insurance policy is owned by someone other than the deceased, the proceeds of that policy are not subject to Federal Estate Tax. For instance, a wife may own the policy on her husband's life and vice versa. Or a small business corporation may own policies on the lives of its two top employees, payable to the company to get it over the hump until a replacement can be found for one of these key people. Sounds like a great loophole, and it is, but there may be problems. Ownership of a policy carries with it the responsibility of paying premiums, the right to change beneficiaries, and the right to choose method of payment of the death benefit, as well as the right to borrow the cash value for emergencies or investments. In a society where the divorce rate approaches fifty percent, one might justifiably be uncertain about relinquishing these privileges to someone who may become another person's spouse before the policy pays off. Or, if the owner happens to die before the insured spouse dies, the policy may revert to the owner's estate with ownership distributed in accordance with the will ("all to my children," for example), or in accordance with the statute of descent and distribution. This can be avoided by naming a successor owner as well as a contingent beneficiary of a life insurance policy. One should be aware of and reconciled to these possible contingencies before signing over one's life insurance to another.

Like the trust, life insurance offers great variety. There are a multitude of ways to arrange for the death benefit to be paid. These include lump sum payments, in which the total value of the policy is paid all at once; fixed period payments, in which the company pays in equal installments over a predetermined number of years; fixed amount payments, in which the company pays a predetermined amount in scheduled payments until the money is gone; life income payments, based on the amount of the policy and the expected life span of the beneficiary, and the interest payment alternative, in which the insurance company keeps the principal and pays the beneficiary regular interest payments at a guaranteed rate.

Combinations of these options are also possible. For example, one might choose a lump-sum payment of half the face value of the policy, with the remainder paid out in fixed amounts or a fixed period. It is worth considering the possibilities. A spouse may receive, income tax free, $1,000 per year interest on the proceeds of a life insurance policy. It may be well worth your while to plan ahead to take advantage of that exclusion. Sometimes, however, the widow or widower may be able to invest the principal and earn more than enough more money to render this exclusion to be no advantage.

Types of Life Insurance Policies   The variety of life insurance policies available is almost dizzying. We'll confine our discussion to the most basic alternatives; you can consult an insurance agent for the latest on the ruffles and flourishes. Each type has a specific purpose which will meet the needs of some people although it may be totally inappropriate for others.

This is one reason it pays to determine who of the insurance salespersons in your area has expertise in estate planning and is familiar with the latest law and alternatives. A professional life insurance person will help, in fact will *insist* that you carefully assess your assets and obligations, and will want to see all existing policies to coordinate his efforts with any insurance you already have in force. The insurance professional should also be well-versed in wills and death taxes and work with your lawyer, trust officer, and accountant to assure that your estate plan is adequate and consistent with pertinent documents. For example, you may decide in your will to put your life insurance in a trust for your children, but two old policies you had forgotten about still name your ex-spouse as beneficiary. The estate would then not be coordinated and many problems could result.

Term Insurance   Term life insurance is bought for a specified period of time, a *term*. The policy expires when the term runs out. Many term policies expire at age 65, others after five or twenty years from date of purchase. Some policies are renewable with increasing premiums to age 95 or 100. There are some expensive obligations in life, such as a house or business, which, if we live long enough will be met by the income from our labors. Many times, persons buy short-term policies to assure the obligation will be met in case they die before "clearing title" to whatever.

For a young person, term insurance is usually quite inexpensive. There is, however, no cash value to the policy. Monthly premiums keep the death benefit in force. But if you happen to survive the term of the policy, you're back to ground zero. The insurance company won the bet mentioned at the start of this section. Term insurance is like paying rent. While you pay, you are covered, but there is no build-up of equity.

Term policies, while inexpensive in one's youth (when your chances of dying are very low), are quite costly in the long run. Premiums increase at each renewal period for the same amount of coverage, and as one approaches age 65 premiums may be very expensive. And, if you haven't died by the specified age at which the policy expires, you have no coverage at all. So, for someone desiring permanent, life-long protection, term is not the answer. Term does, however, meet a real need for some persons at a particular point in their lives when funds are minimal and insurance needs are great.

Whole Life Insurance Whole life insurance provides permanent protection and carries with it certain other benefits. It is more expensive than term if both are bought in one's youth. But premiums for whole life remain constant while term premiums continue to increase and will eventually surpass those for permanent insurance, assuming coverage is the same. The level premiums are possible because the insurance company invests the cash value of your policy and may share the interest with you in the form of dividends. Whole life insurance never runs out. It is always there when you need it.

Whole life also has the advantage of accumulating cash value, like a savings account. This cash value may be borrowed from the insurance company for emergencies or to invest however one chooses. If one should die before the loan is repaid, the policy stays in force and the amount of the loan is simply deducted from the death benefit.

If you suffer financial difficulties and for a time are unable to pay premiums on your policy, several options are open to you. You may borrow from the cash value to pay the premiums, or you may reduce the face value of the policy by using the cash value to purchase a smaller amount of "paid up" insurance. Another possibility is to have the company use your cash value to purchase extended term insurance. All three of these options would still leave you with life insurance protection at a time when you can't afford it but probably need it. Also if you choose to cancel a whole life policy, the cash value—your "savings" account—is yours to take and do with as you please.

The cash value of a policy comes from the premiums you pay. Some of each premium, especially in the period soon after purchase of the policy, is not directly credited to the cash value, because this is the portion that pays for the death benefit. After a number of years, however, most of your premiums will be credited to the cash value and annual or semiannual dividends are paid on this investment, as well. Sometimes the dividends are used to purchase additional paid-up insurance. The buyer of the policy may select how to have the dividends paid. There are about five options.

The "face value" of any policy refers to the amount of the death benefit purchased, $10,000, $50,000, or $75,000, for example.

With a whole life policy, the insured may elect to use the proceeds as retirement income after reaching a certain age. This is essentially an annuity arrangement. The insurance company makes agreed-upon monthly payments to the insured which may decrease the amount of the death benefit, but provide needed support from one's own investment.

All of these and other options should be discussed before purchasing the policy that is right for you. Be certain that the particular policy you select has the flexibility you feel you may need later. Not all policies are the same! Not all insurance companies are the same, either. Some are far more reputable than others. There is a wealth of consumer information available which will help you determine which companies are the best. Take advantage of this information before investing your money.

A Word to the Wise

Educate Yourself

As already stated, this chapter gives but an inkling of the legal and financial details that accompany our living and our dying. Hoping your curiosity has been aroused, I recommend that you read a good, *current* book on legal matters and/or estate planning. While browsing through a family legal guide copyrighted in 1971, I discovered that much of the material was out of date. So be sure to get a recent book. Three good ones—I'm sure there are others—are: *You and Your Will* by Paul Ashley; *Who Will Get Your Money* by John Barnes; and *The Complete Estate Planning Guide* by Robert Brosterman.

Assess Your Needs

After you have assimilated more detailed information from one or more of these texts, examine your own fiscal situation. Determine the present size of your estate. Itemize assets; you may be surprised how much you actually own. Survey and list your debts and your responsibilities. What outstanding loans remain? How many children must be cared for and for how many years? What other obligations (ailing parents, business agreements) must be considered? Then ponder for a time your special concerns and desires regarding the eventual distribution of your estate. Who have you promised to remember in your will?

Seek Expert Assistance

Once you have some idea where you are and what you want, seek out respected trustworthy professionals to assist you in the estate planning process. A lawyer with known expertise in this area will gladly work together with the professionals you choose in insurance, accounting, and trust management. Any one of these professionals will be able to recommend to you members of the other professions with whom they have worked in cases similar to yours. Or ask for referrals from friends, business associates, or others who have used comparable services and were happy with the outcome.

Do-it-yourself wills can be legal, but often are inadequate. Your estate planning team will no doubt ask you questions you never considered and suggest options and contingencies which may amaze and delight or appall you. It helps a lot to be a bit prepared; hence my admonition to read some books. It will save you and your lawyer time, and therefore save you money, if some of these decisions have been considered before walking into the attorney's office.

Keep Up With the Times

It will probably be necessary to revise your will from time to time, most notably when there has been a significant change in life circumstances. Marriage, the birth of a child, divorce, death of a beneficiary, and change in business arrangements are all good reasons to review the terms of your last will and testament. When reviewing your will, take a look at your life insurance coverage, too. Is it still realistic based on the rate of inflation since purchase of the policies? Or, maybe your obligations have diminished, and you are buying more insurance than you really need at that point. It will be worth your spending a few minutes to reevaluate the state of your estate. Also, any future changes in laws affecting estate or inheritance tax may necessitate an alteration in the structure of your estate plan. Ask your lawyer to keep you informed of these changes in the law.

A final note: If you are seeking a lawyer to help in settling an estate, establish in advance how his or her fee will be determined. Some lawyers charge a flat hourly rate, others take a specified percentage of the total value of the estate. There may be a big difference for you between these methods, and it helps to know what to expect before you get the bill!

There you are, a mini-course in death law and life insurance. Now, take the time to get your affairs settled so you can relax and enjoy the rest of your life!

9

What Comes Next? A Look at After-Life and Reincarnation

Humankind has forever been intrigued with the mystery of what happens to the "essence" of a person at death. It seems obvious to us that the body ceases to function, is motionless, cold, unresponsive—merely so much matter. But we yearn to know if there is some continuity of the "force" that once energized and directed the activities of that now lifeless biological organism. If, indeed, we are more than mere mineral and biochemistry, *what* are we? Is this all there is?

For most of us, this is necessarily a matter of faith. We believe the teachings of our religions in this regard, or we attempt to formulate our own interpretation of after-life, or perhaps we dismiss the notion as unscientific and, therefore, preposterous. Although, based on scientific data (or more accurately, the lack thereof) the evidence for after-life is miniscule, we do acknowledge that all the "facts" are not available yet. The chance may be remote, from the scientist's perspective, that consciousness could somehow exist wihout a brain, but there is a chance.

Those less inclined to believe that everything of significance must be weighed, measured, quantified, and verified by scientific methods, take the quantum leap and declare that it is preposterous to assume that somehow we could *not* exist beyond our present constrictions and form. Are we merely an accident of biology with no ultimate purpose beyond perpetuation of the species?

A burgeoning interest in this area has been instrumental in the increasing scientific research now underway to somehow reconcile what for some seems to be an intuitive awareness of our potential for post-death survival with the scientific challenge of proving that potential.

Belief in an after-life presupposes belief in the spiritual nature of persons. How can we *know* there is some part, some essence of us that is capable of existence independent of structural biology? This is a question now being seriously considered by scientists in physics, psychology, and parapsychology. The faithful have taken it for granted for centuries.

The next step has to do with the post-death survival of that essence. If the spirit can exist outside the physical body during life (as in out-of-body experiences or astral projection), does it continue to survive once the body itself is no longer alive? Studies of near-death experiences are beginning to approach at least the threshold of this possibility. Discoveries in modern physics lend credence to the theory.

Just as belief in after-life presupposes a belief in a surviving spirit, belief in reincarnation presupposes a belief in both surviving spirit and afterlife. One might believe in after-life and not reincarnation, but not the reverse. Reincarnation suggests that the surviving spirit can exist independently of a human body and that it may continue its quest for knowledge and understanding by inhabiting other human bodies at future times, as it may have already inhabited other bodies in previous times. As impossible as it seems to prove reincarnation's existence, scientific research into reincarnation is now quite widespread. The findings have been intriguing, if not conclusive.

In this chapter, I briefly discuss each of these three areas, (1) the existence of the soul, (2) after-life, and (3) reincarnation. There is a rapidly growing body of printed information in this area. In the next couple of decades our conceptual framework regarding these issues may have undergone considerable transformation. For the present, this is where we are.

The Autonomous "Soul"

Religion has long courted our fealty by promising a beautiful after-life. We are admonished to "save our souls" before it is too late. What, exactly, are we "saving"? What evidence do we have that there is in fact, something to save?

While absolute proof is still a future prospect, an abundance of recent literature describes the out-of-body experience. Both experiencers and investigators of these experiences have described their apparent characteristics with surprising similarity. The out-of-body experience, OOBE, is also sometimes referred to as astral projection, projecting one's "self" "toward the stars."

Those who claim to have had these OOBEs tell us that they are aware that their consciousness is somehow existing apart from their physical bodies. Most often, it is a one-time experience which happens to an individual at a time of crisis, such as severe illness or a close brush with death. Many persons, however, claim to be able to initiate the OOBE virtually at will, or at least experience OOBEs in a nontraumatic state.

This discmbodied consciousness is sometimes perceived as (or "in") a "second body," which exactly resembles the physical body in appearance, but is described as being so much bluish mist or vapor, capable of easily passing through matter without injury. This ecsomatic* (the term of an English parapsychologist, Celia Green) consciousness is often characterized by heightened mental clarity and incredibly vivid visual and auditory acuity.

The OOBE may consist of nothing more than the sensation of being suspended in mid-air in the same room with one's physical body and being able to perceive it from *outside*. Other experiencers of OOBEs have found their ecsomatic consciousness to be in the home of a friend or stranger, in the company of a deceased relative, or on a totally different plane of existence.

While the phenomenon has not been proved, the wealth of evidential material relating to it is compelling and researchers (Celia Green, Charles Tart, Karlis Osis, R. Crookall, and others) are attempting to scientifically validate the out-of-body experience. Vivid autobiographical versions of such experiences have been contributed by Robert Monroe, John Lilly, Vincent Turvey, and others.

The verification of an ecsomatic consciousness during life does not assure the continued existence of that consciousness after the death of the body to which it "belongs." Perhaps this consciousness somehow derives energy required for its adventures from the physical body and would cease to function when the source of energy died. Those involved in the research tend to feel that this is not the case; that the consciousness can, in fact, exist completely independently of a physical body.

Fascinating contributions to the investigation of consciousness independent of biological attachments come from the fields of physics and brain research. Unsuccessful in his exhaustive attempts to locate and literally excise the unit of memory (engram) from the brains of animals, Karl Lashley and his assistant Karl Pribram were bewildered to discover that memory did not seem to be located in any one part of the brain, but was apparently somehow distributed throughout the brain. How could a memory not be any one place, but be everywhere?

*Ecsomatic: *ec* means "outside," *soma* refers to body.

The amazing discovery of holography by physicist Dennis Gabor opened exciting new perceptual frameworks. Holography is a method of three-dimensional photography without the use of cameras or lenses. Light is reflected onto a photographic plate from two sources, from the object itself, say a rose, and from a mirror which reflects light from the object onto the plate. The image on the photographic plate itself looks nothing like a rose, only an apparently random arrangement of swirls.

Now comes the "magic." When a coherent light source, such as a laser beam, is aimed at the plate, the image of the rose is *projected into space,* a distance from the plate of swirls, in full three-dimensional form. What's more, if any piece of the pattern of swirls is broken off and independently illuminated by the laser, the entire rose would appear in full three-dimensional proportions, just as if the entire plate had been illuminated. That is to say, the image of the entire rose is present in any and every part of the holographic pattern.

Pribram and other researchers have begun to relate the concept of holography to human consciousness. Perhaps thoughts, memories, and ideas exist in holographic form and the brain is "merely" the analyzer of the information stored in the hologram (consciousness). Perhaps the holographic consciousness uses the brain and body to supplement or focus its awareness.

Researchers suggest the mathematical functions of our brain in interpreting frequencies result in our perception of the "real" world as we know it. Here, the holographic theory becomes too complex to explain fully in this limited space. The implications are, however, that the world we see is actually a product of the brain's interpretation of frequencies in our environment, perhaps itself a hologram. Freed of the mathematical confines of the brain, the true "frequency domain" in which space and time are collapsed may be perceived by the true consciousness.

The characteristics of the ecsomatic consciousness coincide dramatically with this theory. Those describing their own OOBEs often shun notions of time and space as being applicable to these experiences. The experiences they describe truly seem to represent consciousness in another dimension, where past, present, and future can coexist simultaneously and location is irrelevant.

Is the soul truly a potentially ecsomatic, holographic consciousness? Stay alert for future developments!

The Near-Death Experience

Raymond Moody's 1975 bestseller *Life After Life* astounded the world with its reports of the experiences of persons who had been declared clinically dead. Soon thereafter, other researchers, Dr. Elisabeth Kübler-Ross and Drs. Karlis Osis and Erlendur Haraldsson, revealed that their own evidence corroborated Moody's findings. Subsequent investigation has been undertaken by cardiologists, psychologists, nurses, psychiatrists, and sociologists. Our ideas about life, death, and after-life will probably never be the same.

Moody's book is based on information gleaned from about 150 cases of persons who were (1) actually declared dead and later revived, (2) had a very close call with death, or (3) reported their experiences as they were dying to a third person who later relayed them to Moody. The bulk of his reports, however, came from in-depth interviews of fifty persons from the first two categories.

Moody is the first to point out that his was *not* a scientific study, but a report of intriguing information of which he gradually became aware. Other researchers have attempted investigations with more stringent parameters. Dr. Kenneth Ring reports his findings of 102 case studies in *Life At Death*. Drs. Osis and Haraldsson did a cross-cultural study of the phenomenon of death-bed apparitions by interviewing medical personnel who observed dying patients having such seeming hallucinations or visions. Their book, published in 1977, is titled *At The Hour of Death*. Michael Sabom, a cardiologist at Emory University authored *Recollections of Death: A Medical Investigation*. John Audette and Michael Gulley are now completing the analysis of their data to be published this year. Audette and Gulley's research was designed to attempt to determine the incidence of the near-death experience (described below) and correlate variables associated with the experience. None of the studies has a perfect design, as it is difficult to approach objectively a topic so inherently subjective.

Bearing in mind the preliminary nature of the research, we will summarize some of the information currently available. Let's begin with a description of the near-death experience (NDE).

When persons come very close to physical death or are actually clinically dead (no heartbeat or respiration) and later recover, some of them (we don't yet know how many) have a remarkably peaceful experience which profoundly affects their attitude toward life and usually erases any fear of death. The International Association for Near-Death Studies gives the following as the principal features of NDEs:

A feeling of extreme ease, peace, and well-being.

Finding oneself outside of one's physical body.

Floating or drifting through a dark tunnel or passageway.

Perceiving a brilliant golden or golden-yellow light which seems to radiate warmth, love, and unconditional acceptance.

A telepathic and nonjudgmental encounter with a "presence" or "being of light."

A panoramic life review.

Entering into a transcendent realm of almost indescribable beauty.

Meeting with (deceased) loved ones or spiritual guides who inform the individual that she or he is to return to earthly life.

Probably not any one individual has experienced all of these features and not any one of the features appears in all accounts of NDEs. But all of them do occur with sufficient frequency to warrant being included as possible components of the "core" near-death experience. While one or several elements may be missing, others will be unquestionably recognizable as part of this newly recognized phenomenon.

Recovered patients say things like:

I felt myself apart from my body. I was sort of hovering over the scene of the accident and could see my body there, trapped under the debris. It seemed silly that everyone was working so hard to save me, because I felt so peaceful and full of joy. Then I heard a strange buzzing noise and found myself moving rapidly through a dark space. There was a beautiful, loving, brilliant light and I wanted to stay with it. But I was told, but not in words, that I still had work to do, that I must go back to "life." Then, somehow, I was back in my body. I don't remember going back, only that I didn't want to.

The reports vary somewhat in details, but the similarities are incredible. Age, religious background, sex, mode of near death, race, and educational level were thought to be potential variables that might affect the nature, depth, or mere presence of what Dr. Ring calls the core experience. The minimal number of cases studied thus far have provided little insight into these variables, but as more research is completed, we may begin to see such relationships more clearly. At present, it seems clear that one's religious beliefs are unrelated to the nature of the NDE, as are standard demographic factors such as occupation, or social status.

Overall frequency of the incidence of the core NDE ranges from 15 percent to 60 percent of those studied, depending on which researcher's work is examined. It should be noted that sampling methods in this area have been imperfect at best and that these figures may not at all represent the proportion of the total population that might expect to have such an experience. Curiously, those who had prior knowledge of Moody's research were *less* likely to have a NDE than those who had never heard about the phenomenon. Both Ring and Sabom found this to be true in their studies.

Ring found the cause of "nearly" dying to have some relationship to the incidence and depth of the NDE, but cautions that his sample may be too small and skewed to draw any firm conclusions. He classed his case studies by three groups reflecting mode of death: illness, accident, and suicide. Women were more likely to have the NDE as the result of illness-induced near death, while men were more likely to have the NDE due to accidents or suicide. The groups, however, were not mutually exclusive.

The nature of the NDE for one who attempts suicide poses an interesting dilemma. The case studies in this area are indeed few and skewed by a number of factors which may alter the findings. For example, a high percentage of suicide attempts are induced by a drug overdose which may impair mental clarity in the perception or memory of the NDE. There are many other complicating factors involved in the study of suicide attempts, one of which is the reluctance of attempted suicides to participate in the research.

Ring's work seems to suggest that those attempting suicide are less likely to experience the transcendent qualities of the NDE. While some researchers had anticipated that survivors of failed suicide attempts might report very unpleasant experiences, this has not been the case so far. Of course, perhaps those who *did* have bad experiences have repressed them or quite simply choose not to talk about them.

One point seems clear. Of those who survive the core experience, whether their near death was due to illness, accident, or suicide attempt, nearly all are impressed with the inherent foolishness of taking one's own life. There is a sense that we are on earth for a purpose, to "learn a lesson," and that if we try to escape the fulfillment of that purpose or the struggle of learning, it is in vain. Eventually, we must learn and do what we have been sent to accomplish. There is almost a karmic* message from these NDE survivors that pain avoided (by suicide) in this life still must be experienced, perhaps in another realm of existence or in another earthly life.

While Ring limited his study to those over eighteen years of age, the phenomenon has been known to occur in young children. Many persons, of all ages, report contact with predeceased relatives or religious figures, often perceived to be coming to "take them away" or

---

*The theory of karma is discussed on pp. 122.

to aid their transition to a new form of existence as the experiencer lies very close to death.

An eight-year-old lay weak and noncommunicative in his hospital bed. For two days, he hardly moved. His parents took turns keeping vigil at his bedside. One evening, as his mother sat beside her pale and listless son, he suddenly sat upright in his bed, extended his arms to an invisible visitor and exclaimed, "Grandfather!" His mother and the nurse who was in the room urged him to lie back down, which he did. He died within minutes.

In a strikingly similar case, a man in his eighties, the last survivor among his siblings, seemed to be speaking to a distant audience, proclaiming, "We're all here but one." Family members thought he might have been referring to the absence of his favorite grandson, who lived several hundred miles away and could not make it to the bedside of his dying grandfather. Moments later his meaning became clear as he sat bolt upright, stretched his hands out and called "Mother," with such relief and conviction that those present were convinced of the familial reunion. He lay back down and breathed his final breath.

Appearance of such apparitions was the focus of the Osis-Haraldsson study. They found that eighty-one percent of their several hundred case studies *did* report seeing an apparition shortly before their death or near-death. Nine out of ten of the persons appearing to the dying patients were relatives of the dying patient—mother, spouse, offspring, sibling, father—in that order of frequency. Some of the apparitions were unknown to the patients and some were perceived to be Christ, angels, the Virgin Mary, or, in India, Yama (the Hindu god of death), Krishna, or some other deity.

In *Life At Death*, Ring reports that these spirits of deceased loved ones appeared to have the function of telling the person it was not yet their time to die, rather than offering to ease the transition. Of course, all of Ring's case studies were survivors and most of Osis and Haraldsson's reported the presence of these "take away" spirits shortly before their actual death.

It is interesting that occasionally an individual will report having seen a dead relative they never knew, or even knew existed. For instance, they may encounter a sibling who died before this person was born and who had never been spoken of by the family. Sometimes, a person sees a mother who died giving birth to them or a grandparent who died long before the person was born. Recognition of the spirit may come only after describing the appearance of the spirit to other relatives who knew him or her.

Long before Moody published his book, it was "common knowledge" or at least common speculation that as a drowning person goes down for the last time, her life would "flash before her eyes" just before death. This panoramic life review has been recognized as part of the NDE by Moody, Ring, and other investigators. It seems to appear in holographic form, with a tremendous quantity of information flashing by, sometimes like a movie, in a very short time or even all at once, in extraordinarily vivid form. Moreover, it is usually just the good parts, with all the negative memories somehow "edited out."

The life review appears to happen more commonly in near deaths due to accidents such as drownings, falls, and auto accidents, although it does occur as well in patients who almost died of a serious illness. As with the other elements of the NDE, the panoramic life review is recalled with positive feelings.

Why do some people have this lovely, tranquil experience when they come close to death and others remember nothing at all? So far, researchers haven't an inkling. Most researchers to date have yet to talk with anyone who described a negative or "hellish" experience, unless it clearly seemed to be a dream and not part of the vivid NDE. One exception is Dr. Maurice Rawlings, a cardiologist who believes some of his patients have had glimpses of Hell. His data, however, are not presented scientifically, and Ring and others find it "too amorphous to evaluate."

Perhaps the most remarkable aspect of the near-death experience is its profound effect on the attitudes and values of those who survive it. While none of them now seek an "early" death, neither are they at all afraid of dying "when it is their time." There is usually a definite sense that life has a purpose and that one should diligently pursue its fulfillment. There is a renewed appreciation of life and its inherent joys and a decided rejection of suicide as a way of escaping problems.

Moody also found a pronounced growth in the recognition of the importance of love for others and the value of continuing to learn. Ring found that material comforts waned in importance as his survivors sought to be more compassionate and of service toward others. It would be interesting to follow these individuals throughout the years to see if this new philosophy of life remains consistent. (Some of the experiencers were in fact interviewed a number of years, even decades, after the event and still felt very strongly about its impact.)

Audette and Gulley suggest that simply coming close to death, whether or not one has the core experience, is itself a profound experience encouraging introspection and a reordering of priorities. For those who do have the NDE, this effect seems to be magnified.

Many questions remain unanswered. Though many explanations have been proposed, such as oxygen deprivation in the brain or physiologically-induced hallucination, no scientifically proven explanation has yet been offered which accounts for the occurrence of the near-death experience. The International Association for Near-Death Studies has been organized to encourage and promote study of the near-death experience and related phenomena. General membership in IANDS costs $15 and entitles one to receive the monthly newsletter, soon to become a magazine. The association is interested in hearing from persons who are doing research in this area, from those who have had a personal near-death experience, and from anyone who wants to learn more about the phenomenon.

Correspondence may be addressed to:

The International Association for Near-Death Studies, Inc.
Box U-20
The University of Connecticut
Storrs, Connecticut 06268

The IANDS telephone number is (203) 486–4170; Dr. Ring's telephone number is (203) 486–4906

Reincarnation

When given the opportunity to rank suggested topics for discussion in our death and dying classes, students *invariably* choose reincarnation and after-life as their number one area of interest. I would consider it foolish and unjust to exclude the topic from the course or from this book. Indeed, student interest has spurred my own study and curiosity in the area, and I believe that reincarnation is at least a notion worthy of our consideration.

The scientific study of reincarnation, like that of after-life, is in its infancy and there is no proof that human spirits sequentially inhabit human bodies in a continuing quest for perfection and understanding, or for the opportunity to atone for injustices of a previous life; neither has the idea in any way been disproved. But the mental exercise of examining the theories of reincarnation may provide us some insights and new approaches to the way we currently think about life.

Recently, I spoke with a midwestern physician whose approach to reincarnation is one of guarded open-mindedness. Nevertheless, he claims to have "an intuitive sense of the continuation of life—dying of flowers in these midwestern winters only to be reborn in our springs, the transformation of the caterpillar into a beautiful butterfly—these seem to be nature's way of reinforcing this notion of life after death, and, perhaps, the existence of yet another life."

While many believe that the spirit survives the death of the body and is rewarded or punished for its earthly deeds in the spirit world, reincarnationists take the idea a step further. Viewed in the vastness of history, seventy years is but an instant. How could we possibly learn all the lessons of life, experience all the necessary joys and pains, in one short lifetime?

Religious Background

Reincarnation has long been accepted by the Eastern religions, and it is not foreign to Western thought from the time of Plato and the Bible to the present. It was taught in early Judaism and Christianity. Millions of Christians continued to accept the notion of rebirth until the time of the Inquisition, when their "Christian" brothers imprisoned, tortured, and burned them at the stake for harboring such beliefs. The Fifth Ecumenical Council of A.D. 553 apparently condemned the work of Origen, a Christian Greek theologian of the third century, whose philosophy on preexistence and rebirth had been previously widely accepted. St. Jerome considered Origen to have been "the greatest teacher of the Church after the apostles."

Owing to the Council of A.D. 553 and the Inquisition, Christian doctrine has in modern history divorced itself from the notion of reincarnation. Many modern theologians, however, do not find it inconsistent with the teachings of Christ. In fact, the reincarnation of Jesus is openly expected in the Second Coming. There are other references to the concept of reincarnation in the New Testament as well. Unfortunately, there is little agreement upon interpretation of a great many Biblical passages, and different translations seem to alter the meaning of a great number of these passages.

Memories of Past Lives

Many persons, when first confronted with the idea of reincarnation, find it curious that we don't remember our past lives, if indeed we had them. Another point that raises questions is the idea that the soul is able to assume different "personalities" and yet retain continuity. Both are simply misgivings, and can be dismissed as solid proof against reincarnation by merely examining the course of our own present earthly lives.

Who among us has but the faintest memories of our existence as an infant and a small child? Does the absence of these conscious memories prove that we did not live as an infant and small child? Of course not. We do, in fact, forget most of the details of our earlier lives as our consciousness becomes absorbed in current interests and tasks. The fact that many, if not most, of these details can be recalled later with the aid of hypnosis provides assurance that, while our conscious mind may not be aware of these memories, they are intact and stored away in our subconscious.

As for the discontinuity that successive reincarnations would seem to result in, we again need only trace our present path in life. We are in a continual transition process, ever growing, ever learning, ever becoming. For a time, we are helpless infants, incapable of all but the crudest form of communication. We learn to speak, to walk, to interpret our environment with increasing ability. Adolescence finds us expressing our new identities, more challenging than those of children. As young adults, we take on new responsibilities and again change our attitudes and lifestyles consistent with the demands placed on us and our perception of our roles. In each successive state of life, we learn and grow. Most of us would scarcely recognize ourselves as the person we were ten years ago, yet we know we are somehow continuous with that person, and that our present personality was very much dependent upon the prior sequence of existence for it to achieve its present characteristics.

In the same way, could we not have had a previous existence, or perhaps several, which are not a part of our conscious memory but which were somehow instrumental in the development of our consciousness as it currently exists? Some persons *do* claim to have memories of previous lives, and others are aided in the recall of these memories by hypnosis. In some cases, there seems to be a rational explanation how the individual would seem to have a memory of a previous life, even though it may not be true. A vivid imagination may be the most common explanation offered. Other cases, however, are too rich in detail and contain incredible information about geography, languages, or skills that cannot so easily be explained away.

One young woman, a college student in Illinois, under hypnosis reported details of a life in a small town in Pennsylvania in the nineteenth century. Because of the wealth of details that might be verifiable, the researcher eagerly began the process of systematic checking of the facts only to be thwarted at the first attempt to do so. None of the maps available showed any town in the state of Pennsylvania by the name she had given. The researcher reluctantly abandoned the case as the product of a good imagination.

The hypnotist's assistant, however, had a nagging feeling about the case. Several months later, while passing through Pennsylvania on a vacation, research led him to the discovery that the town she mentioned did, in fact, exist at the time the young woman said she lived there, but had been destroyed by a flood shortly after her reported previous life. After the flood, the survivors had just moved to a nearby community. The town was never rebuilt, which explained why it had not appeared on any state maps since that time.

A few other details of the account were verified, but most of the town records had been destroyed in the flood, which hampered the investigation. How did this college student in west central Illinois happen to know of the existence of a tiny town in a distant state, a town which had disappeared more than a hundred years ago? Perhaps she read of it or heard of it on TV, but this was such an obscure place that it seems unlikely that it would have been the source of any contemporary literary or entertainment interest.

Many well-known historical persons claimed or intimated having memories of a past life, including Charles Lindbergh, Charles Dickens, Louisa May Alcott, Henry David Thoreau, General George Patton, Alfred, Lord Tennyson, and many others. Albert Einstein and Henry Ford reported no specific memories of a past life, but clearly believed in the concept of reincarnation.

The presence of early genius or the ability to speak a language otherwise unknown in the present life are certainly puzzling, if not proof of previous existence. Another Illinois college student underwent hypnosis and past-life regression and began speaking in fluent French, a language she had never studied in this life. (This was verified by checking her educational background and interviewing her family and previous associates.)

Xenoglossy is the term referring to this ability to speak in languages never before studied. Many other cases have defied logical explanation. Twin American boys puzzled their parents by speaking to each other in a language no one else understood. Finally, it was determined the young brothers were freely conversing in Aramaic, an ancient language spoken when Christ was alive. Another case involves a five-year-old boy in the United States who spoke a dialect of northern Tibetan and described in detail his former school in the mountains of Tibet.

In Columbus, Georgia, in the last half of the nineteenth century, a blind, four-year-old enslaved boy was a genius at the piano. His concert career began at seven and by fifteen he had performed on many stages, both in the U.S. and abroad. His minimal intellectual abilities were far inferior to his inexplicable musical talent.

Those who deny reincarnation might refer to these talents as "gifts" or "miracles." Taylor Caldwell, a famous author of numerous historical novels, offers another approach. Having reported thirty-seven past lives under hypnosis herself, she adamantly refuses to believe in reincarnation. Rather, she attributes her incredible knowledge of historical events, which astounds even herself, to some genetic or racial memory. Perhaps all of the knowledge of the world has become the holographic human consciousness of which we are all a part.

Some of us may be more skilled than others at tapping this information which abides in our collective memory. In essence, perhaps we all potentially share the knowledge of all those who came before us. Why some persons seem to have ready access to this consciousness and others do not is no easier to explain, of course, than is reincarnation itself—which is not to say it couldn't be a viable explanation. There is simply too much we do not know.

Theories of Reincarnation and Karma

People who believe in reincarnation will tell you they do so simply because it makes sense. It affords the spirit the opportunity to reap the rewards of past good deeds and to pay the debts for former indiscretions. There are so many apparent injustices in this world, and reincarnation seems to make some sense of it all.

Consider the hard-working soul who gets little recognition or monetary reward for all his labors and is plagued by health problems and family tragedies. Would it not seem just to find him better situated in another life, in pleasant surroundings and good health as compensation for his past diligence and suffering? And what of the callous murderer and thief who cleverly escapes capture, lives luxuriously on the money of others, and feels no remorse for the grief and pain he has caused?

One apparent injustice that many find troubling is that of people who blatantly abuse their children and are "blessed" with a number of them, while many eager, loving, potentially great parents remain childless. Indeed, often it seems there isn't any justice in the world. Reincarnationists find some comfort in believing that, eventually, we all must learn our lessons and pay for our mistakes.

Critics often dismiss reincarnation as the product of wishful thinking or the distorted ambition to live forever. This is hardly the case. Rather, for those who embrace the philosophy, it seems to be expression of divine wisdom and infinite justice. It gives a purpose and meaning to everything in life, and leads to the inescapable conclusion that we alone are truly accountable for not only our particular lot in life, but also for our every action within the framework of our circumstances.

The law of *karma* further explains the cycle of life, death, and rebirth. Karma is defined in Buddhism and Hinduism as the moral law of cause and effect. It commits the believer to a complete personal responsibility. Our parents, spouse, employer, children, or friends are not responsible for our condition. We have free will to choose our life, but eventually must rectify our misdeeds and learn from our trials, with the ultimate goal of achieving total personal and universal harmony.

Believers in karmic law hold that as souls progress to their stage of personal harmony, they are freed of the need to reincarnate and proceed to a higher plane of existence, where there are new lessons to be learned. How many lifetimes it takes to achieve this perfect synthesis of mind, emotion, and spirit with physical existence depends upon the individual and the paths he chooses. The karmic belief system suggests that it may take many of us thousands of lives to reach this goal, though some may need many fewer, but "all will reach the sunlit snows."

Sylvia Cranston and Joseph Head in *Reincarnation: The Phoenix Fire Mystery* liken the journey to the process of learning to play a musical instrument. Early in our endeavors, we strike many a discordant note, but gradually develop the skill to avoid cacophony and produce only beautiful, harmonic melodies. When our lives and our spirits become perfectly in tune we graduate from earthly lessons to those of a grander nature.

While reincarnation is highly regarded by many great contemporary minds, there is no empirical evidence of its workings. Therefore, theoretical interpretation of the concept varies on certain details. Bearing that in mind, following are some of the more widely held ideas concerning reincarnation.

Ordinarily, the soul may stay in a free-floating disembodied state for a long time between earthly incarnations. Some suggest this might be a generation or a century or more. This time is used by the soul to assess the lessons of the past life and to determine the goals of the next life. One might need to learn patience, compassion, or diligence, for example, and so would choose a life which will provide opportunities for development of that virtue. Reincarnationists believe we do, indeed choose our parents!

The exception to this long free-float period between lives is believed to occur in instances of sudden, early or violent death which came before the spirit had completed the goals for that life. Since the opportunity for learning has been cut short, the spirit soon reincarnates to continue the lessons too quickly aborted. Parents who have lost a child to death have in rare but compelling instances given testimony of the incredible similarities between the dead child and another born to them later. The accounts of numerous "insignificant" idiosyncrasies shared by the children often truly defy any explanation other than that the same spirit has returned to this family.

Did you ever encounter a perfect stranger and feel at once that you knew her or him, although you had never met? Perhaps you have, in another life. Reincarnationists generally believe that we usually choose lives with at least some spirits who are familiar to us and that, in fact, we have some karmic debts to settle with them.

Those who are our parents in this life may have been our children, siblings, or spouses in previous lives. Close friends recur in different roles in our various lives, as well. Believers use this to explain "love at first sight" and the overwhelming feeling lovers often have that they know their partner in intimate ways beyond the experience of their present relationship.

One concept about which there is considerable disagreement is that of the sex of the soul. Most reincarnationists seem to believe, however, that the soul is a pure entity, devoid of sexual identification. In "remembered past lives," persons often have recalled being of the opposite sex from their present personality. Purists say that only by experiencing life from both perspectives do most of us begin to understand the true nature of life and develop a universal love and compassion for our fellow beings, regardless of sex.

The same may be said of race, religion, social status, and other artificial barriers that separate souls from their comrades in the cosmic journey. By experiencing life from many viewpoints, we learn to accept and love each other without reservation. Eventually, we may begin to see the true value of the spirit, apart from its temporal attachments. If we are cruel or cause harm to one who is disfigured or maimed, in a future life we may find ourselves or a loved one so afflicted so that the lesson of compassion becomes more vivid for us.

Certain religious objectors claim that if reincarnation were a fact, there would be no motivation for individuals to save their souls. With an eternity available for ultimate salvation, what's the rush? Those who propose this objection apparently either do not understand karmic law or underestimate the appeal of the eternal peace they offer.

Karma is consistent and inescapable. If one postpones an important lesson or mistreats his fellows, his karmic debt is enlarged and further delays his eventual enlightenment and final reward. Rather than encourage procrastination of noble deeds, one who believes in karma is compelled to do his best in life, realizing his own ultimate responsibility for all that he does.

More than one hundred years ago, in 1881, the crime statistics in India reflected a stark difference between Christian and Buddhist convictions. Among Europeans and Eurasians in India, one in every 391 persons was convicted of a crime; among native Christians, the ratio was one in 799; among Buddhists, one of 3,787 persons was convicted of crime. The Buddhists' deeply ingrained sense of morality greatly impressed the Catholic writer who reported these statistics in 1888.

Methods of Research

The many mysteries of reincarnation intrigue and evade researchers. We seek to understand, to find some scientific evidence that might convince us once and for all of the possibility or impossibility of the idea. There has been a great resurgence of interest in the area recently and a number of approaches are being taken in research.

By far the greatest amount of research into reincarnation has been conducted by Dr. Ian Stevenson, Carlson Professor of Psychiatry at the University of Virginia. To date, he has investigated well over 1,700 cases of recall of past lives and meticulously pursued the verification of the facts remembered. Only a few of his case studies have involved adults. The rest comprised past-life memories of children, usually first verbalized between the ages of two and four years!

His published work, *Twenty Cases Suggestive of Reincarnation*, 1974; *Cases of the Reincarnation Type*, Volume I, 1975, Volume II, 1977, Volume III, 1978; *Xenoglossy*, 1974, and many articles in professional journals have detailed the exacting professional approach he has taken in his work and revealed the startling detail and accuracy of these memories of small children. Realizing the many opportunities for criticism of such an endeavor, Dr. Stevenson has applied the most stringent standards to his research.

The now-famous psychiatrist began his current studies as a search for an explanation for personality characteristics for which no basis in this life could be found. The work has taken him on journeys amounting to some 55,000 miles of travel per year, going to the exact location of the stated previous life, sometimes with the child, to verify the authenticity of his data. His findings have been remarkable and inexplicable, except by theories (collective unconscious, reading of the "astral light") which are at least as difficult to prove as reincarnation.

Dr. Stevenson is interested in hearing from persons who remember a past life or know of someone else who has such memories. He encourages parents to listen to their preschoolers' "imaginative" conversations. He may be reached by writing to:

Dr. Ian Stevenson
Division of Parapsychology
Box 152
Medical Center, University of Virginia
Charlottesville, Virginia 22901

Another method of research used by psychologist Dr. James Garrett and others is hypnosis and past-life regression. The subject is hypnotized and "regressed" to successively earlier times in his present life, then encouraged to recall memories from before he was born into this life. Of course, many persons are not good hypnotic subjects and report no such memories. Others suggest past lives which are either apparently pure fabrication or are simply not rich enough in detail or uniqueness to allow for scientific verification of the memories. For these reasons, Dr. Stevenson and others prefer not to approach the subject by use of hypnosis, although Dr. Stevenson has acknowledged some exceptions.

Occasionally, a hypnotic subject will speak in a foreign language previously unknown to him, or provide such vivid accounts steeped in specificity about a time it would have been impossible for the individual to have knowledge of in any normal way that the hypnotist is able to transcribe the taped session and verify the wealth of information it contains. The story of Bridey Murphy was thus revealed, as was the subject of Stevenson's own *Xenoglossy*.

The public still awaits publication of significant findings derived from this approach, which may soon be forthcoming. Other research methods with less scientific validity are the investigation of "readings" of mediums or psychics regarding past lives and the use of LSD to promote such memories. Neither of these is currently being used to any great extent. Taylor Caldwell's 37 "past lives" were derived from two methods, hypnotic regression and psychic readings, and were recorded in some detail in Jess Stearn's book *The Search for a Soul: Taylor Caldwell's Psychic Lives*. (It should be reemphasized that the famous novelist denies she truly lived these reported lives.)

So What?

Would the world be any better or any worse if we all believed in reincarnation? Of what value is this knowledge in our day-to-day existence? Those who do believe are convinced that the world would become a more peaceful, compassionate sphere if the notion of karma were more widespread. The onus of responsibility for one's actions and thought is clear and unavoidable. "As ye sow, so shall ye reap" was never more applicable. Karma is a system of infinite justice. But can we believe it?

One possible benefit Dr. James Garrett envisions from our eventual knowledge of reincarnation as reported to me in a personal interview, would be the ability to tap previous knowledge and skills for use in this life. If we could somehow consciously recapture a past-life fluency in a foreign language or mastery of a literary technique, perhaps we could build on that base and achieve far more than might have been possible in one brief lifetime.

Of course, virtually everyone is convinced that we would all be better off if only the whole world believed exactly as he or she does. Curious readers are encouraged to ponder the matter, to read Cranston and Head's *Reincarnation: The Phoenix Fire Mystery*, for a massive review of the literature on the subject, and to decide for themselves the meaning of it all.

10

The "Deathless Deaths": Divorce, Disability, and Other Major Losses

In this country, we tend to view death as an alien, an unwanted foreigner whose milieu is strange and frightening to us. And yet before we actually die, we "die a thousand deaths." Life constantly presents us with gains and losses. Perhaps we think we're happier if we pretend that death is the only source of grief in human existence.

Death may be the ultimate loss in terms of our earthly experience, but we grieve for many other losses in our lives. Even many positive changes, such as getting married, starting a high-paying job, or moving to a new home, may be accompanied by surprising feelings of sadness and depression as we part with the familiar and comfortable elements that had been our life and embark on this new adventure, however promising. Part of us must "die" as we adapt, grow, and change and become the "new" us.

As we mature, we learn to cope quite well with most of these losses—roll with the punches, perhaps. And these skills help us when we are faced with an even greater loss. We will consider several major losses and examine the grief and adaptation process involved in each. It should then become apparent that this same coping challenge presents itself in many forms throughout our lives.

Divorce

Imagine meeting two single women at a social gathering. One of the women was divorced six months earlier, the other was widowed about the same time. Would you feel differently toward the women, knowing only this much about them? Many people have more positive, sympathetic feelings toward the widow, although in many circumstances, the adjustment to a divorce can be even more difficult than the adjustment to the death of a spouse.

Death of a spouse and divorce often evoke the same problems for the survivors. All too often, however, divorced persons find far less support and help in adjusting than do their widowed counterparts. Divorce tends to be viewed as a failure, a lack of commitment or perhaps an inherent personality problem. And yet, there may be an injured party in a divorce who is every bit as much an unsuspecting victim as the person whose spouse is killed in an accident.

A friend of mine who is a health professional recently was given a rather abrupt announcement that her husband wanted a divorce. Apparently he had developed "outside" interests while she was furthering her education. She said, "I always jeered when people said 'The wife is always the last to know,' but now I believe it. I thought everything was great between us, then wham! I couldn't believe he was serious."

This *denial* is just as common in divorced partners as it is for widows and widowers. In fact, all the stages of dying (discussed in Chapter Two) are especially apparent in persons confronted with divorce. Anger may be vented at our partner's real or imagined faults or perhaps at our own. We may even blame other people or things, such as an interfering in-law or a too-demanding job. Bargaining comes in the form of a myriad of suggested compromises, "I'll do this if you'll do that," or perhaps "I'll do anything you ask if you'll just keep loving me."

The depression that accompanies divorce may be profound and long-lasting, and has a dimension not usually present in widowhood. That dimension is rejection. Occasionally, a widow or widower has a sense of rejection, "If he had really loved me, he would have taken better care of his health; he didn't want to live with me." Usually it is irrational and short-lived after the death of a spouse, except in cases where the spouse committed suicide. But, if you are the injured party in a divorce, there is no escaping the blatant truth. That person you loved so much and to whom you gave so much no longer wants you. They didn't get hit by a truck or an invasion of cancer, they willingly, eagerly walked away from you. That hurts.

Obviously, we are not speaking here of the individual who seeks the divorce, who wants to walk away. That person has probably already decathected from the relationship and has chosen to try a new life-style. The person left behind, however, has been forced make many of the same adjustments as the widow or widower—being single again, changed financial situation, possible child-rearing complications, altered role responsibilities, perhaps new housing arrangements, not to mention the agonizing absence of this once so very special person. On top of all this is that haunting, aching feeling of being unloved, maybe even unlovable.

Besides the rejection, another aspect of a divorce that complicates the grief process is, strangely enough, that the person *isn't* dead. Making the break, accepting the loss is sometimes more difficult for the divorced person than it is for the widowed. If your spouse has died, there may be some short-lived fantasies regarding his or her return to life, but most bereaved persons recognize its impossibility and, as much as they yearn for that return, they know it can't happen.

For the divorced, however, there is much more of a tendency to do some wishful thinking, to imagine that the wayward spouse will "come to her senses," or "realize what he's missing" and rush back to the abandoned marriage. As long as one harbors these notions, one cannot complete the grief process. "Keeping the home fires burning" and severing emotional ties are simply incompatible tasks. One must choose.

Reconciliations, although infrequent, *do* occur. Those who have experienced one will tell you it is worth the wait. There is no magic formula, however, to predict which relationships will somehow re-kindle after a major freeze. One must decide if it is more important to start fresh and begin to build a new life or to cling to a past that is no more. The widowed have this decision made for them by circum-stances. For the divorced, it is a much more complex situation.

Our society does make some allowances, though not enough, for widows and widowers as they go about the task of coping with their changed circumstances. We offer divorced persons little but our stares and disapproval. When the spouse dies, family and friends unite and offer condolences, casseroles, and camaraderie. Parents, in-laws, friends, business associates—all are sympathetic and do in some way share the loss. An employer will likely expect the bereaved to take off several days "to get themselves together" and fellow employees will probably be understanding if things don't go too smoothly the first few days back on the job. The company many even send flowers or a memorial donation.

Consider the divorcée in the throes of the legal "dis-spousement."

Friends and family may not know how to act, what to say. Some may take sides, others may stay away entirely, not wanting to interfere or show favoritism. In comparable situations, a widow is flanked by many comforters, while the divorcée may find herself isolated and insulted just at a time when she desperately needs support, reassurance, and someone to talk to. Not only does her husband reject her, but so does much of the rest of her world. It is probable she will have to take a vacation day to attend the court proceedings. There is no sympathy or special accommodation for the divorcée. It's business as usual the next day. Forget the flowers and the time to get yourself together.

The effects of parental divorce and death of a parent are very similar to a child. Somehow, we recognize the child's loss in a divorce more than we do the parent's. Dr. Miriam Gofseyeff, child psychologist at the Harvard Community Health Center, says that in children, "the common causes of depression are loss of a significant parent, either by death or through separation or through emotional withdrawal . . . That is the most common, some form of loss of the parent." We expect, or at least consider it normal if children become depressed or hyperactive, withdraw, have problems at school, lose interest in eating for a while, or cry a lot when their parents get divorced or if one of them dies.

While we acknowledge the child's right to some time to adjust to the upheaval in his life, the divorced parent is afforded no such luxury. "Big girls don't cry." The need for time for grief is often just as important after a divorce as it is after the death of a spouse. It is, unfortunately, far less socially acceptable.

Another possible contrast may be found in the financial status of widows and divorcées. The widow may be left with a large trust or life insurance check to ease her pain, while the divorcée is more likely to find herself searching for her first full-time job, another major life adjustment. Of course, there are poor widows and wealthy divorcées, too. The point is that both situations can be very difficult and that each case is different. One cannot say "divorced persons deserve more sympathy than widowed persons" any more than one could say the reverse.

Widowers and divorced men have special problems, too, which we are probably even more reluctant to acknowledge than we are the problems of women and children. If adults are tougher than children, men are supposedly toughest of all. Instead of expressing their grief behaviorally, men often internalize their feelings and end up with ulcers, heart attacks, or high blood pressure. These are, unfortunately, socially acceptable, bonafide ways to get attention and sympathy.

Some divorces, of course, don't have an injured party. There may be a mutual loss of interest in the relationship and agreement that they would both be better off on their own or in other relationships. But don't be too anxious to jump to conclusions here, either. Even so-called easy or friendly divorces involve a big loss. The individuals must accept that their chosen life partner and life plan, perhaps, are not working out as they expected. They must admit an error in judgment or at least prognostication. It is easier to concede these facts intellectually than it is to adjust to them emotionally. After a time in marriage, it may become glaringly obvious that the partners are incompatible. One is a night-owl, the other a lover of sunrises. One wants a big family, the other hates children. One adheres to a devout faith, the other scorns religion. And so on. Living together is simply unbearable, unrealistic, in spite of an underlying concern for the other's well-being and happiness and a strong emotional attachment.

Even in mutually-sought divorces, there is a need for time to adapt to the dramatic change in one's life. Many parts of one's life may be simplified—fewer arguments, more free time, a sense of being unburdened. But the task of "cleaning out our closets" remains. One should take advantage of this experience to reassess values, establish new goals, reevaluate priorities. What do I want out of life? What do I want in a marriage partner? How much am I willing to give to a marriage? How important are children? Because of the necessary time involved in obtaining the legal divorce, many persons accomplish a good deal of this preparatory grief before the final decree is issued.

Because of the sense of failure and rejection generated by a divorce, many persons seem to rush out to search for verification of their own worth and desirability. This is popularly known as getting involved "on the rebound." Friends may be skeptical of attachments formed so soon. They warn of being taken advantage of and being so vulnerable. Of course, caution is always appropriate before getting too involved in any relationship. But these early postdivorce liaisons may be helpful in reestablishing self-confidence.

Maybe it is because divorce is so common today that we tend to minimize its impact on the persons involved. Maybe we think they "got what's coming to them." Losing a spouse through divorce is, however, one of the most significant and stressful experiences any of us may endure. Those who go through it deserve more than a critical review and a cold shoulder. Simply because half the population has a broken leg this month doesn't make my bone heal any faster, my pain diminish any sooner, or help me learn to walk on crutches any more easily. "Safety in numbers" is hardly a comfort when one is freshly bereaved or freshly divorced.

Long-Term Illness, Disfigurement, and Disability

Occasionally something happens in life that seems completely intolerable. Death is one of those things. But many of them are not life-threatening, only life-altering. It is often not a total loss of life to which we must adapt, but a loss of life as we know it. An accomplished gymnast may be stricken with arthritis. An artist may lose his vision. A fashion model may need a mastectomy. Many soldiers lose arms and legs. The list is long. Each of these circumstances necessitates a period of adjustment and grief work—a "death" of the person we were and a rebirth in our new identity.

Because of the remarkable change in our lives, many of these losses are very difficult to handle. This can be an incredibly depressing, wrenching process, especially if the crisis requires that we completely reorder our priorities and our life goals. It may seem at least as painful as a period of bereavement, and the reactions may be very similar.

Progressive Disabling Disease

One of my former students, a professional nurse, wrote the following comments at the end of the term. Part of her job had been to help patients "put their lives back in order" after a severe illness. She felt competent in this professional role . . .

> It was quite a bit different when a doctor told me that I have a muscular disease which in time I know will become disabling. I wondered if you noticed that night as I sat in class, fighting back the tears, and for the most part being unable to do so, as we discussed the Stages of Dying as described by Kübler-Ross. The shock had not quite passed from the news of the morning, although I had diagnosed my problem about three weeks before I even went to the specialist in St. Louis. Somehow I didn't want to hear him tell me I was right. Now *I* was saying, "Why me?" Just at the same time you were telling me this was normal! Why does it have to hurt so bad just to be normal?

This nurse was only beginning her grief process when I knew her. The anticipated changes in her life are many. Her ability to function as a nurse, a mother, wife, cook, housekeeper, and sometime waterskiier will be altered. Her sense of identity and self-worth in each of these roles will be threatened. As she gradually adjusts to the imposed restrictions, she must develop new identities and goals. And I am confident she will succeed in finding appropriate solutions to the new problems posed by her diagnosis. It may, however, be a very difficult and long-term endeavor. I am grateful she has a loving, supportive family.

Burn Victim

Another former student had been severely burned in a fire which destroyed her home. To make matters worse, she was inadvertently responsible for the blaze. Her guilt was aggravated by her family's obvious despair and bitterness over the loss of their home. Consider the magnitude of this woman's losses.

Burns over most of her body caused severe pain and required months of hospitalization. The unrelenting pain resulted in a demoralizing loss of self-control. The burns scarred and maimed her legs causing a loss of function (walking) and a change in body image (ugly scars replaced lovely smooth skin). The lengthy hospitalization required a separation from friends and family (she was in a burn unit in a city a hundred miles from her home). The visits were too infrequent and not very pleasant, at that. Of course, had she not been hospitalized, there would have been no home to go to, anyway. That alone could be a major source of grief.

As she improved physically, the family began to let her know just how disappointed they were in her. Their house was gone, their possessions were gone, and she wasn't even home to help them cope with *their* losses. It was obvious they blamed her for the whole mess and had little sympathy for the agony she endured. Her support system, too, was gone. Who would help with *her* grief?

The long posthospitalization recovery required time-consuming treatments and routines. She had lost her identity as housewife, mother, employee, social person, and gained a new, unwelcome one. She was now "burn victim." Her life necessarily revolved around the rehabilitative, recuperative process. She could not function in her former roles until she regained the strength and mobility these roles required.

Besides the loss of the house and its contents, her financial burdens were increased by the overwhelming expenses incurred in long-term hospitalization. Hospitals don't give discounts—"stay two months, get one month free." Insurance helped with some, but not all of the financial losses. Her guilt feelings with respect to incurring these expenses was worsened by her inability to generate any income.

There were other losses, but these are sufficient to illustrate the devastation one such event can have on a person's life. This woman is now physically able to participate in most desired activities, but she still experiences moderate pain in her legs and has a lot of grief work yet before her. The ordeal has inspired her interest in helping other burn victims to cope with their difficult experience, to let them know someone understands their special problems. This is a prime example of a positive outcome of a tragic event. Because of her pain, others will benefit. I know that her determination will result in many regional public educational programs as well as support and assistance for burn patients and their families.

Birth of Handicapped Child

Imagine the grief of the parents who have just learned that their precious, longed-for newborn infant has a major congenital disease that will require a lifetime of close medical supervision and expensive treatments which will make life only slightly more bearable. Gone are the dreams of Little League baseball, piano lessons, and honor rolls. Whatever fantasies the parents had about this child have been shattered. They have lost the child they anticipated and the life which they yearned to spend with this child. Their parenting roles will be altered. Their identities will be threatened. Instead of being Eloise and Harry, happy prospective parents, they become producers of a defective child. Their self-esteem is endangered.

These are real and serious losses which signal the need for some grief work. The parents must accept the death of the fantasy child and reinvest their energy in the life of the real child born to them. This is often extremely difficult, for the parents not only feel guilty about having a handicapped child in the first place, but also feel guilty for having wanted so desperately to have a "perfect" child. They go through the "why me's," denial, depression, and finally, acceptance.

Once the parents can accept the reality of their loss, they can more effectively appreciate and care for the gift that is theirs, although it was not the gift they sought. They begin to realize that even "perfect" children pose considerable problems, and that despite their inherent tribulations, handicapped children can bring a lot of joy and fulfillment to a family. It is not unusual for parents to misunderstand at first the exact nature and implications of their child's disability. The more they learn about what lies ahead of them, the more real and tolerable the situation becomes. As they learn to cope with their challenges, they cease being "producers of a defective child" and become Eloise and Harry, competent, caring, and confident parents.

Mastectomy and Amputation

For a woman, a mastectomy probably represents one of the most serious threats to self-esteem and personal identity. In this situation, there is a very obvious, physical, undeniable death of a part of that person. This is a very concrete loss of our society's symbol of femininity. Of course, the intensity of any grief process is related to the strength of the emotional involvement with the lost person or thing. For some women, it is an incredibly devastating experience, especially for those who derive a great portion of their sense of sexual identity from their real or imagined physical attractiveness. For any woman, it is a major loss.

Amputation of any part of the body requires a period of adjustment. The young soldiers who had lost an arm or leg in Vietnam often went through a period of turmoil as they had to revise their body image to conform with their new physical limitations. The "phantom" pain they feel in the amputated limb aggravates the confusion about the "real me." It feels like the leg is there. It actually hurts. But a glance below the knee reveals nothing but bed sheets. Eventually the pain subsides, the physical absence is undeniable and the young man must begin to adapt his identity, dreams, and goals to make them consistent with his present capabilities.

Once the initial information sinks in, there may follow periods of denial, anger, and depression. A young woman who had had a mastectomy said "I can't even look at myself in the mirror. How can I ever face my husband again? How could he possibly ever want to make love to someone who looks like this?" A young man whose right arm had been amputated above the elbow lamented, "I have always wanted to be a surgeon. My dad and brother are doctors and I had great plans for going to medical school when I got out of the service. Look what they did to me. What am I gonna do now? My future is ruined."

Given counseling, support, and education, those who endure mastectomies and amputations may discover things weren't as bad as they thought and might even develop a new perspective and deeper appreciation of life. Our would-be surgeon may not make that goal, but it could be altered to perhaps another specialty of medicine where the use of a hand is not as critical. There is at least one blind physician and many with other serious handicaps. Surely the young man who had lost his arm could become a doctor too, if he maintains his dedication. Thousands of people have adjusted quite well to prosthetic legs, some even achieving national recognition for athletic accomplishments with artificial limbs.

A group of volunteer women, called Reach to Recovery, all former mastectomy patients, visit recent mastectomy patients to offer support and help in learning to cope with their situation. Besides the fact of the physical loss of part of the body, and the additional sexual and emotional implications of having a breast removed, the spectre of cancer will have already been raised, and the possibility of its spread will be cause for concern. Although most people probably know very little about it, the word brings with it a horror. We fear that cancer, like spilled mercury, is forever beyond our control. Reach to Recovery volunteers, sponsored through the American Cancer Society, help patients to learn about cancer and its treatment and assist them in adjusting to their new identity. Advice about prosthetic breasts is given, too. This educational and supportive program encourages new patients to recognize and maximize their own strengths and to gain confidence in dealing with this part of their lives.

Contrary to popular belief, cancer is not the worst disease in the world and is not an automatic death sentence. Many types of cancer are being cured or controlled by an ever-evolving armamentarium of medications and treatments. The outlook is not as bleak as it once seemed. Research by the National Cancer Institute and the American Cancer Society, as well as many other scientists has had a significant impact on the prognosis for cancer patients. The American Cancer Society especially is providing information for the general public and individual patients to help us learn how to cope with, if not conquer, this menace.

Common Hurdles

Whatever the source, any significant loss causes us to somehow change our concept of ourselves. We cease to be the person we once were and become a new, and we hope, wiser, person. If the loss is due to divorce, we can no longer think of ourselves in the context of that marriage. If the loss is brought on by a disabling disease, we can no longer cling to the idea of our direct involvement in physically demanding situations.

Each loss requires a special adaptation, further refined by the individual's previous attachment to the value represented by the loss. A person who depends for much of his self-esteem on his accomplishments in long-distance running might adapt more readily to the accidental amputation of a couple of fingers than would a pianist or typist. A woman who has many interests, friends, and activities might adjust to a divorce more easily than one whose entire life has centered around her spouse. Of course, many other factors contribute to the process and it would be folly to predict the magnitude of any individual's loss and grief.

If the loss is perceived by the individual to be significant, it is. There may be individuals who initially deny the importance of the loss and later experience an unexpected depression. In addition to the specific problems already mentioned as they pertain to a particular loss, there are also several nearly universal aspects of sustaining a significant loss. Obviously, the intensity of the response will be related to some degree to the intensity and type of the loss.

The disruption of one's sexual identity is a frequent and sometimes alarming component of the grief response to divorce, long-term illness or disability, or death of a spouse. From the time we are very small, we identify ourselves as a female or male. Nearly everything we do in life is colored by that concept. "I am Ron, a man," affects how Ron relates to all persons. When Ron has a heart attack, his male identity becomes secondary to his condition. The principal self-concept then becomes "I am Ron, a heart patient." The new identity now pervades all his thoughts and behavior. Previously secure and confident in his masculine role, Ron may seek frequent reassurance that others still perceive him as a man rather than a patient.

Another possible extension of the identity change may be "I am Ron, a heart patient, unworthy of respect and admiration." Often there is a sense of diminished value when a significant loss occurs in our lives. Because our culture places such importance on productivity, we are inclined to question our right to affection and pleasure while we are incapable of producing. This is a time when many people desperately need confirmation that they are in fact lovable, even while they are aware that their own ability to contribute to a relationship has been compromised.

A prosperous businessman who was paralyzed from the waist down after an automobile accident felt as if he were floundering in his search for a reason to keep on going after this devastating change in his life. He could only watch as his wife mowed the lawn, chauffeured him everywhere, and did many of the tasks which formerly fell within his purview. He wondered, "How can she keep loving me when I am only half a man? What can I offer her now?" It is difficult to view oneself as virile and desirable soon after such a loss has occurred.

Almost any depression or grief response will have an effect on one's sexuality. We perceive, perhaps in error, changes in our desirability as well as our desire. The energy which might have been directed to sexual interests is diverted to the grief tasks at hand. Sometimes, especially for heart patients, there is a fear that sexual activity may cause pain or adversely affect their physical condition. All of these modifications in sexuality may be only temporary, gradually resolving themselves as part of the resolution of grief. Viewed as a normal reaction, it may be easier for the individual and partner to cope with this temporary change.

Another aspect of the adjustment to a major loss is often the feeling of being on the sidelines. A housewife and mother who was always in charge of the household, juggling schedules and laundry and meals and shopping, feels left out when a serious illness leaves her the helpless observer of all of this activity. The businessman whose stroke has affected his speech patterns feels cheated knowing that others are working out the business deals that used to give him such pleasure and satisfaction. He was once a very well-spoken and influential negotiator. Now he can merely hear or read of the accomplishments of his colleagues. It is difficult to take a back seat when one is accustomed to driving. Those suffering from this reaction eventually must find new sources of accomplishment and satisfaction. Roles and goals must be adapted consistent with the new self.

Society's view of a sick or disabled person as generally incompetent is exceedingly frustrating to those whose problem is only in a very specific area. It is quite common for a stranger or even an acquaintance, while in the company of both the patient and a member of the family to ask the family member, "How is he feeling today?" It would be better to address the question directly to the patient. Patients quite capable of responding on their own are made to feel even more inadequate than they are. Persons in wheelchairs or with other obvious, visible physical problems are most often victims of this sort of perhaps unintentional abuse. It does happen though, to heart attack victims, leukemia patients, and others whose problem is known but not as apparent. This is a frustration that could be eliminated by an increased social awareness that it exists. I doubt that others intend to insult persons in this way. They simply don't stop to think about what they are doing.

A New Life

There is a colorful poster in my friend's kitchen. It says, "When life gives you lemons, make lemonade." It is not an entirely original thought, but it is a philosophy worthy of consideration. When confronted with a terrible loss, we have choices. We can pretend for a while that it isn't happening. We can become bitter and remain bitter, alienating those who once loved us. Or we can, in time, make a new life for ourselves incorporating the necessary changes dictated by the loss.

A successful local businessman watched as his offset printing establishment was enveloped in flames. The fire had started in the room where the essential printing chemicals were stored and spread quickly through the considerable stock of paper in the building. Except for a couple of machines and some furniture they managed to salvage, the building and business were a total loss. Many years of his life were devoted to the development of this place, and, in a matter of hours, it was gone. But his spirit was not tarnished in the blaze. A new building was constructed on the same site, and the company held a community open house a year to the day after the fire destroyed the old one. Meanwhile, the business had operated in makeshift facilities.

Asked if the experience made him bitter, the man replied, "What good does it do to be bitter? These things happen. It aged me about ten years in one year and it was the hardest thing I've ever lived through, but it wouldn't do any good to get bitter over it."

A young couple found themselves unexpectedly financially strapped from inflation and increased obligations. Although content with their current lifestyle, it became apparent that they would either have to generate more income or make some stringent sacrifices. The wife decided to try her skills at a job she thought she "might get into sometime," and within a short time she was very successful.

In an interview she revealed, "If we hadn't been so broke, I never would have gotten into this, at least not for a long time. The fights over the bills and how we were going to pay them were unbearable. I guess if it had gone on much longer, we might have gotten divorced. But now I'm really *glad* it happened. If we hadn't been so miserable, I'd still be doing the same old thing. Not only would we not have had the money, but more importantly, I wouldn't have had the satisfaction and self-esteem of knowing I could make it. There wouldn't have been any motivation to try."

For most people, business and financial losses are not as threatening as personal and physical losses. (Of course, there are exceptions. More than one person has committed suicide over such matters.) Perhaps we view a functional loss as more threatening because of our society's inclination to value physical beauty and vitality above the intangible qualities of character and personality.

We might all be better off if we realigned our values with those things that truly mean the most in life. Most of us never really have to consider the bases of our values, so we don't. But those who have endured a major loss or a serious threat to life must ponder these issues. They can no longer take for granted the health, mobility, and skills most of us have and don't even appreciate. Their grief requires them to reassess the traditional values and seek new ones, which are often deeper.

This national preoccupation with the physical nature of humans pervades our lives. It inspires the post-death preservation of the body and the inordinate time we spend glorifying the body in life. Any physical feat of the human body can be out-performed by some member of the animal kingdom. But no other creature can outdistance humans when it comes to judgment, love, compassion, sense of humor, reasoning, learning, speaking, and listening, to name but a few. Why is it we fail to respect and value these uniquely human traits in favor of physical accomplishments our animal friends can mimic or do better?

Those who have faced a physical crisis often come to realize the derangement of our priorities, as well as appreciate the incredible wonder and capabilities of the body generally taken for granted. It is sad that it often takes a crisis to bring about this insight. Perhaps it is the gift of those who have suffered, although I believe it is a lesson we all could learn, if only we would.

The struggle through a loss can leave us with more knowledge, understanding, and appreciation as well as a new direction in life. Adversity is often the source of new ideas and new satisfaction, if we but endure the decathexis from our previous, comfortable life and prepare to reinvest that energy in living once again.

Some Sources of Help

There are a great many national organizations that conduct research and provide personal assistance to those afflicted with a variety of long-term illnesses and disabilities. The following is a partial listing, but will be a good place to start. A call or letter to one group often will provide you with the names of others which may be more specifically suited to your particular needs. Look for a local chapter first, then write the national headquarters.

The American Cancer Society sponsors a number of programs to help individuals cope with a diagnosis of cancer. Reach to Recovery, Cancer Mount, and I Can Cope are three of the best-known and most popular. ACS also cooperates with the United Ostomy Association and the International Association of Laryngectomies. For more information about these and other programs, contact your local chapter of the American Cancer Society or write to:

The American Cancer Society
Director of Service and Rehabilitation
777 Third Avenue
New York, New York 10017

The United Ostomy Association
2001 West Beverly Boulevard
Los Angeles, California 90057

Those afflicted with multiple sclerosis may find assistance, support, counseling, and loan of equipment such as braces and wheel chairs, by contacting their local MS Society or by writing to:

The Multiple Sclerosis Society
257 Park Avenue South
New York, New York 10010

Persons who have had heart surgery or other disabling heart problems may wish to seek the aid of the American Heart Association, which produces many public education materials and provides support groups for heart patients in many areas. The national address is:

American Heart Association
44 East 23rd Street
New York, New York 10011

Other groups active in helping persons with specific problems include:

Arthritis and Rheumatism Foundation
23 West 45th Street
New York, New York 10036

Muscular Dystrophy Association
1790 Broadway
New York, New York 10019

American Foundation for the Blind
15 West 16th Street
New York, New York 10011

National Burn Victim Foundation
308 Main Street
Orange, New Jersey 07050

11

To Pull or Not to Pull (the "Plug")

Only recently have we become concerned with the meaning of the term *natural death.* In the past, if a person was not killed in an accident or at the hands of another, and did not commit suicide, it was generally assumed that death was due to natural causes. There was little confusion about whether man or nature was responsible for the death, to put it in simplistic terms. Today, however, we are plagued with ambiguities which characterize the mixed blessing of advanced medical technology. There is much talk of "prolonging dying" by use of "extraordinary" medical treatment; some people beg for the chance to die without this "unnatural" interference. There are also those who feel we are morally obligated to use whatever means are available to postpone the moment of death; that *not* to do so would be to play God, to decide when a person *should* die. The arguments are sincere and fervent on both sides of the controversy, at the crux of which is the establishment of criteria for a "good" death. No one, of course, would want a "bad" death. But what constitutes a good death, a death with dignity, is a hotly debated matter.

Defining the Good Death

We have a fancy name for the "good" death, with a litany of pairs of refining adjectives. The name is *euthanasia,* taken from the Greek words for good or easy (*eu* as in euphoria) and death (*Thanatos,* the Greek god of death.) Perceptions of the meaning of euthanasia are, however, clouded, and so we attempt to refine the concept by adding terms like active or passive, positive or negative, direct or indirect, and voluntary or involuntary. To further refine, we can use the adjectives in combination. Thus we may have voluntary active euthanasia, involuntary indirect euthanasia, and so on. The semantic intentions are honorable, but fall short of clarity.

Other terms have been devised that attempt to convey these concepts, too. The first was probably *mercy killing.* Everyone understood mercy killing, whether or not they approved of it. *Antidysthanasia* was a term which surfaced briefly during the Karen Quinlan court case. *Benemortasia* was one author's effort to provide us with a term for good (*bene* as in benefit) death (*mort* as in mortality) without the negative connotations accumulated by mercy killing and euthanasia. Let's try to sort out what all these terms used by writers on this subject mean.

Mercy killing: a deliberate and empathic act to end the life of a person who is suffering terribly from an illness or condition which will probably (though not always) claim her life soon anyway. An example would be giving a patient an overdose of sleeping pills or morphine. It is a merciful mission done with good intent to put a patient out of misery.

To some people, this sounded too callous, too calculating. Then along came—

Euthanasia: a decision not to interfere with the inevitable death process. For instance, a person terminally ill with cancer would not be given drugs to cure pneumonia. The pneumonia then claims the patient's life, sparing the patient further suffering from the cancer. Again, the intentions are merciful but the act is less direct. In the mercy killing example, the sleeping pills killed the patient. In this example, the pneumonia killed the patient, although the pneumonia probably *could* have been successfully treated.

The distinction between mercy killing and euthanasia was never too clear, at least to the public, and so further efforts at clarification have been pursued.

Antidysthanasia: *Dys* means difficult or painful. Therefore, antidysthanasia means against a difficult or painful death. It involves a refusal to allow medical machinery to prolong the dying process; the removal or withholding of extraordinary means so that the person is permitted to die a natural death. This term was mentioned in the case of Karen Quinlan, a 21-year-old woman in a coma whose parents sought to have her respirator disconnected. They felt her life was being artificially maintained. After a difficult and widely publicized court battle, the respirator was disconnected. Karen did not die, although she remains in a coma in a nursing home, six years "after the fact." Antidysthanasia meant simply letting nature take its course, without extraordinary modern medical intervention and its attendant pain and discomfort.

The use of "extraordinary means" has almost gotten a bad name these days, although these are the same means that save thousands of lives. Exactly what do extraordinary means entail? A respirator, perhaps. Respirators as we know them were not around fifty years ago. Also called a ventilator or breathing machine, a respirator is a device which regulates and takes over the job of maintaining air flow to the lungs, when the patient can no longer breathe on his own. It is intended to be used as a stop-gap method of getting the vital oxygen into the blood stream while the patient is temporarily debilitated by a drug reaction or overdose, an injury, or respiratory fatigue brought on by a severe illness. The machine keeps the cells alive while giving a seriously ill patient a chance to regain strength and overcome the source of the original debilitation. It is used to buy some time until the body can recuperate. Many people would not be alive today had a respirator not been available to help them over the rough spots. Doctors do not put patients on respirators so that they will live as "vegetables" indefinitely. It is impossible to tell beforehand which patients will recover and which will not, so the prudent physician gives each patient every available opportunity to regain his health.

So, then, is a respirator "extraordinary"? It is, in that it is a fairly modern medical development. But so is insulin treatment for diabetes. Only thirty years ago, the prognosis for a diabetic was grim. The thought of a person self-administering daily injections of medication would likely have seemed quite extraordinary, although today it is quite routine. Until recently, the idea of taking a kidney out of one person and incorporating it into another would have seemed ludicrous. While the technique is far from perfected, kidney transplants have had incredible success at reprieving the death sentence for many victims of kidney disease.

"Extraordinary," then, is a dynamic chameleon-like concept, changing as rapidly as advances in medical technology make yesterday's miracle become today's commonplace treatment.

Active euthanasia: taking a decisive measure which will lead to early termination of the life of a patient already close to death. An act of commission.

Passive euthanasia: failure to begin or continue treatment which would prolong the life of a terminally ill person.

Direct euthanasia and positive euthanasia: a deliberate act to shorten a life, such as injection of a large volume of air directly into the bloodstream. Most often, "direct" and "positive" are used synonymously with "active."

Indirect euthanasia and negative euthanasia: allowing death to occur unimpeded by medical intervention or continuing ameliorative treatment (such as addictive pain medications) although they may hasten the moment of death. "Indirect" and "negative" are often used synonymously with "passive."

Voluntary euthanasia: the patient consents to, even requests and cooperates in bringing his life to an early end. This is essentially suicide with the knowledge and assistance of others. The motivation would most often be to avoid continued pain and suffering, sometimes the patient's, sometimes the family's, sometimes both.

Involuntary euthanasia: shortening a patient's life for reasons of mercy without her consent, usually because the patient is incapable of communicating because of loss of consciousness, impaired mental faculties, or, yes, even infancy. Severely malformed infants are, with some frequency, allowed to die rather than fed and protected only to endure what those in attendance perceive to be a life of agony, pain, struggle, and even ridicule for child and parents alike.

There are other shades of interpretation, too. Some persons see direct or active euthanasia as having an immediate effect, whereas with indirect or passive euthanasia, death would not follow the action or decision quite so suddenly. Relative morality is also a matter of some confusion. Generally, because it allows nature to take its course, indirect or passive euthanasia is thought to be more moral than an active decision and action to bring an early end to the life of a human being. There are many instances, however, when the passive decision is followed by a lengthy and agonizing, though "moral," death. Consider the plight of a seriously deformed newborn infant. The physician and parents confer, deciding not to prolong the child's life, but to let nature take its course, assuming the child would die within hours or a day or two at most. The parents would feel uneasy about the baby being given an overdose of medication to end its life. They also feel it is in everyone's best interests, especially the baby's, not to subject it to endless painful diagnostic and corrective medical procedures when the prognosis was grim, at best. Suppose that instead of dying quickly, the baby clings to life for three long weeks, slowly weakening from starvation and dehydration awaiting the release of death in his lonely corner of the nursery. Is this a more moral death? The intention was, perhaps. Whatever one's moral perception of the situation, the fact is that few would judge the child's passing as either "good" or "easy."

There is much confusion and disagreement with respect to the differentiation between *active* and *passive*, or *direct* and *indirect*. I once attended a day-long conference on euthanasia where physicians, attorneys, and philosophers presented their most salient thoughts on the issue. At the conclusion of the sessions, many of us were only more bewildered than we were at the start. One philosopher maintained that there is essentially no difference between active and passive euthanasia, that in effect there is no such thing as passive euthanasia. If one makes a decision to allow someone to die rather than to administer readily available life-sustaining treatment, the decision is, in fact, an action. His contention was that we contrive terms such as *passive, indirect,* and *voluntary* merely to assuage our consciences and make us feel somehow less responsible for our actions or lack thereof. On the other side of the argument are thousands of sincere, concerned, knowledgeable individuals who feel that our technology has advanced so far that in many cases rather than restoring life, we merely prolong dying. When this prolonged dying is accompanied by pain, agony, and mental anguish, doesn't it seem just and right, these proponents argue, that we should attempt to halt the suffering which would not have happened had technology not intervened? Does not the golden rule, stated in remarkably similar language in virtually every major world religion, beseech us to do unto others as we would have them do unto us? Would we, would you, want to lie and suffer for days and weeks and months?

Legal Considerations

There are compelling examples which support virtually every position on euthanasia. Indeed, euthanasia is practiced in hospitals and nursing homes many times every day. We seldom hear about the decisions because, most often, they are the result of a quiet mutual agreement of the physician(s) and family involved. Usually, only when there is a strong difference of opinion does a case come to the attention of the public or the courts. When this happens, euthanasia becomes a legal issue, in addition to posing the moral and ethical questions already at stake. In some countries, such as Uruguay, euthanasia, when "motivated by compassion induced by repeated requests by the victim" is not considered to be a punishable crime. In the United States, we simply do not have an adequate legal framework to deal with this unique legal dilemma. In fact, few cases ever get to court and of those that do, convictions are exceedingly rare. Apparently jurors respond to these merciful killings with a compassion not unlike that which inspired the "crime." The most dramatic and publicized case in recent history involved Lester and George Zygmaniak. George, age 26, was in a motorcycle accident on June 18, 1973 and was paralyzed from the neck down. He repeatedly pleaded with Lester, 23, to end his life. Out of compassion and empathy for the plight of his idolized older brother, Lester brought a sawed-off shotgun to the hospital on the third day after the accident, and after reaffirming that it was, in fact George's true wish, Lester shot his beloved brother. This was, in the most blatant way a voluntary, active mercy killing. Lester was acquitted.

The fact is that beneficent euthanasia does not fit the definition for any of the currently recognized homicide charges. The following charges from *Illinois Criminal Law* are typical, but vary somewhat from state to state.

> *Murder:* killing of another person with intent to kill or do great bodily harm to that individual or another. Mitigating factor: the murdered individual was a participant in the defendant's homicidal conduct or consented to the homicidal act.

In a mercy killing, or beneficent euthanasia, there is intent to kill, but, perhaps ironically, *not* to harm. Also, the mitigating factor of the "victim's" consent or participation in the death is often present, as it was in the case of the Zygmaniaks.

> *Voluntary manslaughter:* killing of another person while acting under a sudden and intense passion resulting from serious provocation by the individual killed or another whom the offender endeavors to kill, but he accidentally causes the death of the person killed.

The mercy killer is acting under intense passion, but the act is usually well-considered and not at all sudden. The death, of course, is no accident occurring when one was attempting to kill another.

> *Involuntary manslaughter:* unintentional killing of another person.

Euthanasia does not fit this description, for it is very definitely planned and intentional.

Because of this obvious defect in our laws, efforts have been made to legalize truly beneficent euthanasia, while allowing direct legal recourse against those who might abuse the merciful intent of the concept. The problems inherent in composing such a law are manifold and despite the many such proposals that have been made, only ten states had passed such legislation as of April, 1979. The first to do so was California, whose "Death with Dignity" bill became effective January 1, 1977. This bill provides for the patient to sign a statement expressing his desire not to have his life artifically maintained should there be no reasonable hope of his recovery. This statement must be signed not more than five years before the life-threatening situation arises. There are specific legal safeguards (witnesses, provision for revocation) to protect the patient from the designs of unscrupulous relatives anxious for the inheritance. If the patient is conscious and capable of actively participating in the process, then all of the others involved bear less of the responsibility. If the patient is not conscious, then her signed statement serves as the conveyance of her wishes.

The Living Will

More than a million Americans have signed similar statements with absolutely no binding legal validity, called *living wills*. It should be noted that a living will has *no* relationship to and should *not* be included in a last will and testament which becomes valid upon the death of the patient. There are a number of standard forms for a living will published and distributed by Concern for Dying, the Catholic Health Association, and other smaller groups which design statements to meet their own particular needs. Indeed, anyone could draft and sign his or her own individual statement. The purpose of these living wills is best understood by reading them. Following are the two major documents now in circulation.

To My Family, My Physician, My Lawyer and All Others Whom it May Concern*

Death is as much a reality as birth, growth, maturity, and old age—it is the one certainty of life. If the time comes when I can no longer take part in decisions for my own future, let this statement stand as an expression of my wishes and directions, while I am still of sound mind.

If at such a time the situation should arise in which there is no reasonable expectation of my recovery from extreme physical or mental disability, I direct that I be allowed to die and not be kept alive by medications, artificial means or "heroic measures." I do, however, ask that medication be mercifully administered to me to alleviate suffering even though this may shorten my remaining life.

This statement is made after careful consideration and is in accordance with my strong convictions and beliefs. I want the wishes and directions here expressed carried out to the extent permitted by law. Insofar as they are not legally enforceable, I hope that those to whom this Will is addressed will regard themselves as morally bound by these provisions.

*Reprinted with permission from Concern for Dying. Free copies are available from: Concern for Dying 250 West 57th Street, New York, New York 10019.

To My Family, Friends, Physician, Lawyer and Clergyman:*

I believe that each individual person is created by God our Father in love and that God retains a loving relationship to each person throughout human life and eternity.

I believe that Jesus Christ lived, suffered, and died for me and that his suffering, death, and resurrection prefigure and make possible the death-resurrection process which I now anticipate.

I believe that each person's worth and dignity derives from the relationship of love in Christ that God has for each individual person, and not from one's usefulness or effectiveness in society.

I believe that God our Father has entrusted to me a shared dominion with him over my earthly existence so that I am bound to use ordinary means to preserve my life but I am free to refuse extraordinary means to prolong my life.

I believe that through death life is not taken away but merely changed, and though I may experience fear, suffering, and sorrow, by the grace of the Holy Spirit, I hope to accept death as a free human act which enables me to surrender this life and to be united with God for eternity.

Because of my Belief:

I, _____ request that I be informed as death approaches so that I may continue to prepare for the full encounter with Christ through the help of the sacraments and the consolation and prayers of my family and friends.

I request that, if possible, I be consulted concerning the medical procedures which might be used to prolong my life as death approaches. If I can no longer take part in decisions concerning my own future and there is no reasonable expectation of my recovery from physical and mental disability, I request that no extraordinary means be used to prolong my life.

I request, though I wish to join my suffering to the suffering of Jesus so I may be united fully with him in the act of death-resurrection, that my pain, if unbearable, be alleviated. However, no means should be used with the intention of shortening my life.

I request, because I am a sinner and in need of reconciliation and because my faith, hope, and love may not overcome all fear and doubt, that my family, friends, and the whole Christian community join me in prayer and mortification as I prepare for the great personal act of dying.

Finally, I request that after my death, my family, my friends, and the whole Christian community pray for me, and rejoice with me because of the mercy and love of the Trinity, with whom I hope to be united for all eternity.

Signed _____

Date _____

*Reprinted with permission from the Catholic Health Association. Free copies are available from: Catholic Health Association, 4455 Woodson Road, St. Louis, Missouri 63134.

The living will, while it wields no legal clout, does provide an opportunity to share one's thoughts about a very critical issue with the most important people in one's life. And that is something. At least it makes us think about what we *might* want to have done, if ever we find ourselves in that sort of situation. There are, however, some serious problems associated with the living will. Let's look at three of them.

1. You might change your mind. Consider George Zygmaniak, for instance. His death occurred only three days after his serious injury. It appeared he would probably be quadriplegic, but there was a slim possibility that he would be able to walk again. Had he had enough time after the accident to discuss his chances with physicians, physical therapists, and psychologists, he might have been able to conceive and accept the idea of a life with limitations, but a life nonetheless. He would have been able to laugh with and counsel his children, watch them grow, give his wife love and support. His mind was not damaged in the accident, but he didn't have time to consider things rationally in the immediate aftermath of an overwhelming experience. While his feelings at the time were very real and very strong, he might have felt differently with time to adjust.

To many of us, a life without free mobility might seem worse than no life at all—*until* we are actually faced with that choice. George and Lester accomplished their conspiracy without benefit of a signed document. Assume, however, that you *do* sign a living will and are involved in a multivehicle accident. You are one of seven injured persons and appear to have a broken neck. You lapse into unconsciousness soon after the paramedic does his brief examination. He looks through your wallet and finds a living will and reads the part about "no heroic measures" and "no reasonable expectation of my recovery from extreme mental or physical disability." Since there are six other critically injured persons, only two paramedics and room for three patients in the ambulance at a time, the paramedic may well feel justified in tending first to the victims who had *not* carried a living will with them. Meanwhile you float in and out of consciousness, too weak to speak, acutely aware that something is terribly wrong and wanting very much to cling to life. When the ambulance comes back for its third and final run, it is finally your turn to ride to the hospital. By then, however, excessive hemorrhaging from internal wounds has caused severe irreversible shock, and you die on the way to the emergency room.

The potential for error is great. First, it is very difficult to speculate on our anticipated feelings in a given situation. Only when we are actually in the midst of reality can we accurately identify its impact on us. For instance, we might presume we could never forgive our spouse an act of marital infidelity. However, once actually faced with the prospect of dissolving a long and happy marriage or forgiving a truly repentant loved one, the choice becomes more clear and real and the consequences more vivid and personal. In short, abstract presupposition and hypothetical game playing are useful tools in helping us understand how we think and feel, but are not always an accurate gauge of those thoughts and feelings in a real-life situation.

2. There is room for misinterpretation in the living will. The problem of determining exactly what constitutes "extraordinary" or "heroic" measures has already been discussed. Exactly what is meant by "extreme physical or mental disability"? The individual may write his own living will, specifying precisely the treatments he feels to be inhumane, and the injuries or limitations he considers unbearable. But even then there are problems. It is impossible to anticipate the entire gamut of potential injuries and treatments and, even if we could, there is still the chance that we would change our minds but be incapable of communicating our wishes at the critical moment. There is also the chance that lack of knowledge or maturity may adversely affect the wisdom of the statements we might choose. For instance, a young man in my "Death and Dying" class announced that he would not want to live without one or more of his limbs and that his living will would include instructions not to treat him if the injury or required treatment would necessitate amputation of an arm or leg. He was a very athletic college student who no doubt took great pride in his physique. Even so, I cannot help but believe that as he goes through life his values will change, and he will discover a reason to cherish his life with or without the possible disfigurement of an amputation.

3. There is room for error in medical judgment and, yes, sometimes miracles *do* happen. Suppose the paramedic who found you at the scene of the accident mistook a temporary paralysis caused by swelling and pressure on the nerves to be a broken neck. Had you been taken to the hospital immediately, emergency surgery could have halted the internal bleeding, and you could have recovered completely with no permanent disability in a matter of weeks. But a hasty decision based on an inaccurate diagnosis and a living will might change the outcome entirely.

I remember very clearly a female patient on a medical ward where I, the idealistic, naive, and eager young nurse was working. Mrs. Jensen, in her late fifties, was admitted from emergency and her condition worsened over the next day or so. She suffered from several chronic conditions and this was her umpteenth admission. Watching her go from miserable awareness to restless unconsciousness, hooked up to every conceivable tube and monitoring device, I honestly thought if ever there were a candidate for euthanasia, Mrs. Jensen would be one. Then I went off duty for a couple of days and, upon returning learned that she has been transferred to the intensive care unit. Her prognosis was grim. As the days and weeks passed, we were busy with other patients, and I guess I assumed poor Mrs. Jensen had died. How shocked I was three months later when she waltzed onto the ward to thank the nursing staff for taking good care of her! To think I was ready to write her off, end her misery, and here she was up and about, all decked out, and thanking me. In less than a year, her illness caught up with her and that time she didn't survive. But she did have those months of health and joy, of which I was compassionately tempted to rob her. There are numerous other cases of patients who seem to be going steadily downhill only to inexplicably come around and eventually regain their health. It certainly doesn't happen all the time, but often enough that doctors are understandably hesitant to give up on a patient.

A medical prognosis is based on statistics. As an example, let's say 95 percent of persons diagnosed as having cancer of the x will die within six months with or without treatment, usually surpassing the "five-year cure" standard. Statistically speaking, if your doctor tells you that he has found cancer in your x, you would be wise to revise your will and get your affairs in order. (You would be wise to do that, anyway!) The odds are overwhelmingly against you. But if you happen to be one of the five percent, you would most probably want every chance at that long survival and so decide to undergo whatever treatment necessary to accomplish that goal. Our dilemma is that, while medicine can tell us that five of every hundred people do respond well to treatment, it cannot tell us which individuals will be among them. Thus, many are subjected to treatments that are most likely expensive and very probably unpleasant on the theory that it is better to save five lives out of a hundred than not to try at all. Many of us would agree with this rationale, for if we happen to be one of those five who will survive, it is a 100 percent survival rate from our personal perspective. The point is this: it is easy to say the victims of cancer of the x should not be subjected to these uncomfortable treatments since only a handful of them will survive anyway. Let's just let them die in peace without the interference of modern medical technology. But for that handful, they may be only too willing to suffer the interference of modern medical technology for a chance at a few more precious years of life. And for the other ninety-five, it may buy some time while medical research discovers a better treatment or maybe even a cure.

There are, too, those rare and wonderful occasions when a critically ill patient with virtually no chance of survival miraculously recovers, defying all medical explanations. One such case involved Tyson Baumgardner, who began complaining of bad headaches about a month after the birth of his sister. Only five years old, Tyson's complaints were so persistent his parents were alarmed and took him to a major children's hospital where tests revealed the presence of a large brain tumor. Surgery was only partly successful since removal of most of the tumor would have required removal of part of Ty's brain. Thereafter, Ty received massive doses of radiation, lost his hair and still his condition worsened. The pressure on his brain grew, and he had several operations to relieve this pressure. He lost more than a third of his body weight, going from fifty-five pounds down to a skeletal thirty-three pounds. At one point, the doctors told the Baumgardners to take their son home to die, that there was nothing more they could do for him. His parents, Carole and Larry were understandably distraught, slept on the floor next to Ty's hospital bed for months, and ached at the thought of losing their first-born son. But the Baumgardners sought and fervently prayed for a miracle, for their little boy to be well. Just a year after Ty's headaches began, he started kindergarten and is now as healthy and normal as his classmates. Larry and Carole freely confess they believe they have been blessed with a modern miracle, and indeed there is no logical explanation for Tyson's recovery.

As dramatic as Tyson's experience was, it is not sensible to generalize the possibility of a miracle to all deathbed scenes, primarily because we all die sometime. If everyone who became deathly ill recovered, it would be considered commonplace rather than miraculous, and we would soon run out of room on our planet. Death is natural and inevitable, as much a part of life as sunshine and rain. It is the timing and manner of death that concern and bother us. If a ninety-year-old great-grandmother dies in her sleep, surrounded by a roomful of caring and appreciative progeny, we can say, "she led a long, full happy life and had a painless, easy death." That is not so hard to accept. Harder to accept and understand is the death of a child or a painful, lingering death, especially if it appears that medicine is somehow responsible for the pain and lingering. It is this painful, lingering death that most often engenders thoughts of euthanasia. We are appalled to see human life diminished to an apparently vegetative and impotent existence. Perhaps we are also appalled to realize our own impotence to relieve the suffering, to alter the course of the illness. We do, however, have the power, if not to relieve the suffering, then to end it. Surely there are times when it is truly inappropriate to continue vigorous medical treatment, when it is beyond human dignity to be subjected to procedures and medications which simply delay, prolong, and make agonizing the inevitable.

Discerning when it is or is not appropriate to continue treatment or to attempt heroics is a most complex matter. Each patient's case is slightly different, and establishing criteria that will cover all the possibilities is an immense if not futile task, which is why legalizing euthanasia is such a difficult problem. Certainly it is easier when the patient can actively participate in the decision. Charles Wertenbaker, a journalist, arranged for his own suicide at a time when he felt the discomforts of his cancer had reached unbearable proportions for him. Because we are all different, what was unbearable for Charles Wertenbaker might be quite acceptable to another, if there were other joys in life which outweighed the discomforts. Another person might give up much earlier than he did. Because of the infinite variety of conditions, personalities, and religions involved, it is ridiculous to presume one law could adequately run the gamut without allowing loopholes that might permit unwanted abuse.

There have been proposals before state legislatures suggesting that euthanasia be employed in state mental institutions and nursing homes, to relieve society of the burden of maintaining these essentially vegetative nonproductive members. After all, what joy does a severely retarded person, unable to control his own bladder and bowel, have in life or bring to the life of others? And what of the lonely forgotten old woman, abandoned by her family to a nursing home. Of what value is she to society, and what is her pleasure in life? When we start making decisions that it is all right to end a human life because of compassion, it becomes difficult to start drawing lines. In fact, the ethical arguments for and against euthanasia frequently occur in abortion debates as well.

Help from a Hospice

But maybe our preoccupation with euthanasia is premature. In many of the situations where euthanasia is considered, the physical pain of dying is one of the primary concerns. And this is the area where we are beginning to see remarkable changes. The hospice movement (see Chapter 13) is growing rapidly all across the country in small and large communities. The purpose of the hospice is to provide personal care to the terminal patient and family as a unit, and to provide an environment and medication that allow the patient to be essentially pain-free. The family is given assistance with psychological and practical problems as well as the medical ones, and patients are treated as persons, not as diseases. The result is that terminally ill persons are able to actually enjoy and live the last days of their lives, rather than anxiously watching the clock, anticipating the return of the pain and enduring the time until the next pain shot. Many times, patients are able to stay in their own homes, which often helps to ease the tension. While the hospice alternative still does not relieve us of all the possible euthanasia situations (such as severely deformed infants, patients in long-term coma) it does provide some light in a very, very grey area.

12

Suicide: The Desperate Cry

Sylvia and Leonard Brown descended the bus steps and began the two-block walk to their home, eagerly sharing the events of the day with each other. As they rounded the corner, their house came into view. "Looks like Sandra is waiting for us on the porch," Sylvia remarked to her husband. "Good. Maybe she had a good day and has decided to quit moping around the house. She probably 'aced' that history exam and can't wait to tell us. I told her not to worry about it, she'd do all right."

As they reached the front yard, the parents called their greetings to their college-age daughter. Sandra responded with purpose in her voice. "Hi. I've been waiting for you. Goodbye." With that, she pointed a revolver at her ear and pulled the trigger. In a moment, her life was gone and the lives of her parents and brother were forever changed.

While surveys tell us that virtually everyone has flirted with the notion of suicide, it remains an enigma that very few of us can comprehend. What torment could lead one to actually put an end to one's life? What is so intolerable about our society that some of our members feel compelled to take their permanent leave from it, and by their own hand? Can we do anything to prevent it? In fact, *should* we try to prevent it? Why does it bother us so, why do we stigmatize it as we never would deaths from natural causes?

Motives

The true reasons for suicide are probably as numerous as the people who attempt the act, and are all probably variations on a number of central themes. For the would-be suicide victim, life may have simply become unbearable, *truly* unbearable. Whatever the untoward circumstances, the individual sees no way out of his dilemma. It is hopeless, meaningless to go on living. Nothing and no one can or will make life any better. There are times, of course, when many of us feel this way. Thankfully, most often we see the foolishness in our short-sightedness and eventually things do improve. Some, unfortunately, may be so overwhelmed by despair that all hope eludes them. They kill themselves before time has a chance to heal the wounds.

For others, the underlying agony is primarily the perception that no one loves them or *really* cares whether they live or die. They are desperately lonely. Of course, there *may* actually be one or several persons who do love and care about this individual, but the expression of this concern may be inadequate, misdirected or merely misinterpreted by the presuicide victim. For instance, many teenagers have difficulty discussing anything that really matters with their parents, because they are tired of being put down for their ideas or wishes or behavior. It is easier not to talk than to get embroiled in arguments one always loses. Parents, bewildered and concerned by the teenager's silence may throw up their hands and decide to wait out what they hope is just a phase. But the lack of communication becomes a pattern; the youngster feels emotionally separated from his parents and rationalizes that "they never really loved me, anyway."

Perhaps even sadder are those who are in fact quite accurate in their estimation that no one would care if they did die, not *really* care. That is not to say that this person can't seek and develop new relationships, but at the time this prospect is not as significant as the feelings of rejection, abandonment, or bereavement. The body of one young man was tragically not even discovered in his college dormitory room until more than two weeks after his death, which only confirmed his sad perception that no one ever noticed him. The scorned lover or widow or widower may feel they will never find another who could value them in the way their now-parted lover once did. In his book, *Suicide,* Earl Grollman concludes, "it is the death of love that evokes the love of death."

A twisted sense of revenge is occasionally a motive for suicide. "I'll make them sorry they treated me this way." The vignette at the opening of the chapter is a dramatic illustration of this sort of thinking. Not only did Sandra for some reason want her parents to suffer because, in her perception, they made her life miserable, but she wanted them to remember the horror of helplessly watching her shoot herself.

Rarely, one commits suicide to make life better for one's family. "They'd be better off without me." Perhaps infirmity or disability has made such a person dependent, and he can not bear to be a burden to the family. Unfortunately, he may be overlooking the many valuable contributions he is making to the family, such as love, a sense of humor, and wise counsel in difficult situations. Sometimes, visions of the family with the fat life insurance check in hand inspires a mad, fast drive over a dangerous curvy road. Many such unrecognized suicides are classified merely as accidents. (Many life insurance companies pay a death benefit on the life of a suicide victim only after two years from the date of the purchase of the policy. If the death is determined to be an accident, double or triple indemnity may apply. Some types of policies pay only on accidental deaths, so if the person dies of cancer, the survivors receive no benefit.)

Suicide while enduring painful terminal illness becomes self-inflicted euthanasia. This is probably the most acceptable form of suicide in America, as we seem to identify more readily with physical pain than we do emotional pain.

Emile Durkheim proposed a theory of suicide based on a societal perspective. He suggested four types of suicide, each reflecting the effect of the culture upon the individual: egoistic, altruistic, anomic, and fatalistic. Although his theory does not explain all suicides, it has surprising relevancy even now, nearly a century after its publication.

The "star," the brilliant artist, the creative genius, all hear a different drummer. Because of their special talents, they are, in essence, above or at least apart from society. They are not as likely to be constrained by the rules and mores of society and may find few, if any, sources of support or appropriate counsel in a time of crisis. Their unique position renders them especially vulnerable to an *egoistic suicide.* Such people are extreme examples of those not well enough integrated into society to be subject to its taboos. Less brilliant persons may also fall into this category.

On the other hand are those who are nearly obsessed with the values of their culture, to the point that they would, in fact, die for them. The priest who calmly douses himself in gasoline and ignites it in protest of a social or political injustice is demonstrating this sort of *altruistic suicide.* The hunger strikers of the Irish Republican Army have shown a similarly strong conviction to the values they hold dear, and many have died of self-induced starvation, hoping to make the society better for their sacrifice.

Occasionally, society doesn't function as well as it might. Persons are disappointed and lost when there is an unexpected disruption in the institutions upon which they have depended. The economy begins to fail, factories close down, jobs (and therefore rent and food) are scarce. Under these conditions, *anomic suicide* appears. The individual perceives his problems to be caused by a failing culture and feels helpless to overcome this mammoth evil.

Oppression of a segment of society may lead to *fatalistic suicide.*

Membership in a given minority may seem synonymous with hopeless existence, void of any opportunity for change or improvement. Slavery or life in a dictatorship may engender these feelings of desperation, as does imprisonment in some instances.

Additionally, Durkheim spoke of a society so well integrated that the group almost seems to think, feel, and act collectively. When all is going well, it goes well for everyone. Likewise, a negative or destructive tenor may be represented in each member of the closely-knit group. This could, and has, led to mass suicide and suicide-murders, as well as to less fatal but terribly disruptive and destructive behaviors such as excessive drug and alcohol abuse, rampant violence, and submission to nonfatal illnesses. In A.D. 73, nine hundred and sixty Jews committed mass suicide in the fortress of Masada, rather than be captured by Roman soldiers.

A less understandable mass suicide, also involving over nine hundred persons, occurred in Jonestown, Guyana in November of 1978. This involved a religious cult, American followers of a dynamic and apparently perverse minister who had directed the ritualistic rehearsal of the mass suicide many times. The reason for the tragedy is a mystery, although Jones, the minister, seemed to fear discovery of his methods by the world outside. There was evidence that some members resisted participation in the suicide pact and were coerced to drink the poison or were shot. It is frightening to see the positive, supportive cohesion of a group turned to self-destruction.

Intention

Often, a question arises regarding a death which might have been a suicide. Did the car go out of control, did the driver lose consciousness before the crash, or did she deliberately steer off the cliff? Did he shoot himself or was he murdered and the gun later placed in his hand? Exact determination of intent is frequently impossible after the fact, unless a verifiable suicide note is found. Such notes are found in only a small percentage of all suicides. Edwin Schneidman and Norman Farberow introduced the technique of psychological autopsy to aid in this process. Their recommended procedure has yet to be adopted on a broad scale, but could help to answer some of the many dilemmas inherent in suicide and perhaps help us learn more about, and hopefully how to prevent, the suicide milieu.

Sometimes, even the suicide victim is not consciously aware of his own intent. Of course, wrist-slashing, jumping off a bridge, and Russian roulette require a conscious decision. There are more subtle forms of suicide, though, that are probably *subintended.* This involves participation in life-threatening behaviors which might not have an immediate effect, such as heavy smoking, tendency to take risks driving or crossing the street, excessive overeating *or* undereating, or alcohol abuse.

Any American who doesn't realize that smoking causes lung cancer, and lung cancer causes death in about six months, simply hasn't been listening to the daily news. One often hears, "They say everything causes cancer now, so you might as well live as you choose." It does seem that way sometimes. However, though some cancer-links are speculative, cigarette smoking is unquestionably proven.

The destructive effects of alcohol abuse are likewise common knowledge. Less obvious are the insidious dangers of over- and under-eating. Many young girls have literally starved themselves to death attempting to achieve an idealized image of the thin American. Overeating aggravates high blood pressure, heart disease, diabetes, and other conditions.

Subintended suicides differ from intended suicides in the degree of conscious awareness with which a person seeks his own end, the strength of the self-destructive wish and the speed or efficacy of the chosen method. These are not exclusive qualities, however. For instance, one might drink to excess and carelessly start driving. This behavior is likely to result in a fatal accident that was not consciously sought, but is nonetheless sudden, violent, and equally as effective as if it had been planned weeks in advance.

Who Could Do a Thing Like That?

There is no immunity to suicide, although persons in certain age groups and life styles seem to be more vulnerable. The older you are, the more likely you are to kill yourself. The overall suicide rate increases with age, although there are individual differences between groups.

Married people have a lower suicide rate than the never-marrieds, who have a lower rate than the divorced or widowed singles until the age of thirty-five. After thirty-five, the rate for never-married singles surpasses that of those who once had spouses. The only exception to this pattern is the young marrieds, especially those under twenty, perhaps because they have jumped hastily into marriage at an early age to escape a bad home life or because of an unexpected pregnancy. For older married persons, though, there is apparently some sense of security, purpose, being wanted and needed that protects most of them from self-destructive behavior.

Women attempt suicide far more often than men, but men succeed about two and a half times more often. Perhaps that is because men usually choose more violent, irreversible means, such as firearms, wrist-slashing, jumping from a tall building. Women prefer to take pills or breathe carbon monoxide, both methods which can be reversed if the victim is found in a short time. (Often she is, because she calls someone for help shortly before or after she swallows the final capsule or closes the garage door.)

Race accounts for some differences in rates, too. Whites and nonwhites have approximately similar suicide rates through early adulthood. But in the twenties for women and the thirties for men, whites begin to show a much higher rate than nonwhites, among whom tendency toward suicide diminishes for women, and remains stable for men.

While the *rate* of suicide in young people is lower than for their elders, the *proportion* of deaths due to suicide is greater. This is simply because fewer people die young. Of the deaths that do occur in youth, suicide accounts for a great number of them. Suicide is, in fact, the *third* leading cause of death for those aged fifteen to twenty-four, following motor vehicle accidents and homicide. For the population as a whole, suicide ranks ninth as a cause of death. The suicide rate among teenagers and young adults is highest where these individuals have themselves lost a parent through illness or accident when they were young. Other problems plague young people, too. Pressure to succeed in sports, school, and in personal relationships is sometimes overpowering. Exceptionally bright youngsters have a very high suicide rate, perhaps because they feel or are treated as though they were different, and aren't, as Durkheim might say, well-integrated into their social setting.

Suicide has seasons, too. It peaks in the spring, especially April in the United States, May and June in England. In this country, there is also a peak around the holiday season of Christmas and the New Year. These are supposed to be happy times. In spring, life and beauty are renewed. At Christmas time there is almost a forced gaiety. Such overt joy may bring sharp contrast to the feelings of depression and hopelessness of those contemplating suicide. They can't tolerate the disparity.

Professionals have a much higher rate of suicide than do nonprofessionals. Apparently the stress and responsibility of such positions are beyond the limits of many who pursue such careers. Physicians, lawyers, and especially dentists and psychiatrists are far more likely to die of their own design than are librarians, academicians, or salespersons. This has recently been attributed in part to "burn-out," a point in one's career where the satisfactions have been perceived to have diminished while the drudgery and dilemmas remain. People going through this begin to face their mortality and think, "can I bear to keep doing this much longer? But what else can I do? I can't change now!" In desperation, they escape the question through a drug overdose or run the car off the bridge. They are also more inclined to many methods of subintended suicide, such as alcohol abuse and risk-taking behavior.

The elderly, especially old white men, have the highest suicide rates of all—and very few unsuccessful attempts. The loneliness, purposelessness, and poor health to which many of our senior citizens are subjected are no doubt significant factors in explaining this trend. This is curiously not true of the elderly black population, whose suicide rate is quite low. Perhaps they have learned better coping skills.

In all subdivisions mentioned, there are probably many more suicides than those actually reported as such. Because of the stigma for the family or simply because it is difficult to determine, many times a suicide is classified as an accidental death. In many cases, we will never know. Experts estimate, however, that actual suicides exceed those presently recorded by a hundred percent or more. The fact that our highly industrialized society has become so intolerable for so many people is a tragedy we all bear and a signal to us to take time from our frenzied pace to attend more carefully to human needs.

Historical and Cultural Perspectives

Although treated with indifference in the Bible, and for a while glorified as martyrdom became fashionable, suicide has been viewed by most religions as a sin. In the sixth and seventh centuries, the Christian church proclaimed that suicide victims could not be given a Christian burial or funeral rites and that even those who attempted suicide would be excommunicated. In the twentieth century, religious practice has mellowed a bit toward suicide, favoring compassion over condemnation.

For many years, suicide was considered a crime, as well. In some countries, including England, suicide victims were once buried at the crossroads so as to impede their final rest. Some cultures imprisoned or fined the surviving family of a suicide as a deterrent to others contemplating the act. In some places, a ritual of driving a stake through the heart of a suicide victim was considered apt punishment. There was even a case in London around 1860 in which a man who had cut his own throat but survived was hanged for attempting suicide. When he was hanged, however, the neck wound reopened, allowing him to breathe. It was then necessary for the hangman to bandage the man's throat until he finally died!

Fortunately, modern policies are not quite that insane. Nine states in the U.S. still list suicide as a crime of some description, but rarely enforce the statutes. Emphasis has shifted, however inadequately, to prevention and rehabilitation.

History has also shown an occasional inclination for the "honorable" suicide. In Japan, one condemned to death could regain his honor by becoming his own executioner. The method was called seppuku or hara-kiri, self-disembowelment performed with a sword. Sometimes, servants voluntarily joined their deceased master in this manner.

To some of the ancient Greeks and Romans, especially the Stoics, suicide was considered at the very least a quite reasonable alternative to a painful existence or meaningless life. The Japanese kamikaze pilots of World War II were highly lauded by their countrymen. A now-discouraged Hindu tradition, suttee, required a widow to fling herself into the flames of her husband's funeral pyre.

Suicide for a cause other than relief from one's personal miseries has always met with more acceptance than a mere self-centered self-destruction. The martyrs of early Christendom, the IRA hunger strikers, the self-immolation of Vietnamese Buddhist monks—all of them gained some place in history for considering the needs of others or the perpetuation of their ideals above the value of their own lives. In imperial Rome, people would volunteer to be beaten to death for the amusement of the apparently deranged populace. In exchange for their suffering and death, their heirs were paid a stated sum of money—an early contract with a death benefit.

Some cultures, such as some in the Orient and that of the Vikings, have demeaned a passive death in old age, glorifying an early, violent demise in battle, for example. This is virtually a mirror-image of our society's view.

Obviously, the enigma of suicide has evoked a full spectrum of approaches and will probably continue to do so. Our task is to discern what aspects of our society encourage the notion of suicide among its members, how the survivors can be helped to cope, how we might alter our society to minimize the problem.

Warnings and Clues

There are many myths about suicide. One of them pretends that people who talk about committing suicide don't actually kill themselves. *Wrong.* Eight out of ten eventual successful suicides gave some kind of warning, usually either a verbal threat or an actual suicide attempt. Sometimes the warning signals are subtle and therefore easily missed by the persons who are probably already paying too little attention to the distraught individual.

Probably even if we were attuned to all these messages, there would still be some suicides we couldn't prevent. It is surely worth our effort to try, though. You may have already, by taking time to listen to someone and share your own thoughts, prevented a potential suicide of which you were unaware. By being aware, perhaps we can improve our average.

We will discuss several signals or life situations that may alert us to the possibility of suicide. Of course, nearly all of these things may also occur when self-destruction is not being considered. But if any one of them is very intense or several occur together, the probability increases.

The suicide attempt is, of course, the most obvious and unmistakable warning. Of those who do kill themselves, 80 percent have made a previous attempt. Twelve percent of those who make an attempt will try again and succeed within two years. That does not mean that "once a suicide, always a suicide" is true, however. If the person can be helped through the crisis that precipitated the suicide, he or she may never again consider it. But an attempt is a desperate cry for that help. If the help is not forthcoming, there may be another, more successful attempt.

Many persons give verbal clues to their intent, some as blatant as "I'm going to kill myself," others as subtle as "I won't be needing this pipe anymore." A male colleague recalls an incident that happened several years ago at a university. A fellow faculty member and friend called him one day to ask if he could meet her for lunch. It was an unusual request, as this had never happened before, and he was somewhat puzzled. His schedule, unfortunately, was already full and the luncheon engagement was never arranged. The next day, his friend killed herself. He wonders if things might have been different had he rearranged his schedule to accomodate that invitation.

How could he have known that she was so desperate? They had gotten along well at work, but had never been close friends. She did not indicate by her tone of voice or wording that the lunch was to have been anything other than a casual, work-related get-together. Other than the rarity of the request, there was nothing that he perceived to be unusual or, more to the point, alarming about her call. Without the presence of other clues, one would probably dismiss the call and invitation to lunch as whims. But the illustration serves to alert us to be more aware of unusual behavior in our associates.

Had my friend perceived the desperation in this woman's life, I know he would have immediately cleared the calendar for that day to see if he could help. Apparently she saw him for the compassionate person he is, but was too shy, afraid, embarrassed, or confused in her depression to openly admit her need for help. Suicidal people are not best known for clear thinking and logic. Often, only one option seems available to them when, in reality, there may be a dozen or more ways to handle their problems.

Some suspicious remarks a presuicidal person might make include: "No one needs me anymore," "I'll be gone next week," "Take good care of the children for me," "I've always wanted you to have my mother's necklace; I don't need it now." Sometimes, a person goes through a farewell ritual, visiting those close to him for a final time, perhaps distributing prized possessions or, even money among those he cares for.*

Other danger signals include depression, apathy, and insomnia. A formerly quite animated individual becomes lethargic and loses interest in previously enjoyed activities and work. The lack of sleep only compounds the problem, as already compromised coping skills are further diminished by fatigue.**

Weight loss and anorexia, increased use of drugs, including tobacco and alcohol, may be signs of serious distress. Any sudden personality change may be a warning, even if it seems to be for the better. Sometimes, when a morose, despondent person finally makes the decision to kill herself, she may feel relieved because she has found a solution to her problems. For the hours or days between the decision and the act of suicide, she may seem strangely happier and more relaxed than she has been in months. Family and friends often assume the crisis is over and applaud themselves for having endured the difficult time so well. They are stunned and bewildered when the body is found. "I thought she was feeling better. She seemed so much happier lately. I can't believe she did this *now*."

Situational clues may also provide some insight. As already mentioned, bereavement and divorce are very difficult emotional situations and render those in the midst of these experiences far more vulnerable to suicide. Other serious family problems, financial setbacks, and poor health may also precipitate a suicidal crisis. Life does sometimes hand out more than a person can bear, at least more than he *thinks* he can bear without the support and guidance of someone who cares enough to offer them.

---

*This farewell ritual also happens sometimes when a person somehow senses impending natural death. One young man told me about his grandmother, who one day went to see each of her sons at their respective business offices, then went to a ladies' room and suffered a fatal heart attack.

**A study of perfectly healthy doctors who were on duty for twenty-four hours at a time for emergencies, proved that they began to show progressively stronger signs of psychosis after having been awake and under stress for long periods. The more fatigued they were, the crazier they acted. And these were healthy doctors.

Intervention

Suppose you suspect a friend is suicidal. What do you do? First, you must decide if this person's life is worth an investment of time on your part. Offering help when it is convenient, only to withdraw it when you have better things to do may only confirm the individual's conclusions that he is unlovable and unimportant. Don't multiply someone's sense of abandonment by alternately demonstrating and withdrawing your concern.

Of course, you needn't attempt to solve this monumental crisis by yourself, either. Others who are close to this person should be made aware of the gravity of the situation and be persuaded to be especially considerate and open to the crucial needs of their loved one. Be aware of community resources and take advantage of them or encourage your friend to do so. The community mental health center, suicide or crisis hot lines, clergy, and physicians may be sources of invaluable assistance. While caring, supportive friends and family are so very important to a distraught individual, they may not be able to offer the kind of objective guidance and insight a professional counselor could provide.

On your part, it takes time—time to be there, to care, to listen, to perhaps offer a different perspective. I am constantly amazed at the simple but brilliant solutions my husband proposes for day-to-day dilemmas I thought beyond resolution. He approaches them from a different perspective than I, and he can see alternatives which would never have occurred to me. You might be able to provide this sort of help to your friend. Especially in times of crisis, we have a tendency to put on the blinders, narrowing our mental vision just at the moment we need the broad view.

Avoid judging, moralizing, and criticizing. Your friend's self-esteem is already rock-bottom. Don't bury it completely. If what your friend tells you seems incomprehensible, you might say "I don't understand what you are saying. Could you explain it to me again?" This shows you are open to his feelings, even though they might not make sense to you. Never suggest, "You're foolish to think that way," to a person who may be about to eliminate that "fool," himself. Offering platitudes or scripture is not likely to be of much help. "We all have a cross to bear" may be intended as a statement of identification and brotherhood, but it doesn't answer the immediate crisis.

Persons who feel secure, loved, and worthwhile are the least likely to take their own lives. While we may not be able to prevent every suicide, stronger family units and interpersonal relationships might help to minimize the problem. In our hectic schedules, we often neglect to take the *time* to actually *talk* with our loved ones, I mean beyond the grocery list, softball schedule, and plans for Saturday night. Television probably robs many families of hours they might have spent getting to know each other better. Many of us *care* about each other, if we only stopped to think about it and could *communicate* it. In our busy rush, we somehow assume that friends and family know we love them and that we don't need to interrupt the momentum of our lives to express and share that love.

After the Fact

The family who survives the suicide of one of its members endures a very special kind of grief, probably the most painful of any. These persons may need a lot of special concern and support as they attempt to put the pieces back together after this shattering experience. Guilt is especially probable when a loved one commits suicide, although it may have no more basis in reality here than the guilt survivors may feel after any other type of death. We simply cannot know or experience anyone else's inner torment. We cannot conclude that the tragedy could have been prevented if we had only done this or that, or not done the other thing.

An old friend of mine is fond of saying, "Everything looks clearer through the old retrospectoscope." If only we knew then what we know now. In the light of past events, it is easier to interpret the significance of words or behavior that might have been dismissed as trivial when they were said or done. But we can not go back in time. "It's a lesson too late for the learning," but it can make us more perceptive and aware for the rest of our lives.

Ray of Hope, 1518 Derwen Drive, Iowa City, Iowa 52240, is an organization dedicated to the aid of those surviving the suicide of someone close. A helpful booklet is available from Ray of Hope for $3.50. Another brief but excellent book, *Leaning Into the Wind: The Wilderness of Widowhood*, was written by Betty Bryant, whose husband committed suicide after an unsuccessful struggle with a terminal illness. It is published by Fortress Press.

Rational Alternative or Crime Against Nature

While many contemporary suicides represent a preventable waste of a temporarily overwrought individual, there is a growing tolerance for the practice in the Western world. Many recent books and articles have been published with titles like *Rational Suicide, Common-Sense Suicide;* a group in England has even published a manual detailing a great number of methods for accomplishing the feat successfully!

Much of this trend has grown out of the dilemma surrounding the terminally ill patient and his right to die rather than continue to face the distress of uncomfortable or even painful medical treatment. Some of the change in thinking has roots in the problems of that portion of the modern elderly population who finds little or no joy or purpose in living. The message is: they should have the right to determine their own destiny. We should not condemn them to a painful, meaningless, existence nor should we, who are well and self-actualizing, judge them harshly for attempting to escape their present and probably permanent lot in life.

At one point in history, it was thought that anyone who committed suicide must be insane. That fallacy has long since been disproved. Can we ever consider suicide to be the best of all possible alternatives? I hope not. But we have no authority to judge the actions of others whose misery and anguish we cannot know. Our challenge is to eliminate those sources of inner turmoil in our society so that our brothers and sisters will not be tempted to consider suicide as an option.

Trends in Living and Dying

The incredible accumulation of knowledge, and technology, and the ingenuity of human compassion have fostered the development of some promising, and some seemingly preposterous, prospects for handling life-and-death situations. We'll discuss several of the most noteworthy trends of today and tomorrow.

Cryonics

The prospect of immortality, Robert Ettinger called it, and so titled his book about *cryonics,* the immediate postdeath freezing of a human body. The purpose of this is to maintain the body tissues until some future time when medical science has devised a cure for the specific disease that caused the person's death. At that time, the body would be thawed, revived, and the cure administered, leaving the patient to go his way until he falls victim to yet another "fatal" malady. Then, of course, he could be popped back into the deep-freeze to await the discovery of the cure for that, too.

It sounds like science fiction, but somewhere in the U.S., there are thirty or more bloodless human bodies cooling it at −321F° for a period of years, whose one-time inhabitants hoped they might have another chance at life. The first freezing occurred in 1966. The idea seems to have hit a peak in the early seventies. Cryonic societies were springing up everywhere and eager proponents crusaded for recognition of and support for their cause. Apparently many of the early enthusiasts became discouraged by the multitude of problems associated with a complex technique and philosophy still in its infancy. In his 1972 book *Here Comes Immortality,* Jerome Tucille predicted that more than half a million people will have been cryonically suspended by the end of the 1980s. I doubt that we'll come anywhere close to that figure. As our technological expertise improves, however, there may be a renewed interest in this prospect of immortality—in the flesh, no less.

Any new idea meets with complications and stumbling blocks. Cryonics is no exception. Whether these many objections and scientific hitches can be overcome remains to be seen. We'll discuss some of the most obvious dilemmas inherent in the current state of the art for cryonics.

The most urgent problem is having the appropriate chemicals, equipment, and personnel at the bedside of the prospective candidate at the instant of his death. Perhaps we should say at the instant the death process has been determined to be irreversible. For maximum preservation of tissues in a healthy state, the preparation of the body must begin before the deterioration of cells has begun. Best results would no doubt be obtained if the cryonics team begin their labors actually moments *before* the person died, so that brain cells would have the briefest possible oxygen deprivation. It helps, therefore, to have prior notice of the impending death and to arrange to have it occur in a location where the necessary accoutrements are available.

The technique involves draining the blood from the body and replacing it with an antifreeze solution, such as DMSO (Di Methyl Sulfoxide) with glycerine, to prevent damage from ice crystal formation. Other causes of damage caused by freezing, such as the osmosis of fluid from the cells into the intercellular spaces, still need some work. One technique being explored involves freezing at high pressure.

While there are still technical problems, proponents of the idea hope that by the time science has advanced far enough that we would be ready to thaw our first "suspendee," it would have also discovered a way to reverse not only the damage caused by freezing, but damage resulting from the storage and thawing process as well.

Corneas, skin, bone marrow, and sperm are routinely preserved by freezing for later use. Goldfish have been successfully frozen and revived. Hamsters and other small animals have been maintained at near-freezing temperatures (but not frozen) and survived with minimal damage. As yet, however, we have not been able to satisfactorily keep an entire human organ at a functional level after the freezing and thawing procedure. The challenge of maintaining the integrity of the complete complex anatomy of a human has not been met to date. That does not mean it is impossible, only that we have yet to learn exactly how to do it.

We do know that humans who have been "suspended" in cold water and snow and were thought to be dead, have survived without any detectible damage. Even the delicate cells of the brain appear to have survived unscathed by oxygen deprivation for a half hour or more. The idea of cold storage is not without scientific basis or precedent. The fact that all the facts are not in is no deterrent to Robert Ettinger, who says in *Man Into Superman* that "the probability of revival is not small; it is simply unknown, which is not at all the same thing."

Those who become excited about cryonics are obviously not concerned about the problem of the human soul, spirit, essence, or whatever your preferred term is. Perhaps they simply deny its existence. For those who have confidence in the human spiritual nature, however, cryonics presents a special dilemma. Does the soul remain "trapped" in a frigid shell of a body or is it "released" at the moment of death? If it is released, will it return to the body at the moment of reanimation? Or will another spirit inhabit the body as if it were a newborn? These questions may be of little significance to the scientist embroiled in issues of optimal temperature and cryobiology, but there are many for whom these considerations bear great importance.

Another curious eventuality if physical immortality were commonplace would be the logistical distribution of an ever-increasing population. If no one dies, where do we put all the people? Will mile-high apartment buildings constitute the community of the future? How many people can our planet house and feed? Will new births eventually be outlawed to avoid crowding out those already here? Will the laughter of children no longer ring through the playground? Perhaps, by that time, we will have established colonies on other planets or will have developed remarkable food-production systems and oceanic underwater supercities. As Ettinger says, the fact that we don't know the answers now is not the same as saying that they won't be forthcoming.

In the rapidly changing world we inhabit, complete with bizarre political philosophies, terrorists, cloning, genetic engineering, and test tube babies, who can predict what the earth and its residents might be like in fifty or a hundred or two hundred years, when medical science has finally perfected a cure for the cause of your original demise? Will you awaken in a society even remotely similar to the one you left? Will you be surrounded by friends and family likewise frozen and revived? Or will your new compatriots speak a completely new language, consume nourishment totally foreign to your palate, and abide in an eccentric social structure of which, perhaps, you occupy the inferior caste? Again, no one knows. It might be terrific the second time around, and some people feel it is worth taking the chance to find out. Others are frankly frightened.

About your family—just where do they stand when you are cryonically suspended? Is your spouse considered widowed and free to remarry? Does social security pay orphan's benefits to your children? Suppose your miracle cure is discovered in a short time, say three years, and the technology to reverse the damage of freezing and thawing has caught up as well. When you are revived, what is your status in a society you left only briefly? Has your estate been distributed by means of your supposedly last will and testament? Has it been held in trust for your eventual return or given to your family to ease their bereavement? Will the life insurance company reclaim the death benefit now that you are no longer dead? Do your children's social security payments stop? Will your remarried spouse be glad to see you?

What would the impact on religion be if humanity were to achieve physical immortality? Would our beliefs in Heaven, after-life, and moral standards be modified by the advent of an indefinite lifespan? In *Man Into Superman*, Ettinger foresees a golden age for humanity when we can dismiss our worries about death and direct our energies toward improving life. Of course one man's improvement is another man's woe. Ettinger pleads for society to be open enough to give it a try. If it doesn't work, we won't be any deader for having tried.

Since the mid-seventies, active interest in cryonics has waned. There are still a number of cryonics societies and associations which remain relatively independent entities. Among those still active are the Bay Area Cryonics Society in Berkeley, the Cryonics Society of South Florida, and the Cryonics Association in Oak Park, Michigan, which is an educational organization. The Cryonics Institute, also of Oak Park, Michigan, is a nonprofit corporation which will contract for cryonics services, including perfusion, freezing, and long-term maintenance. The groups in Michigan enjoy the guidance and membership of Robert Ettinger himself.

The Cryonics Institute estimates total cost for all services as of 1977, on a package basis, to be about $29,000. Some commercial firms provide similar services for about $50,000. Prospective suspendees must obviously make prior arrangements for payment, which is usually done by purchasing a life insurance policy for the purpose.

Those interested in more information on the current research and prospects of cryonics may wish to join the

Cryonics Association
24041 Stratford
Oak Park, Michigan 48237

Rates for members are: initiation $25, yearly dues $50, or $5 monthly; for associates: $15 per year.

Members and associates receive a monthly newsletter, *The Immortalist*. Other benefits are available to full members.

At present, it seems unlikely that cryonics will soon reach the widespread use and glory that Ettinger and others once envisioned. In fact, interest among researchers seems to have shifted more toward the pursuit of confirmation of the surviving soul and anticipation of its future adventures in dimensions more grand than our present limitations. For now, it is all speculation, but speculation that helps us examine our values and goals in life. Contemplation of such eventualities encourages a clearer focus on the here and now, too. Perhaps, the problems and challenges posed by cryonics are what make the issue worthy of our mental exercises, even in the absence of any technological certainty about its possible implementation.

Harvesting the Neomorts

Willard Gaylin, president of the Institute of Society, Ethics and the Life Sciences, The Hastings Center, has proposed that we might maintain newly dead bodies, "neomorts," not for their own eventual resuscitation, but rather as an organ transplant bank and realistic practice patients for surgical residents trying a new procedure for the first time. If you are familiar with the novel or movie *Coma* by Robin Cook, you have some idea of the concept. Gaylin, I'm sure, would frown on the abuse of the great potential which was so cleverly and viciously fictionalized by Cook, while acknowledging that the possibility of such abuse is but one reason to proceed cautiously in the pursuit of such an endeavor.

In addition to the uses already mentioned, Gaylin also proposes that neomorts might be used for testing drugs, diagnostic instruments, and antidotes for poisons.

They could serve as manufacturing units, too, for hormones, antitoxins, and antibodies, many of which are laboriously and expensively produced courtesy of our friends in the animal kingdom. We might, for instance, inject a neomort with leukemic blood cells to encourage a generation of antileukemia antibodies which could then be given to living patients as a possible cure. Antiaging procedures could be tested.

The vast opportunities for research and experimentation as well as "manufacturing" and parts-supply with neomorts could make a considerable contribution to the improvement of life for the living. Yet Gaylin has no delusions about our rushing out to set up facilities to accommodate these preserved cadavers. Resistance to the idea may be even stronger than the scientific appeal. The cost in dollars of maintaining a large number of bodies on respirators would not be insignificant. The equipment, buildings, and other expenses, however, are only one drawback, and one that might be mitigated by the advantages to be gained.

The overwhelming objections would most likely be emotional. There are a number of people who donate their bodies to science, and their organs for transplantation so that, even in their death, they might help others to live. But many of us cringe at the thought of dead bodies being ventilated, suspended, intentionally diseased, and experimentally treated, especially if those dead bodies happened to have once belonged to our parents or siblings or spouses or children. There is for many, an emotional tie to the physical remains of a loved one. The mere idea of their indefinite post-death maintenance as human guinea pigs is unsettling.

Society has, however, adapted to many other ideas which had their moments of inspiring incredulity. Transplants themselves took some getting used to, as has the notion of cyborgs, the part-human, part-machine concept now embodied in thousands with pacemakers. Soon, no doubt, we will have developed artificial replacements for many body parts *à la* the Six Million Dollar Man. If cyborgs are here, can the neomort bioemporium be far behind?

When we consider the possible advantage we might gain in finding a cure for cancer, that consideration alone weighs heavily in the favor of Gayin's proposal. It has been nearly a decade since this human recycling suggestion appeared in an article in *Harper's* magazine. To my knowledge, we have yet to see the first bioemporium in operation. Perhaps it is simply an idea whose time has not yet come.

It might be interesting to note that while cryonics and the neomort bank ideas are both related to the advancement of medical and scientific knowledge, their proponents must necessarily fall into mutually exclusive groups. If one anticipates a future healthy life, she would not want her suspended body further compromised by practicing surgeons or potentially damaging drug experiments or the purposeful introduction of a terrible disease so that scientists could attempt (with or without success) to develop a cure for it for others. Those who opt for the altruism of the neomort bioemporium must relinquish any notion of possible personal physical survival. Cryonicists yearn for the presence of those miraculous discoveries, but not at the expense of a human body, most certainly not *theirs.*

Wholly Healthy

In our highly industrialized society, we are quite accustomed to the idea of specialization. No longer are there generic lawyers, engineers, and doctors. There are now attorneys specialized in corporate, entertainment, estate planning, criminal, and other areas of law. There are civic, industrial, chemical, and locomotive, not to mention domestic, engineers. Don't attempt to ask any of them for an answer that falls within the expertise of their esteemed colleagues. The phenomenal amount of knowledge necessary to function competently in even one area is difficult enough to maintain, as can be seen by the volumes of new material continually appearing in journals and trade publications. To expect any one individual to keep up on the latest in a variety of fields is a request for superhuman effort.

We *want* our professionals to be highly skilled. We don't want our ear surgery to be done by a proctologist. We want the *best*. If we expect to get individuals with extraordinary expertise, we must allow, even encourage them to specialize.

The obvious benefits of this system notwithstanding, there are some deficits in the resulting fragmentation of a body of knowledge and attendant skills. We often wind up with a situation in which the left hand doesn't know what the right hand is doing. In the 1981 calendar year alone there were several major calamities resulting from poor design, construction, or materials used in large buildings. The collapse of the elevated walkways at the Hyatt Regency Hotel in Kansas City, the several serious fires in large hotels in Las Vegas, and the crumbling of an apartment building under construction in Florida may have resulted from the failure of the experts in one area to consult with the experts in another area to determine the best and safest way to design and build these mammoth and often beautiful structures. We have paid a high price for the benefits of specialization.

The same sort of fragmentation has occurred in medicine. It is not at all unusual for a single patient to be simultaneously treated by a surgeon, a cardiologist, a neurologist, an oncologist, and the family physician he went to see in the first place. Each specialist views the patient from a different and narrow perspective. The result may be the latest and greatest medicine has to offer in each of the represented disciplines. That, certainly, is our goal, the very justification of the fragmentation from the start.

But whatever happened to the *person* who inadvertently became a surgical patient, a neurology patient, a cardiology patient, and a cancer patient? Is the patient, too, to be fragmented, to consider himself so many apparently malfunctioning departments? Have we lost him in the shuffle of our magnificent knowledge and therapies?

This is *not* a plea to return to the good old days. We must have specialization in order to make the advances and discoveries that will benefit all people. Rather, it is a call to acknowledge the growing evidence that positive health is the result of the comprehensive well-being of the total person. There is increasing awareness of the influence of emotional, stress-related, and even spiritual factors in the breakdown *and* recovery of physical health. Never before has this wholistic approach to health and life been so needed.

One of the most dramatic manifestations of this philosophy has been demonstrated at Carl and Stephanie Simonton's Cancer Treatment Center in Fort Worth, Texas. There, hopeless cancer victims have been shown how to recognize their own role in their illness and ways of fighting back using their own minds and bodies. *Getting Well Again,* the Simontons' book (written with James Creighton), available in paperback, details their techniques and philosophy. I highly recommend it.

The Simontons have demonstrated an undeniable link between stress and the development of cancer. They do not contend that stress is the cause of cancer, per se, but that when we are under a great deal of stress, our immune systems are not as efficient in fighting off the potentially cancerous abnormal cells that our bodies produce from time to time. There are many possible contributors to the development of cancer. Diet, pollution, radiation, smoking, family genes, overexposure to the sun, and certain chemicals have been identified as having such a relationship to cancer. The Simontons utilize existing conventional medical treatments, including surgery, radiation, and chemotherapy, and add their own special weapon—the patient's mind.

The oncologist (Carl, M.D.) and psychotherapist (Stephanie) perceive their patients as whole persons who have the capacity to participate actively in and influence their own health. Patients are encouraged to truly examine their lives and goals, and to assess for themselves the benefits (yes, *benefits*) they derive from their illness. Few of us consciously realize that getting sick has it advantages: we don't have to go to work, we get extra attention and consideration, critical deadlines can be postponed, and we are allowed time to rest undisturbed. In the hectic pace of our production-oriented twentieth century, these are rare pleasures.

Are these pleasures worth their price? Must we get cancer to get rest? Patients must consciously reevaluate their lives' directions. Perhaps cancer could be added to the list of possible subintended suicides. If the pressures get too great, the body essentially says, "I can't take it anymore," and succumbs to the present affront, whether it be high blood pressure, viral flu, a cold, or cancer. This doesn't explain all illnesses, but the relationship of stress to disease has long since passed the stage of mere hypothesis.

Once a person recognizes the importance of his own attitude in his illness, the Simontons teach him to maximize the body's defenses against the enemy. They use relaxation, visual imagery, goal setting, pain management, physical exercise, consultation with one's "inner guide," and positive counseling to mobilize the patient's inherent, but often untapped, ability to direct the healing process. This is all done *in addition* to conventional medical treatment. These are not quacks off on a wild tangent.

While the conventional medical treatment is continued, the Simontons' results outdistance those obtained by using medical treatment alone. They began their studies with a group of medically incurable patients, each expected to survive no more than twelve months. For the patients who died during the first four years of the study, the average survival time was 20.3 months, nearly twice their anticipated prognosis. Of those who have survived, forty-one percent now either have *no* evidence of disease, or their tumors are regressing, while another twenty-seven percent are in a stable condition. Most of the surviving patients are as active as they were prior to their diagnosis.

Because of the many variables involved, the Simontons do not presume to guarantee recovery to those who follow their methods. But the evidence they present has profound significance for our approach to health care. Lifestyle, stress, mental attitude, and emotions can have an incredible impact on "organic" physical illnesses. One of their patients, cured of his supposedly incurable cancer, applied his newly learned skills to the arthritis which had bothered him for years. He had remarkable, though not complete, success.

Like many others, the Simontons have found that the will to live and the will to health are at least as important as medications and treatments in the amelioration of human ills. The amazing powers of the human mind and spirit have only begun to surface and it is exciting to ponder what else we might be able to do when we get around to thinking about it.

The prospect of immortality is not a gift the Simontons offer, but the implications of their offering may benefit us all in this mortal life.

A Better Way Out—The Hospice

When asked where they would choose to die if the choice were theirs to make, all but a few people say "At home, with my family." Some envision a quick, easy death without foreknowledge and the accompanying preparatory grief. While this type of death may be easier for the person dying, it is usually much more difficult for the family to deal with after the fact. Whatever our speculations, most of us, more than eighty percent, die in hospitals and other institutions. Some never make it to the emergency room from the scene of the accident. Two percent are at home with their families when it is their time to die.

If you are sick and planning on getting better, the hospital, with its life-saving orientation and equipment, is probably just the place for you. If you are sick and are not expected to recover, the cool efficiency, tubes, tests, and trials of hospitalization may only compound your pain. The mere acceptance of a terminal diagnosis is a considerable feat. The differentiation between terminal and nonterminal diagnosis is often difficult, as I already mentioned. But many patients seem to sense (perhaps even orchestrate) the final sequence of life. For them to be subjected to the assaults of the "life-savers" on a sterile ward is a mockery and an indignity.

Dr. Cicely Saunders recognized that need of dying patients for a kinder, more comfortable environment. In 1967, she founded the first modern hospice, St. Christopher's, in London. The hospice is as much a concept as it is a facility, and that concept has been embraced and implemented by insightful persons all over the world. There are now several hundred hospices of various descriptions in the United States, and the idea continues to gain momentum.

A hospice is a program which provides palliative and supportive care for terminally-ill patients and their families. In fact, the family is the "unit of care" in a hospice. Hospices may operate on both an in-patient and out-patient basis. The emphasis is on care rather than cure, and comfort rather than rehabilitation. The nature of the care is determined by the family's personal needs rather than by the patient's medical diagnosis.

The goals of a hospice are to

1. keep the patient home as long as possible
2. help the patient to live as fully as possible
3. control pain and other symptoms
4. supplement and coordinate existing services to avoid duplication and confusion
5. provide emotional support for patient and family
6. educate health professionals, as well as the general community about needs of dying patients
7. provide a respite for family caregivers
8. offer bereavement counseling
9. minimize expenses for the dying patient.

With the aid of hospice professionals and volunteers, two-thirds of patients may be enabled to die at home. Occasionally at-home care becomes burdensome for the family and the patient may be moved to an in-patient hospice facility for a time to give the family a break in the routine. The hospice also provides assistance for patients in other settings, such as nursing homes or hospitals.

Thomas Leicht found that fears associated with dying were connected to seven general areas. The hospice attempts to minimize these anxieties by appropriate care. Briefly, Leicht's seven fears of dying include

1. fear of the process of dying, pain, and body changes
2. fear of loss of control
3. fear of loss of one's loved ones and concern for their future well-being
4. fear expressed in the eyes of caregivers
5. fear of isolation
6. fear of the unknown; concern, questions about after-life
7. fear that life will have been meaningless.

If one is experiencing considerable pain, it will be difficult to concentrate on anything else. In a traditional hospital setting, pain medication is usually given p.r.n., "as needed," but no more often than every three to four hours. The patient in pain often lives for the medication, agonizing during the last hour of each wait until it is permissible to have another pill or shot, and yearning for the moments of relief he anticipates. There is an understandable inclination on the part of physicians to use minimal doses as infrequently as possible to avoid the spectre of addiction. That is the story for nonterminal patients. Even so, it doesn't always work too well and we still have a lot to learn about pain control. A man who suffered severe pain from massive burns was abruptly taken off his usual narcotic medication because, now that it appeared he would recover, the doctors feared addiction. The pain, however, continued. He was chided for being a baby when he asked for medication. Even three years after the ordeal, he vividly recalls the agony and his resentment toward the nurses who showed such a lack of compassion.

For terminal patients, the problem of addiction is less troublesome. Starting with that philosophy, hospices began to experiment with approaches to pain control and many have successfully used a modified "Brompton's cocktail," which is a palatable liquid containing morphine, grenadine or cherry syrup, and water. Another alternative is the "Val-Steck" elixir which contains methadone, ethyl alcohol, and flavoring, although there is some speculation that repeated use of methadone may actually shorten the patient's life. Sometimes, amphetamines or phenothiazines are given with the narcotic to counteract the possible side-effects of drowsiness and nausea.

In the hospice program, the patient's pain is carefully assessed, and the liquid medication program initiated. Rather than wait for the patient to request medication for pain, the prescribed dose is given regularly every four hours around the clock. A dose is delayed or omitted only if the patient is sleeping. In this way, the blood level of the narcotic is maintained, and the patient can remain in a relatively pain-free state. If necessary, dosage is adjusted to accommodate changes in the patient's pain level or sleepiness. Often, hospice experience has shown that once patients are aware that they can be free of pain, the anxiety that usually accompanies anticipation of pain is diminished. The dose of morphine can then be decreased, while the patient is still pain-free.

With her new confidence in the freedom from pain, the patient has the time and energy to participate in life and enjoy those around her, making her last weeks and months of life fulfilling and worthwhile, rather than agonizing and debilitating. One woman who had bone cancer had required increasingly large doses of pain killers, lost all interest in eating, slept most of the time, and was afraid to walk. She was started on Brompton's cocktail every four hours. Her appetite improved, she became increasingly alert and able to think more clearly, and she gained strength in her new pain-free state. She was able to spend nearly a week at home with her three children, a precious interlude for which they were all grateful. She died four weeks later, without pain, in a nursing home.

The loss of control one senses when subjected to hospital rules and regulations is eliminated when the patient can stay at home, in familiar, comfortable surroundings with beloved, caring friends and family in attendance. The isolation of a clinical experience is likewise dissipated by the opportunity to participate in family life. Improved mental clarity afforded by pain relief can help the patient work out with his family their plans for existence in his absence. He can contribute suggestions and help them to cope with their impending loss.

Hospice teams offer special help to families in this stage of planning for and coping with life without the deceased. A patient care coordinator in a small hospice in a one-hospital town in the midwest relayed her efforts to help the 34-year-old daughter of a dying man obtain instruction to get her driver's license. She had never been employed and still lived in her father's home. The hospice arranged for her to enroll in a vocational rehabilitation program, too, so that she would learn a skill with which to support herself after her father's death. Her father was relieved of one of his major concerns about dying—leaving his daughter uncared for.

Spiritual guidance and psychological counseling are provided by qualified members of the hospice staff. Hospices can also coordinate and initiate services of which the patient and family may have been unaware. Many community groups will provide rent-free use of hospital beds, wheelchairs, commodes, walkers, and other such equipment that eases the chore of caring for the patient at home. Visits from public health nurses or other visiting nurses assist with necessary treatments and answer questions about medications or the development of new symptoms. The physician, of course, will be consulted as necessary as the patient's condition changes.

Volunteers often provide some of the most important benefits of hospice. They listen and care and are available to help the family with many of their important, but nonmedical needs. Help with errands, transportation to appointments, playing cards and other games with patients, writing letters for them, reading to them, taking them for walks, are all possible contributions a volunteer can make. A training program for volunteers is usually required by the hospice organization.

All hospices provide out-patient services. These are the least expensive to organize and, for the majority of patients, are the most helpful. Hospices also can provide care in a variety of settings. Some have their own separate building for use as an in-patient facility. Here, rules are minimal, and patients are allowed to bring treasured possessions, such as a favorite chair or a pet, to make their environment as comfortable and home-like as possible. Hospice concepts have also been adapted to assist patients in nursing homes and hospitals.

The recognition of the patient as a whole—as a person and not a diagnosis—is crucial to the hospice concept as well as the Simonton's approach to care for the terminally ill. Perhaps hospices will begin to adopt some of the Simonton's pain management techniques and be able to decrease dependence on medications even further.

The compassion and creativity demonstrated in the development of these latest trends in dealing with the final phase of life are an inspiration and tribute to the evolvement of a greater American understanding of life and death.

Toward a Better Understanding

The National Hospice Organization, founded in 1978, provides advice and assistance to its member hospices and seeks to promote the development of the hospice concept. (There are also many fine independent hospice programs which happen not to belong to the NHO.) The NHO will provide information on its member hospices (now numbering around 250) upon request. Write to:

National Hospice Organization
1311A Dolley Madison Boulevard
McLean, Virginia 22101
Telephone: (903) 356-6770

Dr. Austin Kutscher, a New York dentist whose wife had died, was discouraged by his difficulty in handling her death and the lack of skills offered by others in helping him cope. To ameliorate similar dilemmas for others, he established the Foundation of Thanatology, which promotes research and education in the areas of death, dying, and bereavement. Conferences are held at least twice a year at Columbia University in New York City. Membership in the Foundation is $30. Write to:

The Foundation of Thanatology
630 West 168th Street
New York, New York 10032

The Hastings Center, Institute of Society, Ethics and the Life Sciences, is an interdisciplinary nonprofit research and educational organization that studies the ethical, legal, and social implication of advances in medicine, life sciences, behavioral and social sciences, and the professions. An excellent bimonthly journal, the *Hastings Center Report*, is sent to associate members. Membership dues are $21 a year, $17 for full-time students and senior citizens (over 65), $35 for institutions and libraries. The Hastings Center also publishes *IRB: A Review of Human Subjects Research* and various monographs and books. For more information, write:

The Hastings Center
360 Broadway
Hastings-on-Hudson, New York 10706

The Forum for Death Education and Counseling, Inc. was organized in the mid-seventies to promote responsible and effective education and counseling, to upgrade the quality of death education in educational institutions, hospitals, residential care facilities, churches, community organizations, and government facilities, and to improve the quality of counseling in the areas of death, dying, and bereavement. The Forum sponsors national and regional workshops, and coordinates a network of resource people for referral in the areas of educational and counseling needs. The Forum Newsletter is published ten times yearly and many Forum-sponsored books and papers are available to members. Membership rates are: individual, $25; institutional, $50; student and older citizen, $10. For more information, contact:

The Forum for Death Education and Counseling, Inc.
P.O. Box 1226
Arlington, Virginia 22210

14

Aging—Making a Long Life Lively

Aging and death are certainly perceived as among the least appealing of experiences. And the only way to delay the former or avoid the latter is to experience the other. As worshippers of youth, we find it intolerable to approach the other end of the spectrum. There is an attitude, a prejudice against aging and the aged as pervasive as racism and sexism. Robert Butler, director of the National Institute on Aging in Bethesda, Maryland, calls it *ageism.* Persons are stereotyped and discriminated against just because they are old.

Ageism is a self-destructive attitude, however, in addition to the damage it does to the current victims of its fallacious philosophy. If one harbors negative thoughts about members of the opposite sex or of another race, one simply reveals (at least) a lack of insight. Racial classification categories and the two sexes are, generally speaking, mutually exclusive categories. The male chauvinist will not suddenly become a helpless female. The elderly, however, make up a universal population, distinguished from others only by virtue of having been born earlier. It is a fast-growing "minority" which will, in time, have included almost all of us. The ill will we feel toward the aged will someday backfire. Eventually we become the objects of our own disdain.

A study of American children aged three to eleven revealed a tacit acceptance of many of the negative stereotypes of old age. "They chew funny." "They're all wrinkled and short." "They watch TV in their rocking chair." Only one-fifth of the children, however, even knew one older person outside their families. The children had warm affection for their grandparents but had no interest in the possibility of themselves becoming old. In fact, the vast majority stated quite openly "Oh no, not me!" "That's awful, being old is terrible."

Many other cultures approach their elders with reverence, deference, and respect. The Japanese have been especially concerned with integrating the elderly into the mainstream of their lives, with three-fourths of the population over sixty-five years of age residing with their children. Most men in this age bracket continue their employment. Those older men and women who are unemployed have responsibilities for child care and household tasks. Children are taught to respect their elders and value their judgment and advice. The Japanese have traditionally viewed aging with honor and prestige, not horror and prejudice.

In the Abkhasian villages of the Soviet Union where many persons live to be over a hundred years old and nearly everyone is long-lived (by our standards), the elders are valued for their knowledge and their actual physical contribution to the work of maintaining the collective farms. There is no such concept as retirement. The old may rest from their labors more frequently through the day, but they continue working into their nineties and beyond. Even while resting, they may entertain their grandchildren or great-grandchildren by telling stories or making toys. The older Abkhasians feel—and are—needed by their families. Rather than being encouraged to leave their jobs to make room for someone with fresh, new ideas, old people are recognized as capable and necessary members of the labor force.

We will consider the status of aging in America and briefly examine the possibilities of a change in that status. It is a task we cannot too long postpone, for in a matter of decades, the lot may be ours. A little foresight and planning may improve the "golden years" for us all.

Demography

Currently just over ten percent of the population of the United States, more than twenty-four million people, are sixty-five years old or older. By the year 2020, that figure is expected to climb to twenty percent of the population. The fastest growing segment of the population comprises those eighty-five and older, whose numbers tripled to 2.1 million in the twenty-five years from 1953 to 1978 and continue to grow more than any other age group. Mortality rates are declining rapidly as medical science and other factors effect a longer life for many of our citizens.

Only about five percent of the over-sixty-five group live in nursing homes, although about twenty-five percent of deaths in that age group take place there. This indicates an inclination to admit the elderly to such facilities as they appear to be approaching death. If we include all types of institutions (such as nursing homes and hospitals), we find that more than eighty percent of the elderly will die within institutional confines. Gone are the days of the "peaceful passing" in one's own home.

That leaves about ninety-five percent of the elderly population living in the community. About a fourth of them live with their offspring, some with other relatives, but many live alone, maintaining their own households. Independence and self-sufficiency are highly prized capabilities in our society.

While three-fourths of the men over sixty-five are married and live with their wives, only a third of the women over 65 live with their husbands. In 1975, there were two million widowers and 10 million widows in this country. In many ways, the problems of aging are exaggerated for women. Women live longer than men and yet lose their value in the eyes of society even more rapidly as they begin to show the effects of aging.

Nine out of ten elderly people are registered voters, and two-thirds of them vote regularly, a potentially powerful political voice. Eight out of ten are in relatively good health, ambulatory, and can participate in their normal activities. While only twelve percent of those over sixty-five are actually employed, another twenty-one percent are retired but would like to be employed, another thirty-six percent are housewives or do volunteer work, and another nine percent would like to do volunteer work.

The elderly derive income from a variety of sources, by far the most common (a source of income for 94 percent of the elderly) being social security and railroad retirement payments. Other sources include private pensions, government pensions, wages, savings, veteran's benefits, and public assistance. Slightly less than half of the elderly derive income from savings. In 1977, the median family income for the elderly was $9,110, or about 57 percent of the national median income. For the single elderly, median income was $3,829, about 65 percent of the national median for singles. Although about fifteen percent of elderly Americans are officially classified as poor, if we count the cost of the benefits they receive through Medicaid and Medicare as income (since these services free up money that would otherwise go to medical expenses), only six percent fall below the poverty line.

Of course, an income that is 57 to 65 percent of the national median does not indicate great wealth, either. It is some help that some expenses of younger people are outgrown, such as child-rearing, clothing and travel expenses for one's job, and, for some, home mortgage payments. The elderly also receive the advantage of a double personal exemption for income-tax purposes, and social security payments are tax-free. However, there are often added medical expenses (only 70 percent of medical expenses are paid by

Medicare and Medicaid), costs of hiring someone to do gardening, mowing, snow shoveling, and other chores that, as senior citizen and writer Dorothy Hansen pointed out in her local newspaper's letters column, younger persons often do for themselves, and being elderly does not exempt one from paying real estate taxes. And many do not own their homes and are paying rent, or even if they do own their home may still be paying on the mortgage. In our highly mobile society, there will likely be fewer and fewer families who reach old age having lived in any one home long enough to have it entirely paid for.

At any rate, the financial status of the elderly has improved dramatically in the last twenty years. There is still room for improvement, however. These gains must also be safeguarded, now that the social security system seems to be in serious fiscal danger and its future uncertain. The recent proliferation of individual retirement accounts (IRAs) may be an answer for some persons. No doubt other promising suggestions will be put into effect, such as pushing the age for mandatory retirement higher.

The Effects of Aging

Life expectancy today for white women is 77.1 years, for white men, 69.3 years. The rates for blacks are slightly lower. This has risen remarkably from the 47 or so years a child could expect to live at the turn of the century. The change has increased the numbers of persons who live to be old, but has not substantially changed the actual human life-span. In other words, we have eliminated many of the causes of death that prevented people from reaching old age, but haven't appreciably altered the biological effects of aging, per se.

Dr. James Fries of Stanford University believes that the normal biological limit of the body is reached, on the average, at age 85. Under ideal conditions, he estimates that 95 percent of Americans would die natural deaths between the ages of 77 and 93. He optimistically predicts that in the future the average period of diminished vigor will decrease, chronic diseases will be postponed, and the elderly person's need for medical care will decrease.

There is much written about the different types of aging. *Physiological aging* has been further subdivided into "primary" aging, or the inevitable loss of function as time progresses, and "secondary" aging, which is a result of the accumulated stresses of a lifetime and tends to accelerate the primary process. Then we have *chronological aging*, which simply refers to the years we have lived. Other authors prefer to contrast physical aging with *sociogenic aging*, an attitude which has no physical basis, but which imposes "imaginary" aging on older persons.

Aging has also been approached from its social, psychological, and pathological perspectives. While much individual variation exists in the rate of aging, there are certain general, predictable patterns in the elderly as a group. Vision, hearing, and touch all decline in several of their characteristics. The lens of the eye often becomes increasingly opaque and rigid, which diminishes the amount of light reaching the back of the eye and compromises the ability to focus clearly. Colors tend to fade and depth perception is distorted. Hearing problems include difficulty in distinguishing sounds in crowded, noisy places or places with background noise from appliances, TV, or radio. Sounds above the 2,000-cycle frequency are difficult to hear, and there is often a problem locating the source of a sound. Some question exists, however, whether these losses are normal or perhaps influenced by environmental factors. Exposure to loud noises is known to induce early hearing loss, even in young people. In some tribes living in quieter surroundings, the loss of hearing appears at a much later age.

A loss of sensitivity in the fingertips makes it difficult to differentiate textures. Loss of fine muscle control may pose problems opening mail, dialing the phone, or turning pages in a book. The senses of taste and smell often decline, as well, leaving the older person with a diminished interest in food and eating.

Muscle strength and density of the bones begin to decrease at about age thirty. The elderly in the U.S. suffer some 200,000 hip fractures each year, thanks to their weaker bones. Kidneys, too, function less efficiently as the years progress, as does the circulatory system. The heart pumps less effectively, and the vessels are likely to be narrowed by cholesterol plaques and atheroslcerosis. Vital capacity of the lungs diminishes by about one-half, in part because of atrophy of the respiratory muscles.

The immune system, that marvelous mechanism that helped us fight off infections and other maladies, becomes far less competent, making the aged more vulnerable to a host of assaults that younger bodies handle quite easily. The basic metabolic rate goes down. The functional capacity of the liver declines, altering the effects various drugs have on the elderly. The skin becomes rough and wrinkled; lesions heal more slowly. Reaction time slows down, no matter what the task.

All of the basic body functions reach a peak at approximately age thirty, some earlier. At that point, each system functions well above the level necessary to maintain life. This gives us reserve power to call on to get us through periods of stress. Beyond this peak, the senses and biological functions begin a downward trend, some faster than others and with amazing variations from person to person. President

Reagan was declared by his physicians to have the "body of a man many years his junior." Many others continue to live quite active and healthy lives even into their ninth and tenth decades.

There is evidence that some aspects of aging (the secondary type) can be altered by lifestyle changes. For instance, the "law of use," which suggests that by using an asset we will have more of it to use, seems to apply to muscle strength, memory, and mental vigor as well as social skills and libido. If we exercise these functions, they increase. Also, reduction of smoking has a favorable effect on cardiorespiratory function and lessens the incidence of cancer (to which the elderly are apparently more vulnerable because of the breakdown of the immune system). There has already been a decrease in the incidence of heart disease since the mid-1960s, perhaps thanks to low-fat diets, reduced smoking among older persons, more exercise, and better control of high blood pressure. Reducing exposure to the sun minimizes the effect of aging on the skin.

One bright spot in the picture of aging is the preservation of intelligence. The myth about the aged being mindless, docile, and senile is far from the reality revealed by a number of recent studies. Paul Baltes and K. Warner Schaie found that intelligence often actually increased right into the seventies and beyond, at least in several of the most important mental skills, as reported in "The Myth of the Twilight Years," *Psychology Today,* March 1974. Some persons do show a decline in measured intelligence within the five or fewer years before death. The vast majority (at least ninety percent) of the over-sixty-five population is definitely not senile. A few, probably less than twenty percent, experience some sort of memory difficulties. Moreover, the aged are often *less* rigid than their offspring's contemporaries in adjusting to changing mores and lifestyles. Maybe they have to be. Those who are old today have experienced dramatic changes in their way of life. They remember the days of smallpox epidemics and outdoor "plumbing." In a single lifetime they have witnessed the introduction of the first automobile, airplane, television, and refrigerator. They have had to be flexible just to adapt to new technology and new job opportunities.

Boredom is seldom a problem in old age. Various studies have found between thirteen and thirty percent of the aged claim that they haven't enough to do or are bored. The stereotype of the angry, irritable old codger has been refuted by research, too. A variety of surveys have demonstrated that most old people are involved socially with friends, family, church, or volunteer groups and that loneliness plagues only a small percentage.

Older workers have fewer accidents than young workers, and older drivers have fewer traffic accidents than their juniors, especially those under thirty years of age. Those who were heavy drinkers earlier in life tend to consume much less alcohol as they age.

Certain physiological changes appear to be inevitable as one nears the last season of life, but the picture is not entirely bleak and will probably improve as we learn more about these phenomena and possibly how to alter them. The National Institute on Aging and many private agencies are vigorously conducting research to determine how we age and what seems to trigger the process.

The task of separating the effects of aging and disease is not as simple as it might seem. Probably far more often than it should be, the behavior of an oldster is attributed to mental senility when an inappropriate response may have been prompted by an adverse reaction to a prescribed medication or a simple distortion of stimuli by regressing sensory systems. Discontinuing the drug or assisting the perceptual process may eliminate the problem, but often these possibilities are overlooked. The need for increased public and professional awareness and education is obvious.

Extending Effective Life Span

Bernard Strehler and Albert Rosenfeld are the leading optimists in the field of *prolongevity,* which is also the title, in fact, of Rosenfeld's book on the subject. They believe that we are close to finding the key to understanding and effectively postponing aging. Strehler predicts that eventually humans will be capable of living 150 years or more, with the healthy middle age of maximum productivity expanded to between 60 and 80 years. The various theories on aging include the "programmed" theory, implying that our aging is predetermined by genetic make-up at conception, the "autoimmune" theory, which holds that our bodies literally become allergic to themselves and gradually self-destruct, and the "wear and tear" theory, to mention only a few of those now under study.

If we can discern the triggering mechanism, it then remains for us to determine or develop a suppressor for that trigger. We have already realized some things we can do to prevent acceleration of the aging process, such as not smoking, decreasing sun exposure and increasing exercise. But even these have no appreciable effect on lengthening the actual life span, only postponing till closer to the end of life the debilitating loss of function. That, of course, is well worth the effort for most people.

New research is continually unfolding ideas that appear to have merit. For instance, the life span of rats can be increased by between twenty-five and thirty-three percent by reducing dietary protein by one half, starting at age sixteen months, which is comparable to forty-five human years. Many researchers believe a meager diet may be the most effective means of postponing aging. Thymosin, a hormone capable of boosting the human immune system has shown some promise in treatment of cancer and immune deficiencies. Antioxidants, such as vitamin E, BHT, and others, have considerable success in extending the life span in laboratory animals and even in their offspring who were not given the chemicals.

Many will be delighted to learn that mineral-, hormone-, and antibiotic-rich honey and red wines, effective virus killers, are also among the growing list of deterioration-deterrents. A host of other potential deterrents to aging are seriously being investigated, including drugs and treatments.

Continued involvement and satisfaction in one's work and a feeling of usefulness are often associated with a long and happy life. A regular program of stress management, such as meditation, reasonable balance of one's activities, and relaxation exercises, is believed by many to have a positive influence on one's well-being far into old age.

Eventually, of course, the body will succumb to the final beat of its rhythms. If we can, however, improve the body's status in the interim, so much the better for all of us.

Retirement

Retirement is one of those mixed blessings. In a society where people usually live long enough to retire, they may greet the relief from work as a well-earned reward or as an insult to their integrity. Many cultures don't have retirement. They need everyone's work in order to survive. In our American economic system, we have great numbers of young workers eager to replace their still-capable elders on the employment rolls.

January 1979 marked the beginning of a new federal law which forbids companies to insist on mandatory retirement before the age of seventy. Many firms and corporations had routinely retired employees on their sixty-fifth birthday. A host of employers still offer extra incentives to encourage the earlier retirements they can no longer legally force. The incentive may be an extra lump sum payment, a percentage increase in the monthly pension, continued discounts on company products, or use of company recreation facilities.

The abrupt removal of an individual from a life-long occupation occasionally is followed by a difficult period of adjustment, especially if the individual had not prepared for the sudden presence of unlimited leisure time. Some blame the maladjustment on the indelible puritan work ethic which implies that personal worth is directly related to productivity. Others explain it as a grief reaction to the loss of status and a way of life. Another approach, verified by some recent research, suggests that anxiety about adequate income prompts much of the disenchantment with the benefits of retirement.

Retirement income is generally far less than one's income while employed. Boredom and the impact of inflation have sent many retirees back into the working environment, often in second careers and sometimes in menial jobs. Social security payments are based on a sliding scale, decreasing in amount as the earned income increases. In 1981, the maximum wage a person could earn and still receive the maximum social security check was $6,000 per year. For each increment in earned income above that amount, the social security benefits decrease, but by a smaller amount.

The system therefore is said to discourage active employment, since it penalizes those who make money outside the system. As many times as I have heard this argument, I fail to understand it. When individuals work more than the specified amount, their social security benefits diminish, but their spendable income has actually increased. They are still better off financially than they would be if they received the full amount of social security and did not work. With double exemptions and other income tax benefits for the elderly, the penalty imposed by this role seems insignificant. The aged would be foolish to refuse desired employment on this basis alone.

Many new approaches to retirement have been suggested and are being tried in a variety of settings. There are various forms of semiretirement, whereby an employee gradually diminishes his workload until final retirement. This may be accomplished by taking successively longer vacations each year or by working fewer days per week, or by relinquishing certain responsibilities and retaining others. Some companies pay educational expenses to retrain their potential retirees for other types of jobs.

The growing use of "emeritus" status allows an individual to continue contributing his expertise to the community, but outside the traditional framework. For example, a physician who prefers not to subject himself to the stresses of maintaining a private practice may offer to work one or more days a week at a free clinic. A retired school teacher might do private tutoring or become active on the school board.

Part-time jobs and shared jobs seem to have a special appeal to retirees who want to supplement their income but cannot or do not want to work full time. Some retirees start entirely new careers and become quite successful. A retired Air Force colonel made a name for himself in real estate. A retired corporate executive bought his own small business. The self-confidence and usefulness engendered by some form of continued employment are often as important as financial rewards.

Clearly, the retirement picture is changing. New appreciation of the capabilities and expertise of our senior citizens, and the economic difficulties of social security and other pension plans will no doubt result in some rethinking of our present system. Interest has surged in this area and innovations are on the horizon.

Aging Activists

If you thought the old folks were sitting back in their rocking chairs ignoring the attitudinal abuse they receive and their second-class citizenship, take another look. Maggie Kuhn has rocked the boat that kicked her out of her job, and the boat and the ocean will never be the same. Fury and outrage over her forced retirement spurred her to develop the Gray Panthers, an activist group with more than 27,000 contributors. The goals of the Gray Panthers include nursing home reform, elimination of stereotypes of age, and improvement in housing, employment and health care for the elderly, to name a few. The Gray Panthers' offices are at 3635 Chestnut Street, Philadelphia, Pennsylvania 19104.

Others are rocking their boats, too. The American Association of Retired Persons and the National Retired Teachers Association, both at 1909 K Street, N.W., Washington, D.C. 20049, provide a broad spectrum of services for retired persons, including the Widowed Person's Service and Legal Counsel for the Elderly. They boast a very large membership.

The National Institute on Aging is a federally funded research center located in Bethesda, Maryland. Founded in 1974, its renowned director, Dr. Robert Butler, oversees studies in physiological, emotional, and social aging. The goal of the research is to enhance the quality of life and expand the productive middle years.

RSVP, the Retired Senior Volunteers Program is sponsored by the federal government through ACTION. Through it, 250,000 senior citizens participate in close to 700 projects. Illinois RSVP programs list about 150 potential assignments for volunteers, utilizing skills they have mastered over the years. Transportation is provided. Foster Grandparents, also an ACTION program, provides transportation, a meal for each day served, and a small stipend for low-income seniors who provide companionship and guidance for emotionally, physically, and mentally handicapped children. More than 16,000 senior citizens currently serve as Foster Grandparents. Another ACTION program, Senior Companions, provides a small stipend, hot meals for each day served, and transportation to some 3,500 volunteers who work with the frail elderly both in their homes and in institutions to help them achieve and maintain their highest level of independent living. For further information about these programs call your local or regional ACTION office, or call toll-free (800)424–8580, or write to ACTION, 806 Connecticut Avenue, N.W., Washington, D.C. 20525.

There are many smaller but also effective efforts at improving the lot of the elderly. One creative community located a day care center in a nursing home. This gave the residents something important and entertaining to do and gave the children a chance to get some attention from surrogate grandparents who had plenty of time to spend with them. Jim Gillies, a businessman in Orlando, Florida has established nonprofit shelter homes for the elderly. Operated somewhat like a resident-run boarding house, the homes provide housing, meals, transportation to doctor appointments or church services, laundry and maid service, and companionship for a reasonable fee. It represents a middle-stage between outright independence and the need for nursing home care. Gillies hopes that others will start such Share-A-Home projects to provide other communities with the means of meeting the needs of its senior citizens.

The senior citizens center is now a familiar facility in many towns. Meals-on-Wheels and daily phone checks on shut-ins are also common. Many educational institutions offer special "elder hostels" or reduced tuition for regular courses; other forms of senior discounts are becoming widespread.

Now that medical science has permitted so many of us to live long lives, we are challenged with the task of maximizing the joy and productivity of these extra years. Medicine, psychology, business, and government are all working toward this goal—making a long life lively.

Common Emotional Experiences of Aging

While the elderly population is as diverse in intelligence, skills, personality, and philosophy as any other age group, its members are likely to encounter certain common life experiences as they approach the end of life. Let us focus here primarily on the emotional reactions to these common experiences. This discussion is not intended to predict the emotional life of any individual nor describe the majority of the elderly at any point, but, like the explanation of stages of dying, can hopefully provide us with a framework to help us understand these feelings when they do occur.

Grief

Probably at no other time in life are there so many occasions for grief. For many years before his own death, my grandfather often wrote letters to my parents in which he included the newspaper clippings of his friends' obituaries. He was acutely aware of the deaths of his contemporaries. There may be little or no time to adjust to one loss before another occurs. In addition to the deaths of freinds and possibly of one's spouse, there are a myriad of other losses which also require some grief work. For some, the grief is engulfing, overwhelming. For others it is at least bearable.

These other losses might include declining health and sensory acuity, financial or physical dependence, loss of self-esteem, loss of the satisfactions of employment, geographical and emotional distance from children and grandchildren, and diminishing pleasure from previously favored pastimes as functional capacities decline. For example, failing eyesight renders reading a frustration, clumsy finger dexterity or pain make needlework impossible. And then there is the loss of their support systems (family has moved away, friends are deceased or disabled) to help with their grief. Of course, preparatory grief in anticipation of one's own death is not unexpected at this stage of life.

Guilt

The accumulation of a lifetime of unresolved guilt sometimes forces the elderly into a last effort at expiation. There are new sources of guilt, too. Often a healthy senior citizen feels guilty simply for having survived or escaped senility when he sees his friends and loved ones die or suffer. Many feel ill at ease with their excess leisure time. The deeply ingrained puritan work ethic makes them feel they *should* be working, doing something productive. Retirement can be a significant source of guilt for the individual with strong feelings about the value of a day's work.

Loneliness

While many old people remain socially active, others feel desperately lonely, especially if they have survived the deaths of a spouse and close friends. There is a fear of isolation, of having no one who really cares. Even those involved in casual church or activity groups may ache for the closeness and understanding of those who truly shared their lives.

As with younger persons, the loneliness of bereavement may ease with the establishment of new, satisfying relationships. But the energy, time, and opportunities available for establishing such liaisons may have dwindled. Decreased mobility and communication problems due to diminished hearing and vision or slowed reaction time interfere with the development of new friendships. It is hard to get to know people when you can't understand what they are saying or discern the expressions on their faces.

The need for affection and attention does not diminish with the decline in strength of the senses, muscles, and kidney function. And, contrary to the popular clichés, sexual desire often remains constant and even increases in many individuals. The main deterrents to fulfilling such desires are the negative attitudes in society toward sex among the elderly (which perhaps the elderly, too, have adopted) the lack of privacy in institutional settings, the unavailability of an interested and interesting partner and, occasionally, the limitations of poor health.

Deanna Edward's song, "Folks Don't Kiss Old People Anymore,"* reveals the poignant plea of many a silver-haired soul:

I still need the loving arms you put around me long ago,
When you were just a little child of four;
I still need your happy laughter and your kiss upon my brow,
But folks don't kiss old people anymore.

My hair has turned to silver and my face is lined with age,
Where the traces of the years have gone before;
I still need the reassurance you longed for as a child,
But folks don't kiss old people anymore.

When will you understand that I'm not really old at all,
Thoughts that fill my mind are young as Spring;
I can't erase my need for love or take away the pain
Of loneliness that each new day may bring.

It would only take a little time from busy chores you do,
How I'd love to see you standing at my door;
I need to feel your gentle kiss upon my wrinkled face,
But folks don't kiss old people anymore.

Depression and Anxiety

The weight of grief, guilt, and loneliness may combine to produce a profound depression in the elderly. The added anxieties related to declining physical integrity and other changes in one's life often

*Reprinted by permission from Franciscan Communications Center, 1229 South Santee, Los Angeles, CA 90015.

compound the problem. The depression may be expressed through despair, lethargy, loss of appetite, and insomnia. This is a serious personal and social problem. For white males, the rate of suicide peaks between the ages of seventy and eighty. In fact one-fourth of *all* suicides in this country are committed by persons over 65 years of age.

Many others would welcome the end of life, but find suicide an unacceptable answer to their problems. One lovely eighty-year-old lady—there must be thousands like her—had arthritis and was nearly blind. A widow for three years, she found little joy left in life and often spoke her desire to "join her husband." For all the annoying physical ailments she endured, her constitution was nonetheless basically strong. She survived yet another two years, hoping each meaningless day would be her last. She had lived a full life, raised a loving, successful family, and had many wonderful memories. But the combination of her grief and the humiliation of physical difficulties were simply too much for her to bear. She withdrew and resigned herself to half an existence, anxious for its culmination.

If someone is available to help ease the grief process (see Chapter 7) the depression may be minimized or shortened, although circumstances vary considerably. It is at least safe to say that a loving, supportive friend, child, or grandchild would provide a positive experience in the midst of so much sorrow. Sometimes joining a widows' and widowers' support group helps those in this predicament to cope better. It is heartbreaking to watch someone you love go through this personal struggle, especially when all of your efforts to assist them fail. Grief takes a long time for even young persons to complete. For the elderly, the strength and the time to manage this ordeal may just not be there.

Sense of Impotence and Helplessness

Loss of financial independence and physical mobility lead many elderly to feel as if they have lost control of their lives, that they have virtually no power over what will happen to them. A widow who, after her husband's death, made a too-hasty decision to move into an "old folks' home" later regretted her commitment. Elizabeth Hughes told this woman's story in the September, 1974 issue of *Human Behavior* magazine. In return for guaranteed life-long residency, she had signed over all of her assets to the home. She was given an allowance of $20 per month. The first couple of weeks were very difficult. Still grieving her husband's death, she felt trapped.

> If I complained or found fault, Mrs. Pierce would tell me to get out and find another place. But where could I go without money? Being so

helpless in this place made me feel angry and desperate. I tried to control myself by saying, "Angelina, behave." It's so hard to keep fighting when you are alone and existence seems suddenly without purpose.

. . . It became increasingly apparent to me that we were at the mercy of the institutional staff. They controlled whether we got an extra piece of toast for breakfast or a clean towel each day. But even more important, they controlled how we felt about ourselves.

Even persons living in their own homes may be uncertain how long they will be able to stay there and feel that, when the time comes, someone else will probably decide what's best for them. Living on a pension, unable to work or drive, they feel helpless to improve their economic status. The reality sinks in, "There is nothing I can do to change my life."

For those dealing with the elderly plagued with such thoughts, it may be helpful to create situations in which they can exert some control. Even if it seems minor, it may mean a lot to the individual. For example, if someone else must prepare most of the meals, it might provide an ego boost to give the oldster responsibility for planning the menu for one or more days a week, preferably the same day or days. "Wednesdays are *my* days to choose the menu" is a somewhat better outlook than "I must always eat what they choose to fix." There are many other possibilities. Seek their advice on household mainte-nance questions such as "Should we paint this year or have siding put on the house?" or "What shall we plant in the garden?" Participa-tion in even small decisions gives the individual at least some sense of control and value. That is better than total helplessness.

Rage

Like the rest of humanity, old folks sometimes get angry about things. But the stereotypical old person is docile and has no original thoughts, so when one of them expresses a normal emotion it is often interpreted as psychosis or senility. Why can't they occasionally get mad like everyone else does?

The widow who moved to the old folks home was admonished for giving her room personal touches. Her decorating was her small attempt to personalize a tiny cream-colored cement block room with rubber tile floors. Nevertheless, the drapes made it difficult for the housekeeper to clean the windows. The scatter rug interfered with floor-mopping and the bookcase was too big and cluttered the room. A committee came to the room to inspect these infractions. She deeply resented the intrusion.

I can still feel the anger rage inside me. It was hard for me to keep my chin up and maintain my pride. In my own home, I was queen, but here I felt like a child. I told Mr. Ford, the administrator, that I had done nothing wrong. The bookcase did clutter the room, but I didn't want to give up my books. Without them I would die! After looking around the room, Mr. Ford nodded his head in approval and the inspection party left. Fighting back the welling tears, I sat rigid on the edge of my bed. I resented being put into such a humiliating position. Maybe I did regard myself as being more "cultured" than the rest. But without a feeling of self-worth, I would never survive.

Certainly this woman's rage is understandable. Who wouldn't rebel in similar circumstances? A sincere effort to understand the source of the rage and the provision of a free atmosphere for its expression may help in the discovery of a solution for the problem. Bottled-up anger increases stress and is self-destructive. Openly expressed anger may allow others to see the situation from another perspective and perhaps alter it for the better. If anger is met with recrimination and ridicule, the aged may be humiliated into remaining silent and becoming increasingly resentful.

Aging and Dying

Growing old might be seen as un-American, just as dying does not fit into the American dream. If we can eventually accept the reality and inevitability of death, perhaps we could assimilate a greater respect for *all* of life, even life that doesn't meet our standards of perfection, but is nevertheless valuable. Remember the doctor in Chapter 3 who helped his patient salvage her plant and her life for all they were worth? And consider the amputees and heart patients and burn victims who treasure the life they have despite the imperfections. Aging, too, has its problems, as losses accumulate and energy wanes, but there *are* still potential joys and meaning and capabilities. Each day and each life have an intrinsic and unique value. Our challenge is to grasp that value while we have the opportunity. If we will allow ourselves to make peace with death, we may discover how to truly make love to life.

15

Appreciatory Living

This book is dedicated to the husband and daughters of Annette Herms, my first cousin and a wonderful, incredibly sensitive woman. She died very suddenly and unexpectedly at the tender age of twenty-five. Vivacious and loquacious one moment, lifeless and silent the next. While the rest of us were stunned by her death, she seemed to have been aware that the ticking of her own internal clock was approaching its final hour. She gave us signals—the matter-of-fact purchase of a life insurance policy, expression of "feelings" that she would not live to see her children in school. (Her older daughter was four years old.) It seems somehow eerie that an errant gust of wind should choose the spot she was standing in on the back of a barely moving pick-up truck and throw her body onto the pavement. The tragedy has left those of us who loved Annette with many questions and mysteries, perhaps a few insights and a lot of grieving—especially for Ron, Lanita, and Mary Lee, as well as her mother and sisters and brother. How could she be taken so soon, while they all had so much love and life yet to share with her?

We are not privileged to know. Yet perhaps we can learn from Annette's death and her life. This woman, a child in many ways, had a special thirst for life. We found her eagerly approaching the well when she might have "better" spent her time in more "productive" pursuits.

When Annette and Ron were married, I remember wishing she had waited until she finished college (a goal she was still pursuing part-time while caring for her little family). Had she postponed her marriage as long as I had, she never would have had her beautiful children. That alone has been a lesson for me in imposing my life's values on others.

There are other, more important lessons. Annette was not the first to die an early death. In fact, it happens often, all around us. We are, it seems, almost constantly reminded of the tenuous nature of our existence, although many of us go about our lives as if it weren't so. We would like to think that death happens only to other people, other families. We are safe. We won't die. Our loved ones won't die. And so we never truly appreciate the finiteness of this life.

But it is the *finiteness* that makes life so very precious. Have you ever been on a long-awaited and very enjoyable vacation when suddenly you realized you had only another day to stay before you had to go back home, back to your routine? You consciously decide to savor each moment of that last day, soak in all the sun, see all the sights, catch all the fish you can—whatever it is you enjoy, you make a special effort to drink it all in. Those hours are remarkably sweet.

If vacations lasted forever, they would cease to become vacations. The special pleasure comes from knowing it is a special, limited opportunity for us. An eternity at Disney World or on the ski slopes or at the beach house would appeal to very few. It is the change of scenery, the chance to rest that makes a vacation fun.

Life is itself a special, limited opportunity. If you are now twenty years old, probably better than a fourth of your life has already passed. If you're forty, it is more than half over. This is it. What are you going to do with it?

Dr. Michael Gulley, whose work was discussed in Chapter 9, was impressed by the stark sincerity of the patients in his near-death research. Having come so close to death, many of them were brought up short by their previous nonchalance about life. "I've wasted all these years without understanding what was really important." Must we face a near-crisis, or an actual one, to make us stop and think?

Must we become terminally ill to marvel at the sky's azure hues, the intoxicating scent of the honeysuckle, and the incredible power of human love? We are all terminal. You would think those of us who aren't ill would have even more to appreciate than our somehow wiser friends who are so close to death.

Orville Kelly spent the last years of his life sharing this urgent message with the world. The cancer that finally claimed his life, though, may have inspired the insight leading to richer, fuller lives for the thousands of persons who were touched by Kelly's simple words, "Make Today Count." Annette seemed to inherently grasp that concept. She, like Orville Kelly, seized those gifts of moments and made the most of them.

We live in a hectic society with some curious values. It is a world full of stresses and not terribly conducive to the quiet contemplation of the true meaning of life. But the stress takes its toll, and the impoverished mind and spirit show up in many a physician's office, manifesting this "dis-ease" in a myriad of physical complaints. Many doctors now recognize the phenomenal effect of stress as well as the fact that more than medication and surgery are needed to restore the healthful harmony of body, mind, and spirit.

If we will but listen to the body's "dis-ease" and slow down enough to consider what is really important, we might discover a better approach to the task of living. Look at your life. Decide what you want, what you don't want. Education, travel, material wealth, service to others, participation in sports, parenthood, marriage, hobbies, professional endeavors—how do these rank in your personal value system? Are you living consistently with your values? If you continue as you are now, will you approach your own deathbed wishing you had done things differently?

Like that lovely vacation, the moments of your life are rapidly passing by you. Claim those moments and make them yours. Even if the reincarnationists are right, and we return for yet another adventure on this planet, this is the last chance for *these* moments, for *this* very special life. To squander such a treasure would indeed be foolish.

Appreciate your life and your loved ones and all the wonder and joy there is in being alive. If you can't find the wonder and the joy, ask someone who is dying for help. How often do we hear it said, "I didn't appreciate what I had until I lost it?" Why are we so blind to the beauty and obsessed with the travails of life? Let us listen to the message of the Annettes and Orville Kellys of the world who seem to have sensed the deeper values of life.

A very dear friend, Frank Goldburg, a gentleman in his seventies, was recently quite disturbed by the death of his older brother, Ariel. Although the brothers lived a thousand miles apart, they remained quite close through the years, and Frank's son, Richard, was also quite close to his uncle.

Ariel Goldburg was a remarkable man, a rabbi whose humanitarian efforts won him many awards. His funeral was attended by many persons of every faith and race.

His death occurred within a week of Frank's last visit and the news, while not a surprise, hit harder than Frank had imagined it could. A third brother, Norman, also a rabbi, wrote this letter to Frank and his wife, Maxine, soon after their brother was buried. In his obvious pain, the equally obvious undertone of gratitude for and appreciation of life is clear. For the Goldburgs, and I hope for you, the pain will subside while the treasures of life are sustained.

Well, Frankie dear boy:
What can one say?
We, the close relatives, the survivors what can we say?

Ariel was, as we know, and will always remember a very special person. No other rabbi like him in America or anywhere else.

The Rabbi Spiro said it all. This feeling of bereavement, of loneliness is shared by all of us.

I have letters from relatives and classmates and friends of Ariel.

Frank, what can I say? What can I write. It is hard for me to contain the grief, to control the tears.

Well . . . I do want to say this, Frank and Macky, the presence of your Richard Burt meant so much to us. What a wonderful boy he is and how proud we all are and how grateful for Richard's long-time devoted attachment to the uncle in Richmond during that most important period of his life. . . .

Well, Frank and Macky, what am I trying to say? I guess I would sum it up with the simple yet deeply meaningful statement "thank God for the years of Ariel's life," allotted to *him* and to *us*.

I guess the ancient phrase sums it up, "The Lord has given: the Lord has taken: blessed be the name of the Lord." Though stricken by grief, we can and do say "Almighty, we thank you for the days and years of our beloved Ariel's life." Amen.

Love to you all,

Norman

Love to you all,
Elaine

Appendix

The following resources are mentioned in the text with specific reference to the nature of their purpose. Some are sources of printed information, some are research groups, others provide direct assistance to individuals, many offer a combinaton of these services. The reader is referred to the chapter for more complete information for each listing.

National Kidney Foundation
315 Park Avenue South
New York, New York   10010
(Chapter 3)

Celo Press
Burnsville, North Carolina 28714
(Chapter 4)

Continental Association of
    Funeral and Memorial
    Societies
Suite 1100
1828 L Street NW
Washington, DC. 20036
(Chapter 4)

Make Today Count
P.O. Box 303
Burlington, Iowa 52601
(Chapter 5)

National Association of Widows
P.O. Box 109
New York, New York 10024
(Chapter 5)

Widowed Persons Service
c/o American Association of
    Retired Persons
1909 K Street NW
Washington, DC 20049
(Chapters 5 and 14)

The Compassionate Friends
Box 1347
Oak Brook, Illinois 60521
(Chapter 5)

The National Sudden
    Infant Death Syndrome
    Foundation
310 South Michigan Avenue
Suite 1904
Chicago, Illinois 60604
(Chapter 5)

Ray of Hope
1518 Derwen Drive
Iowa City, Iowa 52240
(Chapters 5 and 12)

American Cancer Society
Director of Service and
  Rehabilitation
777 Third Avenue
New York, New York 10017
(Programs: I Can Cope, Cancer
Mount, Reach To Recovery.
Chapters 5 and 10)

Candlelighters Association
123 C Street SE
Washington, DC 20003
(Chapter 5)

Mothers Against Drunk Drivers
  (MADD)
5330 Primrose
Suite 146
Fair Oaks, California 95628
(Chapter 5)

Parents of Murdered Children
1739 Bella Vista
Cincinnati, Ohio 45237
(Chapter 5)

The International Association for
  Near Death Studies, Inc.
  (IANDS)
Box U-20
The University of Connecticut
Storrs, Connecticut 06268
(Chapter 9)

Dr. Ian Stevenson
Division of Parapsychology
Box 152
Medical Center, University of
  Virginia
Charlottesville, Virginia 22901
(Chapter 9)

The United Ostomy Association
2001 West Beverly Boulevard
Los Angeles, Californa 90057
(Chapter 10)

The Multiple Sclerosis Society
257 Park Avenue South
New York, New York 10010
(Chapter 10)

American Heart Association
44 East 23rd Street
New York, New York 10011
(Chapter 10)

Arthritis and Rheumatism
  Foundation
23 West 45th Street
New York, New York 10036
(Chapter 10)

Muscular Dystrophy Association
1790 Broadway
New York, New York 10019
(Chapter 10)

American Foundation for the
  Blind
15 West 16th Street
New York, New York 10011
(Chapter 10)

National Burn Victim Foundation
308 Main Street
Orange, New Jersey 07050
(Chapter 10)

Concern for Dying
250 West 57th Street
New York, New York 10019
(Chapter 11)

Catholic Hospital Association
4455 Woodson Road
St. Louis, Missouri 63134
(Chapter 11)

Cryonics Association
24041 Stratford
Oak Park, Michigan 48237
(Chapter 13)

National Hospice Organization
1311A Dolley Madison Boulevard
McLean, Virginia 22101
(Chapter 13)

The Foundation of Thanatology
630 West 168th Street
New York, New York 10032
(Chapter 13)

The Hastings Center
360 Broadway
Hastings-on-Hudson, New York
10706
(Chapter 13)

The Forum for Death Education
and Counseling, Inc.
P.O. Box 1226
Arlington, Virginia 22210
(Chapter 13)

The Gray Panthers
3635 Chestnut Street
Philadel,ɔɩia, Pennsylvania
19104
(Chapter 14)

National Retired Teachers
    Association
1909 K Street NW
Washington, DC 20049
(Chapters 5 and 14)

American Association of Retired
    Persons
1909 K Street NW
Washington,DC 20049
(Chapters 5 and 14)

ACTION
806 Connecticut Avenue, NW
Washington, DC 20525
(Programs: Senior Companions,
Foster Grandparents, RSVP.
(Chapter 14)

Bibliography

Alvarez, A. *The Savage God: A Study of Suicide.* New York: Random House, 1972.

Ashley, Paul P. *You and Your Will: The Planning and Management of Your Estate.* New York: New American Library, 1977.

Barton, David, ed. *Dying and Death.* Baltimore, Maryland: The Williams and Wilkins Co., 1977

Becker, Ernest. *The Denial of Death.* New York: The Free Press, 1973.

Bugen, Larry A. *Death and Dying.* Dubuque, Iowa, Wm. C. Brown Co., 1979.

Caine, Lynn. *Widow.* New York: Bantam Books, 1975.

Colen B. D. *Karen Ann Quinlan: Dying in the Age of Eternal Life.* New York: Nash Publishing, 1976.

Concern for Dying. *Euthanasia: A Decade of Dying.* New York: Concern for Dying, 1979.

Cox, Harold. *Aging.* second ed. Guilford, Connecticut, Dushkin Publishing Group, 1980.

Evans, W. E. D. *The Chemistry of Death.* Springfield, Illinois, Charles C. Thomas, 1963.

Ferguson, Marilyn. *The Aquarian Conspiracy.* Los Angeles: J. P. Tarcher, 1980.

Garfield, Charles A. *Psychosocial Care of the Dying Patient.* San Francisco: McGraw-Hill Book Co., 1978.

Grollman, Earl A., ed. *Concerning Death: A Practical Guide for the Living.* Boston: Beacon Press, 1974.

Grollman, Earl A. *Suicide: Prevention, Intervention, Postvention.* Boston: Beacon Press, 1971.

Hardt, Dale V. *Death: The Final Frontier.* Englewood Cliffs, New Jersey: Prentice Hall, 1979.

Head, Joseph and Cranston, S. L., ed. *Reincarnation: The Phoenix Fire Mystery.* New York: Julien Press/Crown Publishers, 1977.

Heifetz, Milton D. and Mangel, Charles. *The Right to Die.* New York, G. P. Putnam's Sons, 1975.

Hendin, David. *Death as a Fact of Life.* New York: Warner Books, 1974.

Hollingsworth, Charles E. and Pasnaw, Robert O. *The Family in Mourning.* New York: Grune & Stratton, 1977.

Jury, Mark. *Gramp.* New York: Grossman Publishers, 1976.

Kastenbaum, Robert J. *Death, Society, and Human Experience.* St. Louis: C. V. Mosby Co. 1977.

Kohl, Marvin, ed. *Beneficient Euthanasia.* Buffalo, New York: Prometheus Books, 1975.

Kohl, Marvin. *Infanticide and the Value of Life.* Buffalo, New York: Prometheus Books, 1978.

Kohl, Marvin. *The Morality of Killing.* Atlantic Highlands, New Jersey, Humanities Press, 1974.

Kübler-Ross, Elisabeth. *Death: The Final Stage of Growth.* Englewood Cliffs, New Jersey: Prentice-Hall, 1975.

Laas, William. *Monuments in Your History.* New York: Popular Library, 1972.

MacDowell, Douglas M. *Athenian Homicide Law, In the Age of the Orators.* Manchester: Manchester University Press, 1963.

Mannes, Marya. *Last Rights.* New York: William Morrow and Co., 1974.

Mitford, Jessica. *The American Way of Death.* Greenwich, Connecticut: Fawcett Publications, 1963.

Moody, Robert A. Jr. *Life After Life.* New York: Bantam Books, 1977.

Neale, Robert E. *The Art of Dying,* San Francisco, California: Harper and Row, 1973.

Oden, Thomas C. *Should Treatment Be Terminated?* New York: Harper and Row, 1976.

Olshaker, Bennett. *What Shall We Tell the Kids?* New York: Dell Publishing Co., 1971.

Osis, Karlis and Haraldsson, Erlendur. *At the Hour of Death.* New York: Avon Books, 1979.

Oyle, Irving. *The Healing Mind.* Millbrae, California: Celestial Arts, 1979.

Palmore, Erdman, ed. *Normal Aging II.* Durham, North Carolina: Duke University Press, 1974.

Quinlan, Joseph; Quinlan, Julia; and Battelle, Phyllis. *Karen Anne.* Garden City, New York: Doubleday & Co., 1977.

Rosenfield, Albert. *Pro-Longevity.* New York. Alfred A. Knopf, 1976.

Ruitenbeek, Hendrik M., ed. *Death: Interpretations.* New York: Dell Publishing Co., 1969.

Schoenberg, Bernard, *et al.* eds. *Anticipatory Grief.* New York and London: Columbia University Press, 1974.

Schoenberg, Bernard, *et al.* eds. *Loss and Grief: Psychological Management in Medical Practice.* New York and London: Columbia University Press, 1970.

Segerberg, Osborn, Jr. *The Immortality Factor.* New York: E. P. Dutton and Co., 1974.

Tolstoi, L. *The Death of Ivan Ilych.* New York: Health Sciences Publishing Corp., 1973.

Veatch, Robert M. *Death, Dying, and the Biological Revolution: Our Latest Quest for Responsibility.* New Haven and London: Yale University Press, 1978.

Veatch, Robert M., ed. *Life Span.* New York: Harper and Row, 1979.

Vaux, Kenneth, ed. *Who Shall Live?* Philadelphia: Fortress Press, 1970.

Verzar, F. *Lectures on Experimental Gerontology.* Springfield, Illinois: Charles C. Thomas, 1963.

Wambach, Helen. *Life Before Life.* New York: Bantam Books, 1979.

Weisman, Avery D. *On Dying and Denying.* New York: Behavioral Publications, 1972.

Werner-Beland, Jean A. *Grief Responses to Long-term Illness and Disability.* Reston, Virginia: Reston Publishing Co., 1980.

Wertenbaker, Lael Tucker. *Death of a Man.* Boston: Beacon Press, 1957.

Wilcox, Sandra Galdiert and Sutton, Marilyn. *Understanding Death and Dying.* Port Washington, New York: Alfred Publishing Co., 1977.

Zarit, Stephen H., ed. *Readings in Aging and Death: Contemporary Perspectives.* London: Harper and Row, 1977.

Index